Stories Without Borders

Stories Without Borders

The Berlin Wall and the Making
of a Global Iconic Event

JULIA SONNEVEND

OXFORD
UNIVERSITY PRESS

OXFORD
UNIVERSITY PRESS

Oxford University Press is a department of the University of Oxford. It furthers
the University's objective of excellence in research, scholarship, and education
by publishing worldwide. Oxford is a registered trade mark of Oxford University
Press in the UK and certain other countries.

Published in the United States of America by Oxford University Press
198 Madison Avenue, New York, NY 10016, United States of America.

CIP data is on file at the Library of Congress
ISBN 978-0-19-060430-1 (hpk.); 978-0-19-060431-8 (pbk.)

9 8 7 6 5 4 3 2 1

Paperback printed by Webcom, Inc., Canada
Hardback printed by Bridgeport National Bindery, Inc., United States of America

To my father and in memory of my mother

Contents

Stories Without Borders

Introduction

THERE WAS NO Berlin Wall, and it never fell. In this book I show that these claims are not in any way radical. My book is neither about conspiracy theories, nor about the fragile nature of truth. Instead, it considers the ways in which we recount and remember news stories of historic significance. It also looks at how we, quite understandably, imagine events that are larger than life. History, like life, is a process—in which occurrences are intertwined with one another in a dense mesh we often call "context." At the same time, history is often incredibly repetitious. Still, some events distinguish themselves in our minds. They split off from the regular rhythms of daily life and stand out in memory as unique, marked as uplifting or traumatic. We isolate these occurrences from whatever came before and after, strip off their contradictions and complexities, and discard their webs of causes. In the stories we tell, such events become stand-alone items, compressions of time and space, elevated above the repetitive flow of time.

Consider, for example, the fall of the Berlin Wall. This event enjoyed extensive international media coverage and its anniversaries are ritually remembered around the world. The special status of the fall of the Berlin Wall seems obvious; its significance is uncontested. Who would deny its power? Who would say the event was "banal" or even a "colossal misunderstanding"? Well, almost nobody, at least nobody living many years later. But both descriptions—"banal" and a "colossal misunderstanding"—come from journals in 1989. "Banal" is how Alonso Alvarez de Toledo, the last Spanish ambassador to East Germany, described the event in his journal *News From a Country That Has Never Existed*.[1] The second label, "colossal misunderstanding," comes from the American historian Robert Darnton, who happened to be in West Berlin at the time, and who collected his memories in *Berlin Journal 1989–1990*.[2] Both authors wondered about the banality, awkwardness, and accidental nature of what may well have been the most significant historic event they had ever personally experienced.

On November 9, 1989, the "fall of the Berlin Wall" had yet to be constructed. Of course the storytellers did not entirely *invent* the fall of the Berlin Wall. No one crossing the border that night, or watching other people crossing the border on television, will ever forget that day. Families were reunited; strangers hugged each other with a sense of trust they had never before experienced, and that they never would again; and political leaders, once powerful, were speechless. Relatives of the Berlin Wall's victims gained some belated justice and hope. But a single night, no matter how emotional, can be forgotten over time if we do not fix it in place with powerful words. And even among powerful words, we need to select the right ones. We have to strike a delicate balance between the "experience" of that night and its "story"—for one cannot work without the other.

The question that propels this book is how storytellers build up certain events so that people in many parts of the world remember them for long periods of time. Focusing on journalists covering the fall of the Berlin Wall and on subsequent retellings of the event, from Legoland reenactments to anniversary celebrations to slabs of the Berlin Wall installed in shopping malls, I discuss how stories of particular events turn into global social myths, while others somehow fade out. What events come to be known and seen as "global iconic events"?

Global iconic events are news events that the international media cover extensively and remember ritually. Although they cannot resonate with everyone around the world, global iconic events like the sinking of the Titanic, D-day, the atomic bombings of Hiroshima and Nagasaki, the fall of the Berlin Wall, and 9/11 become reference points in multiple countries and regions. Many iconic events are national: they do not cross their "local" boundaries to become global stories. And conversely, many global events are not iconic: they capture the international audience's attention for a moment, but fail to become lasting icons. Global iconic events both transcend national boundaries and do so in a lasting way.

Global iconic events are *never* universal. They are readily transportable but not necessarily transported by everyone. Global iconic events touch many hearts, but they do not have the same meaning for everyone. International news events enter a strongly fragmented political and journalistic space, which makes it hard for them to get unequivocal international recognition. While 9/11 was a deeply traumatic historic event for the West, in many other countries its meaning is more nebulous and contested. While the Srebrenica massacre constituted the largest mass murder in Europe since the Holocaust, Serbia still finds it hard to accept the event's significance and the responsibility of its perpetrators. Even the Holocaust, the moral of which seems universal to most, does not have the same moral for everybody. No historic event gets universal celebration or mourning. Global iconic events are always contested or ignored in some place.

Powerful state-influenced counter-narratives can destabilize the meaning of a potential iconic event in a lasting way. Consider the conflicting international interpretations of the Armenian genocide, China's attempts to suppress the memory of the Tiananmen Square massacre, or the international disagreement about the recent uprisings in Syria. Yet such counter-narratives may also vitalize or revitalize the construction of an iconic event. The urge to refute them can impel narrators to redouble their efforts to build up a myth.

These multifaceted dynamics that define the viability and longevity of international news events are the focus of my book. I start with a theoretical chapter that examines how "events" have been discussed in the field of communications. I focus on the most influential book, Daniel Dayan's and Elihu Katz's *Media Events: The Live Broadcasting of History* (1992). After reviewing *Media Events* and other relevant international media research on events, in my second chapter I draw the contours of a new understanding of global iconic events. My approach examines the dynamics in which iconic events are formed in transnational contexts. It suggests that global iconic events have five narrative dimensions: (1) foundation: their narrative prerequisites; (2) mythologization: the development of their resonant message and elevated language; (3) condensation: their encapsulation in a simple phrase, a short narrative, and a recognizable visual scene; (4) counter-narration: their competing stories; and (5) remediation: their ability to travel across multiple media platforms and changing social and political contexts.

After the theoretical introduction, I present an extended case study of the formation of a global iconic event. In five chapters I examine the five elements of my concept of global iconic events in the developments of November 9, 1989—what came to be known as the fall of the Berlin Wall. Throughout these chapters I analyze the event's narration in four national contexts, using three languages, showing fragmentation in international narration. First, I look at the fall of the Berlin Wall's narrative prerequisites in the imagination of East and West. Then I examine the event's initial narration in West German and American television and press, and show how the event's mythical message of "end of division" was developed. Later I track the Western condensation of the event's story into a simple phrase ("fall of the Berlin Wall")—a short narrative of freedom with a recognizable visual scene. I also describe the event's alternative narrative, as told by the East German and Soviet media. Finally, I highlight how the story of the fall of the Berlin Wall travels across multiple media platforms and gains currency in changing social and political contexts from China to Hungary to the United States. In my concluding chapter, I also consider three ways in which global iconic events may shape individuals and societies enduringly: global iconic events as frames of mind, as what I call "predictive pictures" for future events, and as tools to confront late modernity. Overall, I hope to demonstrate how the fall of the Berlin Wall came to be constructed as a social myth for the global community.

The fall of the Berlin Wall as a global myth successfully crosses national and temporal boundaries, but it does not prevent us from building new "walls" of division. Approximately forty new separation barriers have been built worldwide since the fall of the Berlin Wall. More than thirty of these walls have been built since 9/11, fifteen in the year of 2015. Many more separation walls, barriers, and fences are being built while I am writing these lines. Still, this powerful "story without borders" (which is also a story *about* borders) remains our main reference point when we discuss separation barriers all around the world, regardless of substantial variation among them. The Berlin Wall's story is painfully relevant *again* as we are experiencing the biggest humanitarian crisis since the Second World War in the numbers of people being displaced from their countries and regions worldwide. Millions of people face deadly barriers as they try to cross borders, and we simply lack answers to them and to ourselves in how to address this challenge. The myth of the fall of the Berlin Wall may provide us with some hope and perspective.

This book defends the "goodness" of banality and attacks the tyranny of details. It shows the power of condensation in transnational storytelling and in the construction of global iconic events. Condensation and the related narrative tools of simplification, smoothing, and packaging tend to get a lot of "bad press" in media research. They are criticized for eliminating nuance, strangling the local, and making media users immune to the inherent complexity of social life. But what if condensation is our *only* chance to keep an event alive in the international context? What if this often negatively portrayed narrative practice provides us with resonant myths that help us navigate the labyrinths of contemporary life? Condensation may help us communicate social meanings in a lasting way that a dense web of facts and details would never be able to do. Surely we want to remember everything, but none of us can. Global iconic events as cognitive shortcuts maybe help us remember at least "something" about a historic occurrence and connect it to issues that are relevant to us today.

In writing this book I have hoped to provide readers with an "event" as well—their own travel through time, space, and media. Readers interested in social theory and transnational storytelling will want to read the first two chapters that build up a new concept of "global iconic events." Those interested only in the case study of the fall of the Berlin Wall are welcome to start the book with Chapter 3. I hope all readers will see, regardless of which chapters they skip, that constructing a lasting transnational narrative borders on the impossible. It is as daunting as building the Tower of Babel. Global iconic events are miracles and shocks, moments of relative consonance in continuous dissonance. They are exceptional, totemic—and very vulnerable to the destructive powers of forgetting.

Julia Sonnevend

New York, Berlin, Budapest, Ann Arbor, Jerusalem

1

Events in Media

EVENTS "OCCUR," "HAPPEN"—THEY fall on our heads and we try to navigate our lives around them. Some events we remember fondly, like the births of our children, the election of a beloved politician, or a successful revolution leading to a more democratic order. Other events are recalled as traumas, such as a diagnosis of a dangerous illness, the assassination of a president, or a devastating terrorist attack. Humans have always "followed" events on media or embodied events in media. Our age is no different in that desire, perhaps only in scale. Public events can now attract the interest of even billions: people watch, listen, and comment, and some viewers even broadcast to faraway others.

Events seem powerful, influential, and often "life-changing." But somehow, they are still powerless in media research. Very few media researchers dare to tackle events systematically. Do media researchers have good reasons to be cautious? Are events unique occurrences that resist typification? Should we avoid them at all costs? Maybe. But many disciplines are less respectful of the uniqueness and fluidity of events, and try to find repetitive and stable features in them. The study of "events" is one of the hot topics of contemporary continental philosophy. Thinkers in phenomenology—for instance, Jean-Luc Marion and Claude Romano, post-Marxists like Alain Badiou, and proponents of poststructuralism, like Jacques Derrida and Gilles Deleuze—have all presented influential theories of events.[1] While highly diverse in their understanding of events, these recent theoretical formulations seem to have a few common features. They tend to consider events both as transformations of situations and as sites for the emergence of new meanings. They mostly regard events as singular entities that cannot be replicated in the exact same form. And they are skeptical of causality, resisting the temptation of connecting events with one or even multiple causes. [2] Overall, what we see in continental philosophy is a recent proliferation of theories and controversies around the concept of the "event"; as Alain Badiou put it, event is a term "common to most contemporary philosophers."[3]

Somewhat disillusioned by the study of patterns, statistical regularities, and other social science–inspired approaches, historical scholarship has also *experienced* a recent "return to the event," as French historian Pierre Nora phrased this renewed interest in exceptional moments in history.[4] Since the 1970s many historians have started to question whether social structures and long-term social processes are fully capable of explaining historical change.[5] These historians became skeptical of the structuralist explanations of the *Annales* School in France, Marxist historiography, and the "new social history" in the United States. At the same time, historiographical scholarship has been less radical and active in the *systematic theorizing* of events than philosophy. A notable exception is American historian William H. Sewell Jr.'s by now canonic article from 1995.[6] Sewell outlined a theoretical concept of the "historical event" and refined it with the help of a case study, the storming of the Bastille. He defined historical events as a "ramified sequence of occurrences that is recognized as notable by contemporaries, and that results in a durable transformation of structures."[7] In his view, each event begins with a rupture or break of routines, which then touches off a chain of occurrences that transform previous structures and practices in a lasting way.

Sociology, a discipline that—to use Daniel Bell's words—"specializes in generalization," has also tried to consider the general within the singular in this context.[8] Perhaps the most extensive sociological theorizing of the narration of events has come from American sociologist Robin Wagner-Pacifici, who underscored the challenges of naming and narrating "restless" events.[9] Wagner-Pacifici developed a model of "political semiosis" to describe the semiotic mechanisms that construct and deconstruct events. In her view political semiosis consists of three parts: (1) performative (a speech act or other performative that changes the world/social order), (2) demonstrative (that situates the event at a given moment and space and draws the boundaries of "us" and "them"), and (3) representational (pictures and other symbolic renderings, "copies" of the original exchanges). By adding the representational feature, Wagner-Pacifici also considered the temporal and spatial travel of events: "[e]very eventful transformation involves representational features—copies of the event, or aspects of the event, need to be generated and sent outward into the wider world of audiences and witnesses at a distance."[10]

Of course, media researchers have not been entirely silent either, even if a comprehensive theory of events has failed to emerge. Scholarship on the media coverage of exceptional events has discussed the Eichmann trial, the Kennedy assassination, the Vietnam War, the Watergate scandal, the protests of the New Left, and 9/11.[11] Some scholars have moved beyond the particular and singular, and defined larger genres of media events. These genres include, for instance, pseudo-events, discursive or conflicted media events, media scandals, disaster marathons, media spectacles, and social dramas of apology.[12] European media researchers and historians have tried to historicize our understanding of media events by examining the media coverage of events before the rise of television, for instance the media representations of the 1911 South Pole conquest and the 1912 Titanic disaster.[13] A substantial body of scholarship has examined diverse journalistic practices in the media coverage, commemoration, and witnessing of events.[14] Edited volumes have attempted to provide a comprehensive understanding of the interrelation between media and memory or journalism and memory.[15]

These various pieces of research, however, have not coalesced into a comprehensive theory of events in and beyond media. They all considered crucial aspects of the media narration of events, but mostly took the existence and definition of events for granted. In other words, what *constitutes* an event was not central to their analysis. There is one exception: Daniel Dayan and Elihu Katz's *Media Events: The Live Broadcasting of History*, published in 1992.

Media Events: The Original Concept

Very few pieces of media research have received the kind of sustained attention that has been bestowed upon *Media Events* since its publication. The possible reasons for the still broad appeal and hard-to-resist charm of this canonic book, which dealt with the kinds of staged, scripted, and live TV ceremonies that take on the character and function of national, or even international, rituals, are manifold. Eric W. Rothenbuhler has argued that the book benefited from bringing together a "social scientist of the American tradition and a humanist of the French tradition."[16] Indeed, perhaps the best way to read *Media Events* is to picture Dayan and

Katz in an endless dinner table conversation about those televised events that interested them the most.[17]

In addition to being charming, *Media Events* also performed a particularly compelling intellectual feat. The authors reframed a key topic of media research: they moved "events" out of the critical-skeptical universe of Daniel Boorstin's *The Image*, which presented most of the events covered by contemporary mass media as manufactured "pseudo-events."[18] In contrast, inspired by the work of Durkheim, Handelman, Lévi-Strauss, and Turner, Dayan and Katz applied the anthropology of ceremony to mass communication, giving "weight" and appreciation to media occasions of public life. The book wondered aloud whether Walter Benjamin's "aesthetization of politics" provided the only possible framework for thinking about ceremonial events that attract the attention of political communities. The authors also highlighted the power of the singular in a field that had, thus far, mostly been fascinated by the statistical study of processes and effects, the average and the ordinary.[19] Finally, taking their cue from film studies, Dayan and Katz illustrated the necessity of a genre theory for television.[20]

Media Events came up with a narrow taxonomy of events—the authors themselves called their approach "parsimonious."[21] An event would qualify for inclusion as a "media event" only if it fulfilled eight requirements. It had to (1) be broadcast live, (2) constitute an interruption of everyday life and everyday broadcasting, (3) be preplanned and scripted, and (4) be viewed by a large audience. There should also be (5) a normative expectation that viewing was obligatory and (6) a reverent, awe-filled narration; and the event had to be (7) integrative of society and (8) mostly conciliatory.[22] This list includes only the core requirements; throughout the book, the authors restricted the definition further.

Replicating Max Weber's distinction among rational-legal, charismatic, and traditional authority, Dayan and Katz presented three basic scripts of media events. These were *contests* (for instance, the World Cup, the Olympic Games, the presidential debates, and the Watergate hearings), *conquests* (such as the landing on the moon, Pope John Paul II's visit to Communist Poland, and Egyptian President Anwar el-Sadat's peacemaking visit to Israel) and *coronations* (for example, the funerals of President Kennedy and Indira Gandhi, the coronation of Elizabeth II, and the royal wedding of Charles and Diana).[23]

Media Events also formulated a firm worldview, a certain taste of social optimism, as the authors acknowledged from the start.[24] The neo-Durkheimian framework served the book's argument in a functional way; it made a claim for the collective and binding nature of media events in contemporary societies.[25] But the framework's employment also suggested that the authors believed television to have the power to contribute to national and even global social *integration* on exceptional historic occasions.

While a powerful account of a particular genre of events in media, *Media Events* had some important limitations. I will focus on three of those in particular: *Media Events'* present-centric view of events; its limited understanding of fragmented interpretational spaces (by which I mean conflicting narratives in the global context); and its inattention to how the narratives and imageries of media events travel across multiple platforms—a feature of what we would now call "media convergence." As I will show in this chapter, scholars who have attempted to rethink events often speak of a need to "update" *Media Events* in a globalized digital age. But these technological arguments for revision are misleading. Certain revisions were crucial even back then in the "stone age" of the 1990s. Discussing these limitations of the book is essential both for understanding the *Media Events* debate and for preparing the reader for a new concept of "global iconic events."

Critique of *Media Events*

The event that inspired Dayan and Katz was the visit of Egyptian President Anwar el-Sadat to Israel in 1977. The visit was filled with hopes for peace: it marked the first time an Arab leader visited the Jewish State. As the authors explained in their introduction, "[f]or more than a decade, we have boarded and reboarded Anwar el-Sadat's plane for the flight to Ben Gurion Airport, trying to understand the magic of the event."[26] The formulation was precise. Dayan and Katz imagined traveling back in time, but they did so without reflecting on the act of time traveling itself. Their eyes were focused on the event in its own historical moment; the years *between* the event and the moment of Dayan's and Katz's reflection on it were not part of their consideration. Perhaps due to the authors' interest in the live television coverage of events, *Media Events* froze events in time, blocking out their pasts and their futures.

The concept of collective memory came up in the book only sporadically, as if it were just one more topic mentioned at the dinner table. In their introduction, Dayan and Katz argued that they thought of media events "as holidays that spotlight some central value of some aspect of collective memory."[27] In this case collective memory refers to something from the past that helps bind a particular society together and that is invoked in the media event itself: "[o]ften such events portray an idealized version of society, reminding society of what it aspires to be rather than what it is."[28]

In a chapter on the effects of media events, collective memory came up in a different sense; there it referred to the collective memory of the media events themselves. But even in this case the topic was featured on two short pages only—and in a somewhat contradictory manner at that. The section started with the claim that "[t]he memory of President Kennedy will forever evoke the image of the funeral as seen on television."[29] The next paragraph was already much more nuanced: "[t]o members of the same generation, media events provide shared reference points, the sense of a common past, bridges between personal and collective history."[30] Again, a diachronic understanding—of how stories of media events change, endure, or fade over time—was missing from Dayan's and Katz's canonic book. While *Media Events* examined events from the past, it looked at them as if they were from the present.

Media Events also paid little attention to the fragmented nature of interpretive spaces. The book employed two core concepts of space: national and "coherent" international.[31] *Media Events* did acknowledge that some events attract large international audiences:

> The live broadcasting of these television events attracts the *largest audiences in the history of the world*. (. . .) Some of these ceremonies are so all-encompassing that there is nobody left to serve as outgroup. "We Are The World" is certainly the appropriate theme song for media events.[32]

Media Events also emphasized that particular nations can come together in a common viewing experience. But only on a few occasions in *Media Events* did Dayan and Katz acknowledge the existence of any other constituencies than the nation and the world.[33] The problems with this concept of space do *not* stem from the fact that Dayan and Katz failed to consider globalization; they did, after all, pay attention to what they called "world communication." But they mostly looked at both the global and the national as single and unified interpretive spaces. Indeed, the question of "counter-narration" is strikingly absent from the book. In a chapter on the pathologies of media events, the authors considered cases in which organizers disagree about the meaning of the event, or in which the audience rejects the original script.[34] But cases in which different (national) media have *contrasting* interpretations of an event got little mention. And, when the possibility of difference or variation did come up, its significance was played down.[35]

This minimization of counter-narration is particularly salient in their treatment of the moon landing:

> Consider, the moon landings, for example. They began as a Contest between the United States and the Soviet Union when the first Sputnik was launched into space. Ten years later, as advertised, came the American Conquest of the moon. Finally (but long anticipated) the astronaut heroes were crowned and recrowned by society and the media (Wolfe, 1980).[36]

But by which society and which media? In the narration of Dayan and Katz, the controversy is present at the beginning and mysteriously disappears by the end. Their reference is to Tom Wolfe's *The Right Stuff*, a book that focuses on the early phase of the American space program and barely discusses the Soviet efforts. The moon journey, presented as a "giant leap for mankind" to the American audience, had a far less enthusiastic coverage in the Soviet Union. This fragmentation of interpretation among and within nations continues to be the case today—*not* due to "increased globalization" or "emerging media," but because we have always interpreted stories in very diverse and conflicting ways.

Media Events also had a limited interest in how events travel from one medium to another. Already at the time of the book's publication, media content traveled across multiple platforms; media events received coverage from television, radio, and the printed press. But *Media Events* paid attention to television ceremonies only: "[t]his book is about the festive viewing of television."[37] If the book's title was somewhat confusing in this respect—suggesting, as it did, a more general interest in the media coverage of historic occasions—then the subtitle, *The Live Broadcasting of History*, oriented the reader a bit more specifically.

No book can cover everything, and no reviewer should expect the impossible. Still, this focus on television had the effect of isolating the media events under discussion from their larger media contexts. Telling the story of an event is never the privilege of one single medium, even if one particular medium dominates the setting of the tone. The story of an event has always differed slightly from one medium to the next, and has evolved as it traveled between them. This feature of the media coverage of events may have become more obvious because of digital and global media research, but it is not a new feature.

In its inattention to media convergence, *Media Events* made itself vulnerable to the criticism that it was only the product of a particular time in media history. It is easy to argue, even if it is by no means true, that *Media Events* has little to offer in a digital era. *Media Events'* television-centrism allowed it to "age" quickly. Had the book paid at least some attention to how the stories of events travel across television, radio, and print, it might not have been labeled a "television book." That label does not do the book justice: its main intellectual achievements are not bound to television, and it is relatively easy to expand *Media Events* backward (to radio) or forward (to digital media) without compromising its basic tenets. While contemporary students would not recognize the "old" case studies of *Media Events*, except perhaps for the moon landing and the royal wedding of Charles and Diana (as "historic" parents of Prince William), they can still understand the concept of a "media event." When reading about contests, conquests, and coronations, they might think of the most recent Olympic Games, the inauguration of the first African American president, or the wedding of their favorite celebrity. They may or may not watch television any more. But they still know the feeling of being immersed in a nationally or transnationally shared event.

Regardless of some gaps in theorizing, *Media Events* provides us with an exceptionally compelling and—in my opinion—rather loveable book on "events." No scholarly writing on events since its publication has achieved similar depth or magnitude. While originally a presentation of a particular genre of events, *Media Events* over time has become the "constitution" for researchers of events in media—a constitution that is, nonetheless, ripe for amendment.

Rethinking Media Events

Dayan and Katz have offered multiple reflections on *Media Events*. An important "defense" of *Media Events* was embedded in their analysis of Kurt and Gladys Lang's essay, *The Unique Perspective of Television and Its Effect: A Pilot Study* (1953). The Langs' essay focused on the difference between an event as personally experienced on the ground and as represented on the television screen. The essay's case study was the enthusiastic welcome event organized for General Douglas McArthur in Chicago, after President Truman recalled him for having overstepped his authority in the Korean War. Fifty years after the prize-winning essay, Katz and Dayan analyzed what the Langs did and did not see about the emerging genre of "media events."[38] In their view, the Langs saw the ingredients of the genre, most importantly television's power to live up to the expectations of the audience better than the real event. But Lang and Lang did *not* see the new genre of ceremonial "media events." Moreover, while the Langs regarded television's representation as a distortion of reality, Katz and Dayan saw in television's coverage a *different* representation of reality. This review essay underscored the achievements of *Media Events*, but did not yet offer a revision of the concept.

In 2007, Elihu Katz, with co-author Tamar Liebes, published a journal article that radically revised both the definition and the worldview of *Media Events*. Katz and Liebes included "dark" events in the "media event" concept, distinguishing these unexpected, disruptive events from the carefully scripted, integrative events that had been the sole focus of *Media Events*.[39] They also argued that disruptive events—like disaster, terror, and war—have in fact upstaged "classical" ceremonial media events.[40] The authors mostly blamed this shift on the cynicism, disenchantment, and segmentation that were undermining attention to, and interest in, ceremonial events, as well as on the mobility and ubiquity of television technology and the downgrading of scheduled programming.[41]

Katz's and Liebes' arguments for the need to include disruptive events in the original concept of media events were ample and convincing. The case they made for their increased pessimism was far weaker. Consider for example the following paragraph, cherry-picking events that seem to justify a more pessimistic perspective on media events:

> The live broadcasting of "historic" ceremonies has lost its aura. Nixon's landslide triumph is soon followed by Watergate; drug scandals and hints of corruption have tainted the Olympics, not even to speak of the tragedy at Munich in 1972; the sentimentality induced by the Royal Wedding of Charles and Diana in 1981 is tainted by divorce and death; the stardom of John Kennedy, Anwar Sadat, and Yitzhak Rabin all end in assassinations.[42]

Each of these events could have been interpreted in a more hopeful way. Perhaps Watergate represented a democratic ritual of renewal after

Nixon's "polluted" landslide triumph;[43] the Olympic Games still attract enormous audiences despite the continuous scandals; the tragic fate of Prince Charles and Princess Diana has been softened by the hopeful stories of their children; and even after Kennedy, Sadat, and Rabin, charismatic figures continue to rise on the political scene.

Moreover, since the publication of Katz's and Liebes' article, at least five major global media events have challenged the authors' claim that disruptive events have upstaged integrative ones: the first Obama inauguration (2009); the Michael Jackson memorial (2009); the wedding of Prince William and Kate Middleton (2011); the Queen's golden jubilee (2012); and the Nelson Mandela memorial (2013). The global appeal of such integrative events strongly challenges the pessimism of Katz's and Liebes' article. In addition to these ceremonial media events, unexpected revolutionary events can also unite large international media audiences in a common experience of hope. A relatively recent example is the live-covered resignation of Egyptian President Hosni Mubarak during the "Arab Spring" in 2011 that people watched in many parts of the world.

Katz and Liebes were of course aware that hopeful revolutions might undermine their concept. After describing in detail the three types of disruptive events that were the focus of their article—namely war, disaster, and terror—they briefly referred to protests: "[a] fourth type, which might be called Protest and that may, however also include Revolution, deserves attention as well, though we will not elaborate here."[44] Revolutionary events did not fit their distinction between integrative (preplanned) and disruptive (unexpected) events. These events often seem to convey a message of hope and enthusiasm, while being cast as unexpected, or even miraculous.

Overall, Katz's and Liebes' article provided a more flexible taxonomy than *Media Events* and introduced a pessimistic, critical perspective on the chances of integrative events in our time. It succeeded in showing that media events need not be integrative; it failed to show that disruptive media events are displacing integrative ones over time.

Dayan's rethinking of media events took a slightly different route. In 2008, Dayan challenged the worldview that he and Katz had originally espoused and opened up their initial definition of media events so as to make it more inclusive. He did not offer, however, a firm judgment regarding the relative strengths and merits of integrative versus disruptive events. Dayan's chapter title already expressed his shifting worldview: the title included three words starting with either "dis" or "de": *Beyond Media*

Events: Disenchantment, Derailment, Disruption. Dayan did not propose a hierarchy among integrative and disruptive events in the way Katz and Liebes had done. But his piece was still shot through with disappointment:

> Media events have stopped being "irenic." Their semantics is no longer dominated by the theme of reduction of conflict through mediation and resolution of differences. (...) Media events still mobilize huge audiences, but they have lost a large part of their enchantment. Bureaucratically managed, they are an exploited resource within a political economy of collective attention. Their magic is dissipating. They have become strategic venues.[45]

Dayan explained his shifting worldview by reminding us that *Media Events* was published in 1992, an exceptional moment of global hope, the same year that Fukuyama's *The End of History and the Last Man* hit the bookshops. In contrast, our time is characterized by segmentation and disenchantment. These changes limit the potential of shared media events that he describes as having four major features: insistence and emphasis; an explicitly "performative," gestural dimension; loyalty to the event's self-definition; and access to a shared viewing experience.

Both Dayan and Katz opened up the original definition, but introduced a more critical view on the potential of having integrative events on the national or global level. Their revisions were published in a time of despair, after 9/11, the second intifada, and the London bombings and before major conciliatory events like the first Obama inauguration, the royal wedding of Prince William, and Nelson Mandela's funeral. The shadowed times in which these revisions were born rendered both articles darker than our contradictory reality. The authors mistook a moment for a permanent reality; they failed to recognize their own location in historical time.

Many other scholars have revised the original *Media Events* concept. Some of these scholars participated in various *Media Events* seminars organized by Katz and Dayan at the Hebrew University of Jerusalem and the Annenberg School of Communications at the University of Southern California during the decade the book came into being.[46]

Eric W. Rothenbuhler, who was connected to the media events discussions in Los Angeles, wrote his dissertation on the living room celebration of the Olympic Games as a form of civil religious activity. Based on nationally representative samples and waves of phone interviews, he tried to track how people "worshipped" the 1984 Olympic Games in their homes in a diversity of rituals. Rothenbuhler also examined the values and beliefs viewers attach to the Olympic Games.[47]

Barbie Zelizer participated in media events discussions at the Hebrew University and wrote her master's thesis on the broadcast of Sadat's arrival in Jerusalem.[48] But her first book moved beyond the narrowly defined genre of media events and analyzed both the Kennedy assassination (which did not qualify as a media event according to Dayan and Katz) and the Kennedy funeral.[49] Nearing the 30th anniversary of the Kennedy assassination, Zelizer pointed out that by acting as authoritative spokespersons of the event, journalists made the assassination story as much about themselves as about Kennedy. She also analyzed the retellings of the assassination, showing that journalists promoted themselves as the preferred narrators of the "assassination tale" over independent critics, historians, and even the Kennedy family.[50]

Paddy Scannell criticized *Media Events'* problematic attitude toward media history as early as 1995, when he argued that the book lacked historical depth. Scannell pointed out that many of the characteristics Dayan and Katz attributed to televised events could in fact also be found in the radio coverage of pre-television events.[51] He showed that various broadcasters within *one* national context provide distinctively different narratives of the same event to highly diverse audiences. Scannell also emphasized that many "magical moments" would not fit the strict definition of Dayan and Katz, but are nonetheless memorable media events, as was, for example, Nelson Mandela's unforgettable walk into freedom. Inspired by Dayan's and Katz's *Media Events*, in 2014 Scannell also published a powerful and original monograph on "television and the meaning of *live*," in which he contemplated the question of existence and the role of "events" in our social and mediated lives.[52]

James W. Carey argued convincingly for the inclusion of rituals of shame, degradation, and excommunication into the concept of media events. Carey emphasized that negative rituals like the judicial hearings of Watergate and the House Un-American Affairs Committee, or the hearings for Robert Bork's failed Supreme Court nomination, are bitter and intense, performed with the aim of sending "villains" into "internal exile."[53] Carey's suggestion to include these rituals into the concept of media events over time resonated with both Katz and Liebes and Dayan.[54]

Monroe E. Price and Daniel Dayan co-edited a volume that focused on the 2008 Beijing Olympics and revisited the concept of media events through the lens of this spectacular event.[55] The book's introduction listed globalization, the establishment of a stronger global civil society, the technological changes that were shaping public opinion, and China's special place in the geopolitical order as reasons for placing this event at the center of analysis.

So far, the most substantial piece of rethinking has come from Europe. In 2010 Nick Couldry, Andreas Hepp, and Friedrich Krotz published a co-edited book entitled *Media Events in a Global Age* with an introductory theoretical chapter by Hepp and Couldry.[56] The editors intended to update the media events concept within an analysis of translocal media cultures. In their scheme of thought *media cultures* refer to "all cultures whose *primary resources* of meaning are accessible through technology-based media," while *translocal* stands for cultures within or beyond national cultures.[57] These cultures may utilize relatively centralized or decentralized media platforms.[58]

Inspired by Émile Durkheim's link between ritual and social integration and Edward Shils' concept of a "sacred center," Dayan and Katz highlighted media events' contribution to social integration through the reassurance of shared beliefs.[59] In contrast, building on Couldry's earlier work on media rituals, Hepp and Couldry spoke of a "mediated center," the myth that powerful and hegemonic media are the key sites for articulating what matters in our societies.[60] In their view, media events play diverse roles in the construction of a mediated center. Therefore we need to critically analyze processes of power construction and centering in each case of a media event and contrast the media representations with the everyday appropriation and understanding of the event.

Combining Dayan's four defining elements with a "translocal" understanding of media cultures, Hepp and Couldry also came up with a new definition for media events in a global age: "media events are certain situated, thickened, centering performances of mediated communication that are focused on a specific thematic core, cross different media products and reach a wide and diverse multiplicity of audiences and participants."[61] One of the most important inventions of their definition was its lack of medium-specificity. They used the broad and flexible term "mediated communication" and emphasized media events' ability to cross media platforms. The authors did not limit the event's message in terms of integrative or disruptive meanings either: the event only had to have a "specific thematic core." Live-ness was no longer a requirement, clearing the space for meaningful events that did not receive live coverage.

Moreover, Hepp and Couldry also opened up the definition for constituencies beyond and within the nation and allowed for multiple "we's" in the global context.

While these revisions are powerful, the definition's first part is more complex. For instance, "centering performances" stands for media events' participation in the construction of a mediated center. "Centering" highlights that the thematic core of the event is central to the narratives of the events. "Centering" also signals that the thematic core is linked to the center of a community, a society, the world, or some other social entity. In this definition, the "magic" of media events has somewhat gone missing.

In sum, all these scholarly writings in communication studies grasped important aspects of the media narration of events. They are like puzzle pieces that did not come together in one picture that would show *how stories of events travel in fragmented interpretive spaces, over time and across media.* My next chapter will try to put these various puzzle pieces together and provide a new understanding of events in media. Instead of freezing events in one moment in time, in one country, and in one medium, I hope to show how they travel through time, space, and media.

2

Global Iconic Events

THE FIVE DIMENSIONS OF TRANSNATIONAL STORYTELLING

EVENTS BECOME GLOBALLY significant through processes of transnational narration. Chains of occurrences, which may or may not have "larger" social and political significance, gain symbolic importance through our universalized stories. Consider, for instance, one of the most powerful myths of Western history, the taking of the Bastille. This event was *not* the most important military occurrence in the French revolution. According to historians, it was the bloodless capture of the Invalides that was the "decisive military action."[1] Still, through processes of signification, the "taking of the Bastille" quickly became the most essential representation of the complex process we call the 1789 French revolution. As William H. Sewell Jr. pointed out, three short days after the storming of the Bastille, the popular newspaper *Les Révolutions Paris* already called the attackers "citizens" and the chaotic urban militia "soldiers of the nation," and characterized the bloody and confusing events as liberation from despotism. Never mind that the soldiers of the nation liberated only seven prisoners, including four convicted forgers: this is *not* what we remember. We remember a spectacular moment of liberation. So how do events, like the storming of the Bastille, come into being from a network of messy happenings? What characterizes the narration of lasting international events?

The framework I would propose starts with a new name: "global iconic events." *I define global iconic events as news events that international media cover extensively and remember ritually.* Global iconic events are not universal, but they have historic significance and meaning in more than one country and in more than one region. In other words, global iconic events are manifestations of what Daniel Levy and Natan Sznaider call "cosmopolitan memory:" they are condensed stories with lasting international resonance.[2] They are not bound to a particular nation or social group. They travel through temporal and spatial boundaries and cross from one medium to another. While my definition does not directly refer to audiences, both the name "global" iconic events and the requirement of "extensive coverage" indirectly suggest audiences that are substantial and actively engaged in their viewing and reading experiences. These audiences serve as witnesses to global iconic events.[3]

The term *iconic* is overused—we apply it casually to just about anything, from soft drinks to designer bags. In the case of global iconic events "iconic" refers to three qualities: resemblance, salience, and sacredness. Global iconic events *resemble* certain aspects of the original event, but they come to represent something larger. They express the mythical in the modern, communicating messages like loss, destruction, division, and freedom. Global iconic events are also *salient*: they are exceptional. These events are major social dramas with lasting presence on the world stage. Finally, iconic also expresses *sacredness*: people want to touch and worship the "myth," making the event's story contagious in the transnational space as these events get recycled in new narratives and replicated in contemporary social performances.

Covered extensively means that the coverage of these events is not limited to short news items; they get substantial media attention as they unfold or over time. The events and their narration can be far away in time. Just consider the Warsaw ghetto uprising during the Holocaust, a major historical event that international media barely reported in its own time, which is certainly extensively discussed and ritually remembered now.[4] Similarly, "Watergate" was transformed into a "scandal" only over long months.[5] This scandal was indeed a "long national nightmare," as President Gerald Ford put it. And Masada offers a compelling example of the belated social construction of events from the ancient world. Masada, a fortress built on the top of a mountain in the Judean desert, served as the last refuge of the Jewish resistance against the Romans in 73 A.D. When it became clear that the Roman invasion of the fortress was inevitable, the leader of the Jewish rebels convinced his community to commit mass suicide. After almost two thousand years, this simplified and universalized heroic myth has become one of the most resonant stories of Zionism and plays a crucial role in the nation-building of modern Israel.[6] As Israeli novelist Avraham B. Yehoshua put it, "[t]ime has passed and Masada is no longer the historic mountain near the Dead Sea, but a mobile mountain which we carry on our back anywhere we go."[7]

Remembered ritually highlights that international media frequently refer to these events, and in some cases even strictly commemorate them at anniversaries. Forms of ritualized media memory include the coverage of official ceremonies as well as new journalistic pieces and special editions or broadcasts devoted to commemorating the event, for instance op-eds, interviews, essays, surveys, blog posts, oral histories, and documentaries.[8] A powerful example for ritual remembrance is the anniversary coverage of 9/11, when the American and international media report on official and private ceremonies, the victims' families, the changing visual appearance of Ground Zero, and the steps to prevent similar attacks.[9]

The media coverage and remembrance of global iconic events need to be sustained at a significant *transnational* level. For instance, while Masada grew into a national iconic event over time, it has failed to achieve lasting international resonance. Masada is not an exception in this respect: there are many similar "local" events that do not travel across national borders and cultural distinctions. They might become celebrated national or regional events without being turned into a transnational symbolic occasion.

While iconic events can be built up over time even if the original coverage did not signal their significance, the reverse is not true: if an occurrence received extensive media coverage initially or at a given time in the past but has since faded from memory, we cannot call it an iconic event until its ritual remembrance begins. There are also what we might call "rollercoaster" global iconic events that international media cover extensively and remember ritually for a while, but that subsequently lose their significance. To take a complex example, the significance of the Hungarian anti-Soviet revolution of 1956 was widely recognized in the West during most of the early Cold War. In 1989, the event went through a revival because its local official interpretation shifted due to the Hungarian political transition from communism to democracy. However, after 1989 the event's significance faded from international memory as the West moved on from the Cold War discourse in the early nineties. Events can shift in and out of global and national salience: a flexible application of the definition of global iconic events is needed to consider these challenging cases.

I deliberately do not provide a definition of *media*. To understand why, consider the example of Théodore Géricault's famous painting, the *Raft of the Medusa*, from around 1818–1819. The painting was inspired by a major news event of that time: the wreck of a French naval frigate off the coast of present-day Mauritiana. Géricault collected as many news stories, public documents, and eyewitness testimonies about the expedition and the shipwreck as possible. He read the bestselling accounts of two survivors, carefully examined all related journalistic images, commissioned the surviving carpenter of the *Medusa* to build him a model of the raft, and even had body parts delivered to his studio so he could "smell" the event. The outcome of his careful research was the large-scale visual condensation of the event now known as the *Raft of the Medusa*.

The 450-square-foot painting became a successful attraction when it was exhibited in London, partly because a theatrical play that was being performed only a few blocks away about the same event provided extra publicity for Géricault's painting. In Dublin, however, Géricault's painting fared far less well. Why? Because there it was met by a strong visual competitor—a 10,000-square-foot spectacular moving panorama, *The Wreck of the Medusa*.[10] Even as early as the 1820s, there were events that were narrated and visualized transnationally, using technologies that are often excluded from contemporary definitions of news media.[11] By adopting a broad and flexible definition, I hope to open up a space for discussion about historic news events—and formats—that may be atypical for the general discourse on media events.

Do we need modern mass media for global iconic events? No, we do not. Narrative practices that create global iconic events have always characterized human life.[12] For instance, Biblical stories successfully traveled well before the age of mass media. But mass media alter the ways in which the narratives and visuals of the events are built and spread. As Karl Marx summarized this process in 1871, albeit from a critical perspective:

> Up until now it has been thought that the growth of the Christian myths during the Roman Empire was possible only because printing was not yet invented. Precisely the contrary. The daily press and the telegraph, which in a moment spread inventions over the whole earth, fabricate more myths . . . in one day than could have formerly been done in a century.[13]

Contemporary mass media can accelerate meaning-making processes around events; they may spread the event's message faster and further. Mass media also elevate occurrences into events, thus shifting meaning and significance.

While a concept of global iconic events has to have historic depth, it also needs to pay attention to present-day changes in the news ecology. Is it possible to require extensive coverage and ritual remembrance of global iconic events given the fragmented and diverse, "new" and "social" media landscape of our time? As I argued in my review of Katz and Liebes' article in Chapter 1, certain international news events still manage to interrupt the flow of time and bridge the disparities between cultures, gaining the attention of many professional journalists, amateur storytellers, and large audiences.[14] Powerful examples are the royal wedding of Prince William and Kate Middleton, the inauguration of the first African American president, the memorial of Nelson Mandela, and major terrorist attacks (for instance the 2015 Paris attacks). Has everybody watched these events? Have all journalists covered them? Have all media outlets paid equal attention to them? No, of course not—but that has never been the case with media events, not even in the heyday of "integrative" television. And while audiences might follow the story of an event on multiple media platforms, they are still paying attention to the same exceptional event.[15] Fragmented audiences even try to gather in shared "places" to discuss the events, for instance under popular hashtags on Twitter.

Events, of course, have a way of outsmarting social science. A definition of global iconic events has to be flexible enough to accommodate events that trick the system and still manage to become iconic. The definition is deliberately vague so as to invite, rather than exclude, creative empirical studies that can accommodate each of the definitional elements. In addition to the definition outlined above, I propose that five narrative dimensions be considered in connection with the transnational narration of iconic events (Fig. 2.1). These narrative dimensions are *not* "criteria": the relative significance and weight of each of these dimensions will depend upon the nature and circumstances of any specific event.

Foundation: Narrative Prerequisites of the Event

Foundation refers to the knowledge we already have about the event's context, place and history. In other words, when narrating an event, we build on the event's *symbolic hinterland*, on its preexisting symbols. Knowing about the Twin Towers helps to strengthen the story of 9/11. Understanding the Syrian crisis makes it somewhat easier to follow the refugee crisis of 2015. Knowing the preexisting symbolic moments of the fall of the Berlin Wall, for instance the Berlin Airlift, the erection of the Berlin Wall, and

---

GLOBAL ICONIC EVENTS

1. Foundation: Narrative prerequisites of the event

2. Mythologization: The development of the event's resonant message and elevated language

3. Condensation: The event's encapsulation in a "brand" of a simple phrase, a short narrative, and a recognizable visual scene

4. Counter-narration: The emergence of alternative narratives that reinterpret the event

5. Remediation: The event's travel across multiple media platforms and diverse social and political contexts

---

FIGURE 2.1 The five dimensions of transnational storytelling.

John F. Kennedy's "Ich bin ein Berliner" speech, makes the story of this event more resonant to us.

When analyzing the narration of lasting international news events, we also need to consider the complex process in which narrators strip an "event" down to its unique, exceptional, once-in-a-lifetime qualities. In the case of the 2008 Beijing Olympics, for example, we have to understand how narrators managed to elevate it above the long and complex history of organizing Olympic tournaments in a wide variety of countries. What makes this an "event" rather than simply "one moment in a repetitive process"? Monroe E. Price addressed this narrative challenge: "[e]verything about Beijing 2008 had to be spectacular, superlative, outsized. [. . .] Even the smog, reframed as just another barrier for the powers that be to overcome, would be turned into a sign of what Beijing could and would accomplish."[16]

All events require some form of effort to be set apart from the ordinary, to rise above their "smog." All *events* have to become more powerful than the *process* that they are part of. For instance, if a revolution is the object of our analysis, then we must consider how narrators elevate this "event" above the underlying and ongoing process of "political transition." Take the 2011 Egyptian revolution. Egypt had already been going through some level of political transition before that specific event—and it certainly did so afterwards. To turn the revolution into an event, narrators had to argue that it was not simply one of many steps in a long process of political transition, but that it was a stand-alone item. Or, to consider a very different sort of event, the 1969 moon landing is not remembered as simply one moment in the complex history of the space race: it is an exceptional, magical event that requires a separate and considerable storytelling treatment.

In thinking about the narrative prerequisites of an event, we must also consider the balance between the power of the *occurrence* (the "stuff" happening on the ground) and the power of the occurrence's story as an *event*. This distinction has also fascinated philosophers and historians in their understanding of events. For instance, French philosopher Gilles Deleuze differentiated between "incident" and its "meaning" within a larger category of event, and American historian William H. Sewell Jr. drew attention to the crucial distinction between a "sequence of occurrences" and their "meaning" as an event.[17] The question we repeatedly need to ask: how much power does an occurrence possess inherently and how much is provided by its narration? Of course, occurrences do provide some boundaries for their narrators; the past can resist its storytellers quite powerfully. But within these boundaries narrators still have quite a bit of leeway in shaping the story.[18] Both the "raw" occurrence and its constructed story matter if we want to understand why particular occurrences become "events" while others do not. In other words, our consideration should always include the delicate power balance between the "occurrence" and its story as an "event."

Mythologization: The Development of the Event's Resonant Message and Elevated Language

When narrating global iconic events, journalists lift their sights from the earth-bound detail to lofty universals. Journalists engage in mythmaking: they communicate internationally resonant social meanings, like division, renewal, loss, and hope.[19] According to historian and scholar of religion Mircea Eliade, the term "myth" has two main meanings. First, an invented fictional story; as the Greeks put it, contrasting *mythos* with *logos* and *historia, mythos* is "what cannot really exist." Second, a sacred, exemplary, and significant story that describes "the various and sometimes dramatic breakthroughs of the sacred (or the 'supernatural') into the World."[20] I use *myth* in the second, "positive" sense, not to denote something skillfully manufactured with the intention of distortion.[21] I take mythmaking to be a process of simplification and universalization that enables large and diverse international audiences to relate to an event. Myths describe and create realities and highlight the power of the sacred in our lives and histories.

To build the mythical story of an event, journalists have to eliminate incomprehensible facts, confusing processes, and messy webs of actors. They have to turn an occurrence into an occasion and replace the actual with the symbolically potent. Like other social myths, the stories of global iconic events are powerful and resonant because they speak to our hearts rather than convincing our minds. While specific facts may alienate those unfamiliar with the exact context, mythical stories appeal and attract by touching on the relatively universal. To be sure, "universal" does not mean that anyone without any knowledge of the context would immediately understand a particular event in all its aspects. These events are not interpreted identically in distinct parts of the world. Nonetheless, differing degrees of knowledge and interpretation often retain the core social meaning of a global iconic event unaltered.

The speed at which journalists develop a mythical language for a given event and the language's duration can vary. As Michael Schudson has shown, after 9/11 American journalists used a strongly elevated language for about two weeks.[22] However, by September 28, 2001, they had largely returned to their regular, factual, and objective reporting style. In the case of the fall of the Berlin Wall, as this book argues, West German newspapers made this shift after ten days, around November 19, 1989. The events of the Holocaust, to give a third, more complex example, present a particularly challenging puzzle in this respect, as it took around two decades to develop and spread their mythical core message. In April 1945, they were described simply as "atrocities" in the pages of the American printed press and on the radio, placed among many brutalities of a world war. It has been a long way to get from there to the Holocaust's current status, with its moral connotations widely recognized and accepted in the West.[23]

When constructing the mythical story of the event, journalists generally reside in the "sphere of consensus" as opposed to the "sphere of legitimate controversy," to use media scholar Daniel C. Hallin's distinction.[24] In the sphere of consensus, journalists speak in the name of an imagined "we," employing a language of shared values and assumptions. Later, when they are ritually remembering the event—at anniversaries, for instance—journalists occasionally move back to this sphere of consensus, replaying or recycling the event's original language.

Condensation: The Event's Encapsulation in a "Brand" of a Simple Phrase, a Short Narrative, and a Recognizable Visual Scene

Global iconic events become lasting symbolic reference points if they can be easily referred to. Therefore, they need narrative "branding." While complex and confusing at first, through repeated acts of storytelling global iconic events are condensed over time into a *simple phrase*, a *short narrative*, and a *recognizable visual scene*. The simple phrases enable us to easily refer to the event and recycle it in new contexts. The short narrative pushes the event's mythologization even further, presenting the transnational message of the event in a more condensed and stabilized form. The visual scene contributes to quick recognition and to the event's reproduction in a variety of formats and embodiments. For instance, the "atomic bombing of Hiroshima and Nagasaki" offers a short narrative about technological apocalypse and we recognize the mushroom cloud as its representative imagery. Similarly, the "fall of the Berlin Wall" has a concise narrative of freedom and also a sequence of memorable images. "9/11" provides us with a contemporary version of the Biblical story of the Tower of Babel along with an unforgettable set of images of the burning and collapsing World Trade Center. Condensation into a simple phrase, a short narrative, and a recognizable visual scene thus helps us quickly and directly refer to confusing and multilayered events.

Like powerful theatrical performances, global iconic events also need key figures, objects, and places. The stories of global iconic events become more poignant if they include symbolic persons, symbolic objects, and symbolic places. These symbolic persons, objects, and places help embody the social meaning of the event, and aid its condensation into a simple phrase, a short narrative, and a recognizable visual scene. For instance, when we think about apartheid, we often think of the "hero" Nelson Mandela. Stories and images of the imprisoned anti-apartheid activist and first democratically elected president of South Africa have become symbolic condensations of the entire tragic event called apartheid. Similarly, Mahatma Gandhi worked strategically on becoming the symbol of nonviolent social movements, whether in India or elsewhere in the world. The "digital revolution" also proudly immortalizes the memory of its symbolic person, the legendary Apple innovator Steve Jobs. "Villains" can embody an event as well; prominent examples are Richard Nixon for Watergate, Pol Pot for the Cambodian genocide, and Slobodan Milošević for the wars in former Yugoslavia.[25]

Symbolic objects, too, can play a significant role in the narrative and the imagery of news events. In the context of the Rwandan genocide, for instance, the machete has become a recognizable and memorable object: the physical wounds inflicted by the weapon are symbolic proxies for the genocide inflicted upon individuals as well as on society at large. We also often remember a symbolic building or a symbolic place when we remember news events: recalling the visual appearance of the place helps us connect to the event itself. The 2008 Mumbai terrorist attacks, for example, have been captured in thousands of digital photographs that circulated online, on television, and in newspapers; yet while we might not specifically remember an individual photograph, we do remember the Taj Mahal Palace & Tower, the site of the attacks. The building's distinctive architectural features made it a memorable symbolic place. Similarly, Tahrir Square is central to the memory of the 2011 Egyptian revolution, Ground Zero is the locus of 9/11 and the Normandy coast is a site of memory for D-Day. All these examples show that symbolic figures, objects, and places can contribute to the narrative branding of events and can serve their transition into a format that is readily transportable across boundaries.

Through the processes of textual and visual condensation, global iconic events also become compressions of time and space: they often come to stand for something that lasts longer and is larger than themselves. The atomic bombings of Hiroshima and Nagasaki meant not "only" the first act of using an atomic weapon; this event also stands for eternal fears of a global nuclear war. Similarly, the fall of the Berlin Wall represents more than one historic night in which East and West Germans embraced; it also serves as a shorthand for the end of the Cold War—something larger and more durable than what November 9, 1989, could offer. Finally, 9/11 does not simply denote a tragic day on a calendar; it stands for a game-changing event in world politics, the beginning of what was once called "the war on terror."

Overall, condensation is a process of crystallization, clarification, and re-presentation. During condensation, the event's contextual details, contradictions, and confusions are increasingly edited out to make the event's meaning accessible. Condensation also refers to the global iconic event's encapsulation in symbolic persons, objects, and places. These easily recognizable representations strongly support the lasting resonance of global iconic events.

Counter-narration: The Emergence of Alternative Narratives That Reinterpret the Event

Next, global iconic events have alternative stories that interpret them in a different light. Global iconic events might even have strong counter-narratives that refute their significance or that even question whether the event "in fact" took place. The mythological character of global iconic events makes them particularly vulnerable to such practices of counter-narration: it is precisely an event's elevated story that those with contrasting interests single out for counter-narration, revealing its inherent inaccuracy.

Some counter-narratives do not question that the event took place, but interpret it in contrasting ways. For instance, while 1948 means the War of Independence for Israelis, the same year is marked as Nakba ("catastrophe") in the Palestinian consciousness. Other counter-narratives deny the scale of an event, questioning its significance. A prominent example is the 1915–1918 Armenian genocide perpetrated by the declining Ottoman Empire. Many countries accept it as "genocide," while others, led by Turkey as successor to the Ottoman Empire, find this label excessive and ahistorical. Even a hundred years after the event, choosing a label for mass murder remains a global political issue with high diplomatic stakes.

Counter-narratives can also shift responsibility, changing, for instance, the perpetrator of a crime. A famous example is the Katyn Massacre. In April and May 1940, after the Soviet invasion of Poland, thousands of Polish military officers and civilians were murdered. The victims were rounded up by the Soviet army and murdered by the NKVD, but the official Soviet narrative blamed the Germans for the crime until as recently as 1989. In fact, the very first Russian leader to place a wreath at the burial site was Vladimir Putin in 2010, seventy years after the event.[26]

Painfully different narratives of an event can develop even within *one* society. For instance, traumatic events that were perpetrated by one group of a society against the other inevitably trigger contrasting stories. An infamous example is the Cambodian genocide from 1975 until 1979, in which approximately one-fifth of the country's population perished. Still, the genocide's chief perpetrator, Pol Pot, denied the mass murder until his death in 1998.[27] In 2013, Cambodia even had to introduce a law against genocide denial, an indication that these denials may still frequently occur.

Conflicting narratives can also arise *within* the group of perpetrators or victims. Just consider the heated debate about the Warsaw ghetto uprising in Israeli newspapers in 2013, on the seventieth anniversary of the event. Authors debated the exact number of rebels, the length of the uprising, and the proper meaning of the event for future generations. As one of the authors put his position in an article tellingly entitled "The Warsaw Ghetto Myth": "[t]he ghetto fighters may have been brave, but they didn't fight as long as has been depicted. And what right did they have to decide the fate of 50,000 others?"[28] These debates both crystallize *and* destabilize the meaning of an event, helping and complicating its condensation into a simple narrative.

Counter-narratives can also be developed and enforced by the ruling political power. A striking example is the Hungarian communist party's narration of the 1956 Hungarian revolution until the democratic political changes in 1989. The Hungarian local party press focused on a few, exceptionally violent hours of the, as the regime called it, "counterrevolution," when protesters murdered several defenders of the Budapest party headquarters. Journalists constructed iconic personalities of this event: the martyrs, the mourning families, the few survivors, and also the heroes, who saved lives. Republic Square, where the murders occurred, became the iconic place of the counterrevolution, and the victims' bodies were presented as iconic objects. These icons as symbolic condensations served as powerful journalistic tools that represented the framing of the events as counterrevolutionary and furthered the regime's desire to erase the vernacular memory of the event.[29]

As all these examples show, a careful analysis of how events travel through time, space, and media must pay attention to the existence and structure of the events' competing stories. These competing stories can strengthen or limit an occurrence's potential to become a global iconic event.

Remediation: The Event's Travel Across Multiple Media Platforms and Diverse Social and Political Contexts

Finally, the event's simple phrase, short narrative, and recognizable visual scene travel through time, space, and media and get reused in distinctively different political, social, and cultural environments. Forms of remediation are diverse and strongly change from one event to the other. In this book I will highlight four forms of remediation: *recycling, reenactment, possession,* and *memorialization*. Recycling happens when the phrase, narrative, and visual scene of the event are recalled in connection with seemingly similar events. Reenactment is the term I use for social performances that imitate the "original" event or its imagery. Possession, as with the pieces of the Berlin Wall collected and preserved as relics, is also a common way people connect to myth. People want to "touch" the event, relating to it in an elementary, corporeal way. Finally, memorialization is the event's commemoration in anniversary journalism, memorials, and exhibitions.

The "dimensions" of condensation and remediation are not easily separated; they overlap considerably. Also, the package of simple phrase, short narrative, and recognizable visual scene may break down as the event travels: its components do not always appear or reappear together. Often, the package does not travel through time, space, and media accidentally; direct promotion can enhance the event's portability and mobility. Commemorative ceremonies, memorials, monuments, rituals of remembrance, and campaigns need promoters as well: the politics of remembrance is key to any study of global iconic events.

Overall, remediation contributes to what historian Alison Landsberg called "prosthetic memory," the emergence of solidarity and identification with an event that we (or our families) may not have experienced personally.[30] The story of the event starts to travel, finding home in diverse locations and hearts in distinct parts of the globe. Through remediation, the event's condensed story begins to act like a contemporary myth. The event is expressed through narratives, performances, and objects, and with the support of these embodiments, it remains alive for extended periods of time.

Why Do We Need a New Concept of Global Iconic Events?

New theoretical frameworks are useful if they help us better understand a crucial aspect of social life. What kind of insight, then, does this new concept of global iconic events offer? The concept of global iconic events enhances our understanding of the cultural dimensions of globalization. In his critique of the discourse of globalization, American sociologist Jeffrey C. Alexander has argued that while we frequently discuss the unprecedented compression of space and time in the "global age," our understanding of the compression of *meaning* is far less developed.[31] Paying attention to the compression of meaning in transnational communication, in this book I ask whether and how a news story, resonating over a long period of time, can function as a social myth for global civil society. With the concept of global iconic events I also expand Daniel Dayan's and Elihu Katz's *Media Events* by considering how the stories of events travel through time and media in highly fragmented interpretive spaces.[32]

Throughout this book I argue that the *only* opportunity for a local incident to acquire long-term resonance globally is if it becomes a simple and readily transportable myth. This happens first through the development of a mythical journalistic language that builds on already existing narrative prerequisites. Then, through condensation, the event becomes a "brand" of a simple phrase, a short narrative, and a recognizable visual scene. Next, the event's simple phrase, short narrative, and visual scene start to travel globally, together or separately. Finally, throughout the event's remediation, I argue, counter-narration, narrowly factual storytelling, forgetting, and other factors can create *roadblocks* to travel that some events are never able to overcome.

Is it possible to describe this process as media distortion, as a violent attempt of global media to silence and simplify local meaning-making? It is certainly possible in many cases. No doubt distant suffering is often sensationalized and simplified for Western consumption at the expense of local context and nuance. Media researchers have to be sensitive to this misuse of power. But we need to think *much* harder in assessing condensation. We cannot presume that local meaning must be richer and more fragile, that Western representations must be strategic, and that the fundamental contest is *always* between the two. For instance, in the case of the most covered and remembered event of the collapse of communism, the fall of the Berlin Wall, West German narrators were simultaneously Western and local. They described events they were intimately connected with, adapting them into a simple and readily transportable format for their local (and, through further mediation, international) audience. The contest was not between powerful Westerners and hesitant locals, but between the mythical and the narrowly factual. Moreover, Western narrators built on the story of the Berlin Wall that was *co-developed* by East and West, as I will show in my next chapter.

This book thus focuses on the desire in *all of us* from East, West, North, and South to construct and remember events that are larger than our messy lives and confusing histories. Media scholars like to discuss the violent and habitual practices of international media, with central metaphors of "squashing," "silencing," and "cannibalizing." I recommend equally carefully describing a cooperative process, which succeeds only rarely, using central metaphors like diffusion and remediation. Instead of cherishing local experience in *all* cases, we may, at some occasions, celebrate the surrender of the local to the universal.

Global iconic events structure time and provide us vulnerable humans with lasting orientation points. They shine like the star of Bethlehem to help us find our way. Global iconic events are also compressions of social meanings—simplified stories with resonance and endurance that help us interpret the challenges of our time. As quick reference points, they can serve the same function myths served for traditional societies. However, the social construction and maintenance of global iconic events require substantial narrative and promotional effort. Moreover, global iconic events operate in fragmented and hybrid interpretive spaces.[33] There will always be those who will under-narrate, counter-narrate, or simply ignore them. Therefore, global iconic events will remain rare. They will always be exceptional wonders for the individuals and societies inhabiting this confusing space we call the "global."

3

Foundation

MY FIRST TWO chapters drew the contours of a new concept of global iconic events. In the next five chapters, I will consider this concept in connection with the "fall of the Berlin Wall." With the selection of this spectacular and uniquely consensual event, I hope to show that an event as magical as the fall of the Berlin Wall is still a result of strong narrative and performative effort on the transnational stage. The fall of the Berlin Wall had to be *constructed* as a global iconic event, and its construction was not easy. Throughout these chapters the concept of global iconic events will provide the framework for the presentation of empirical details. Each chapter will highlight one dimension of transnational storytelling—foundation, mythologization, condensation, counter-narration, and remediation.

This first chapter is thus dedicated to the first dimension of the global narration of the fall of the Berlin Wall: foundation. When you narrate an event, you emphasize those aspects of the event that you would like others to remember, and hide the ones you do not find useful. As German historian Reinhart Koselleck argued, "[e]very historical portrayal represents a *selection* from the potentially limitless field of things endured or enacted in the past."[1] At the same time, "occurrences" of the past will also limit your imagination: they will set some boundaries for your creative storytelling.

Narrating an event like the fall of the Berlin Wall requires at least two major narrative steps. First, the story of the fall of the Berlin Wall has to build upon the story of the Berlin Wall itself—and become its happy ending. Second, storytellers need to set the event of the fall of the Berlin Wall apart from the slow and transitional process that was at play in East Germany in 1989. Storytellers need to elevate the event above the process and the regular: it has to become independent and magical, marking the end of the Berlin Wall era. This chapter gives brief analyses of the Berlin Wall story and that of East Germany in 1989. To understand how journalists and other storytellers narrated the fall of the Berlin Wall, we must consider these narrative prerequisites and contexts.

Foundation I: How the Berlin Wall Became a Symbol

Late on a cold November night in 1989, due to the erroneous announcement of a new travel regulation, the immense confusion and agony that pervaded the East German political leadership, and efficient communication by some West German broadcast media, crowds were able to cross the border between East and West Berlin. Calling this event the "fall of the Berlin Wall" was possible only because both the East and the West were already speaking of the Berlin border in metaphorical, rather than fact-oriented, terms.

The Berlin Wall as a single, coherent wall dividing a nation is an abstraction, an imagined entity, whose name was somehow accepted from the start. In reality, the Berlin Wall was a multifaceted border-control regime with a continuously changing material presence and an ever-shifting aesthetic design. If we want to understand the Berlin Wall as a symbol, we must consider its real material qualities. In particular, we need to ask how the complex East German border-control regime looked in its physical reality, as compared to the simple Berlin Wall symbol featured in Western memory. In other words, we first have to draw a mental map of all the elements of the German border-control regime in order to grasp the symbolic power of the "Berlin Wall."

The Berlin Wall differed from most famous fortifications in two important ways: it divided *one* community and it was designed to keep people in, not out. The Berlin Wall was erected to block emigration from East Germany. Between the founding of East Germany in 1949 and the erection of the Berlin Wall in 1961, an estimated 2.7 million people had left the East German state to the West. Although many of them decided to emigrate for political reasons, economic factors played an important part in the mass exodus as well. While West Germany experienced an economic boom in the 1950s, East Germany, due to its policies of economic centralization and agricultural collectivization, was faced with shortages of consumer goods and housing.

Hoping to stop the massive waves of emigration, East Germany had already sealed its border with West Germany in 1952, except for the borderline between East Berlin and West Berlin. On August 13, 1961, East Germany closed the only remaining open section of the border: we call this section the "Berlin Wall" Fig. 3.1). Was the Berlin Wall immediately a wall? No, it was not. In its very first form the Berlin Wall looked more like Berlin Barbed Wire. So much barbed wire was needed, in fact, that a Socialist Unity Party (SED) internal memo expressed concern that the country just did not possess enough material to do the job. Indeed, as German art historian Leo Schmidt has noted: "[w]hat could be more typical of East Germany than that the wall's history began with a supply shortfall?"[2] Only barbed

FIGURE 3.1 West Berlin, 1961. A boy standing in front of a barbed-wire fence holding an issue of *Berliner Morgenpost* announcing that East Berlin is closed off. Georgi/The Granger Collection, New York.

wire made it possible to finish the job within the five short hours between 1 a.m. and 6 a.m., August 13, 1961. But this provisional sealing required more work.

There were *four* distinct generations of the Berlin Wall during its 28-year existence.[3] The first-generation wall was approximately two meters high and consisted mostly of square cinderblock elements. Where buildings stood in the way of the Wall, residents were evacuated and their windows were bricked up (Fig. 3.2). Although this first-generation wall was no longer a barbed-wire fence, there was still confusion about its name. For instance, a famous documentary shot during the first two weeks of the Wall was titled "Die Mauer" (The Wall). But its sequel, showing the fortification and augmentation of the wall through the end of December 1961, was called "Stacheldraht" (Barbed Wire).[4] And the West German studio that broadcast right from the Berlin border to the east side was named "Studio am Stacheldraht" (Studio at the Barbed Wire).[5] But over time, the Berlin Barbed Wire began to look more and more like a Berlin Wall.

A second-generation wall was built in 1962. This wall was largely a fortification of the previous barrier, not exactly a new design (Fig. 3.3). Heavy concrete slabs replaced many of the cinderblocks to discourage escapes with vehicles. Then, in 1965, East Germany erected a more professional, third-generation wall that consisted of "fairly narrow concrete slabs inserted horizontally between H-sectioned posts of reinforced concrete; it was then topped by lengths of concrete sewage pipe, rendering it virtually impossible to scale."[6] Finally, in the mid-1970s, a fourth-generation wall, the Border Wall 75, sought to solve all previous problems with a physically and aesthetically perfected design (Fig. 3.4). Border Wall 75 resulted from a long research and design process that had even included the erection of test walls. This fourth-generation wall needed no foundations and was so strong that virtually no vehicle would ever break through. The surface of the Border Wall 75 was smooth and white, conveying coherence as well as power.

The story of the four generations of the Wall is a story about progress in design. But the four types of wall can also be regarded as symbols for the changing international image of East Germany. From 1961 to 1965, the period of the first- and second-generation walls, the East German state was isolated from the field of international relations. In 1949, when the German Democratic Republic (GDR) and the Federal Republic of Germany (FRG) were founded, the West German FRG did not recognize

FIGURE 3.2 West Berlin, September 24, 1961. An East Berliner, 77-year-old Frieda Schulze, escaping out of her apartment window to the western side of the city, as the West Berlin fire brigade stands by. Ullstein Bild/The Granger Collection, New York.

the East German GDR as a state. Beginning in 1963, however, West Germany's policy of political isolation gradually began to soften; the two German states over time negotiated border passes for West Germans and started ransoming East German political prisoners. The Berlin Wall continued to remain impermeable for East Germans. In 1969, when the Wall

FIGURE 3.3 Berlin Wall, June 17, 1963. People standing on ladders in West Berlin, looking over the wall toward East Berlin. Von der Becke/The Granger Collection, New York.

was in its third generation, Willy Brandt became West German chancellor. He was the candidate of the Social Democratic Party of Germany and came to power after twenty years of Christian Democratic Union leadership. Brandt introduced a more collaborative "Ostpolitik," aimed at easing the pain caused by the Wall by accepting the division.[7] In the German–German basic treaty of 1972, West Germany finally recognized East Germany as an independent state. The third-generation Wall witnessed a shift in East German political leadership as well, as Erich Honecker

0110373   BERLIN WALL, 1976.
Credit: Rue des Archives / The Granger Collection, New York

FIGURE 3.4 Berlin Wall, 1976. Viewed toward East Berlin. Rue des Archives/The Granger Collection, New York.

succeeded Walter Ulbricht. By 1975, when the fourth-generation Wall arrived, East Germany was admitted to the United Nations Educational, Scientific and Cultural Organization (UNESCO) and established diplomatic relations with France and Great Britain. It was a relatively hopeful time for East German politics, and the Wall's design reflected a newly gained confidence. At the same time, the increasingly professional and expensive Wall also helped to conceal the economic realities of the GDR: it was meant to hide the country's growing despair and highly inefficient economy.

Telling the story of four generations of walls brings to light the changing aesthetics of, and politics around, the Wall. That said, the idea that there were *four* generations reflects a Western perspective.[8] This narrative of a "single wall" focuses only on how the Berlin Wall changed over the years as seen from the *Western* side; it pays little attention to the physical obstacles on the Eastern side of the border. Even the metaphor "generation" is inaccurate, since the Berlin Wall of the 1980s was a strange blend of design, including design "features" of previous times.

The "real" Berlin Wall was not one but *two* walls and a myriad of obstacles between them. The border-control regime looked so different in distinct locations and changed so much over time that providing a "universal" description of it is challenging. Generally, the would-be escapee first saw warning signs and the inscription "Frontier Area—Passage not allowed" in German, English, French, and Russian. Thereafter came in many places the eastern wall, the so-called Hinterland Wall—which was in fact the frontal, most important wall that stopped most escapees. From the Hinterland Wall began the very wide "death strip." First the escapee entered a narrow area right in front of an electrical signaling fence. If touched, the fence would immediately send an alarm to the nearest command post. Anyone who managed by some lucky chance to scale this elastic fence landed on other obstacles like long sharp spikes. In some areas, after passing the fence an escapee would be even confronted with dog runs.[9]

Border guards monitored the entire border area closely and had orders to "arrest or exterminate" border violators. They carried automatic rifles, had military training, and were constantly watched by infiltrated secret police members to prevent desertions. Watchtowers and command posts helped them detect movement on the death strip and beyond, while light strips provided plenty of light for them even during the darkest nights. A telephone network also connected the border posts, enabling continuous communication. After the border guards' patrol road came a wide control strip, covered with sand to retain footprints. The next barrier was an antivehicle trench, followed by a wide strip. Finally, at the end of all these obstacles, there was the Border Wall, that *one* wall we generally have in mind. Although East Germany continued to reshape this system of obstacles throughout the Wall's existence, most of its elements were already in place at the time of the twentieth anniversary of the East German state, in 1969.

Over time, the name "Berlin Wall" came to stand for this multilayered and multigenerational border-control regime that included, among other things, barbed wire and concrete; antivehicle crash obstacles and control strips; self-activating searchlights and patrol roads; watchtowers; and heavily armed border guards. Moreover, it also came to stand not just for the Wall running through populated areas, but also for the border along rail embankments, marshland, fields, and waterways. In these areas, the wall was often no more than a line through a lake or a river or even a bridge; nonetheless, it was "the" Berlin Wall.[10]

Even photographs of the various generations of the Wall, capturing it in all of its alternating states, have come to represent the Berlin

Wall. For instance, the most widely reproduced Berlin Wall photograph depicts the young East German border guard Conrad Schumann's leap to freedom—or more precisely, his jump over a barbed-wire fence two days after the erection of the Berlin Wall. Peter Leibing's photograph of the jump is now the central image at the Berlin Wall Memorial in Berlin. On Brunnenstrasse, a few steps away from the Memorial, a citizen-initiated sculpture embodies the photograph as well (Fig. 3.5). The sculpture includes a piece of barbed wire to represent the "wall"; while being barbed wire, it is nonetheless *seen* as a "wall."

So how do we account for the exceptional consensus in calling an elaborate and ever-changing system of obstacles "the" Berlin Wall? And why do we still use that name today? There are at least two quite distinct reasons that could help explain the perseverance of the concept of the Berlin

FIGURE 3.5 Sculpture by Michael and Florian Bauer, and Edward Anders entitled "Mauerspringer" (Wall Jumper) at Brunnenstrasse 142 in Berlin. Erected in 2009. Photo: Julia Sonnevend, 2015.

Wall. Neither of them stands alone, but together they may help solve the puzzle. The first reason is aesthetic and has to do with the changing architectural design of the Wall. The second is political and relates to effective propaganda from both sides.

As described above, the four generations of the Berlin Wall progressed toward a coherent wall image. Looking from the west side, the provisional, rough, and shoddy "patchwork wall" over time began to look more and more like a professionally designed wall system. East Germany aimed to make the wall look smooth and flat for the West. The wall's professional appearance on the Western side turned the whole border-control regime more and more into *one* wall, at least in imagination. Still, the changing, consolidating design of the Wall therefore cannot fully explain the perseverance of the Berlin Wall concept. Perhaps a look at the propagandistic representations of the Wall will provide some answers. The Berlin Wall was a powerful propaganda object for both sides: maybe neither side had an interest in seeing it as complex and ever-changing.

In the mind of East German party and state leader Walter Ulbricht, the border regime existed as a Wall months before its birth. At an international press conference on June 15, 1961, Ulbricht famously announced: "Niemand hat die Absicht, eine Mauer zu errichten" (Nobody has the intention to build a wall). His announcement, which is still frequently reprinted on Berlin postcards, pictured a "wall" and engraved this image in memory well before the wall even came into being. But even *after* the official birth of the "Berlin Wall" on August 13, 1961, for some time the "wall" remained only an image, while most of the border fence was made of barbed wire. In a meeting around a month after the official erection of the Berlin Wall, the East German military still advocated against a wall, and suggested keeping and extending the barbed-wire fence instead. The military believed that border guards, rather than physical obstacles, should be catching any would-be fugitives. For the military, an actual physical wall seemed like a meaningless barrier—one that potentially might even "hide" escapees from the border guards' prying eyes.[11]

Erich Mielke, who was the Head of the Ministry of State Security throughout the Wall's existence, expressed a different opinion at that meeting: "the security measures at the border have a big political meaning."[12] In fact, by the time of the September 1961 meeting a physical wall was already under construction at a few *very visible* locations: in the city center, between the Brandenburg Gate and the Potsdamer Platz, and between Checkpoint Charlie and the Spree.[13] On August 13, 1962, a whole year after the date we have come to associate with the construction of the Berlin Wall, physical walls protected only twenty percent of the Berlin–Berlin border, and only five percent of the entire border of West Berlin. Nevertheless, by this time the *concept* of the Wall went uncontested: those percentages were enough to make it represent a reality that did not yet exist.

So how did the Eastern Germans narrate this "wall" that did not yet fully exist? In 1961 East German propaganda immediately started to call the border barrier the "Anti-Fascist Protective Rampart." This choice of name was not a subversive or idiosyncratic one; after all, antifascism had been the central founding myth of the GDR. Struggling to construct a legitimate national identity, the GDR used antifascism as the main justification for its existence.[14] As political myth, antifascism made the founding of the new German state seem morally and historically desirable.[15] East Germany presented itself as embodying both the resistance against national socialism and the better traditions of German history.[16] The name "Anti-Fascist Protective Rampart" was perfectly in keeping with East Germany's widespread antifascist propaganda campaigns. East German propagandists called the 1953 uprising by East German workers demanding the resignation of the government a "fascist putsch"; its posters depicted the anticommunist West German Chancellor Konrad Adenauer as the "Hitler of today"; and its slogans emphasized West Germany's failure to go through an efficient process of denazification. East German propaganda also used antifascism to discredit Western criticism of the GDR. Attacks by the West German press were compared to the propagandistic efforts of the *Völkischer Beobachter*, the infamous newspaper of the Nazi party.[17]

The Anti-Fascist Protective Rampart was advertised as an effective barrier that kept out provocateurs, fascists, aggressors aiming for armed conflict, and immoral economic activities like pornography, smuggling, and human trafficking. While this combination of unwanted elements might seem awkward or arbitrary to the contemporary reader, it fitted the antifascist narrative. The GDR understood fascism in the terms offered by Georgi Dimitrov: "fascism is the power of finance capital itself."[18] Barring capitalism and barring manifestations of fascist politics were equally important.

In visual representations, the Anti-Fascist Protective Rampart was generally reduced to one single image: that of the Brandenburg Gate.[19]

FIGURE 3.6 Members of the "Combat Groups of the Working Class" lined up on the West side of the Brandenburg Gate on August 13, 1961. Bundesarchiv, 183-85458-0001, photo: Heinz Junge.

This central photograph of the East German visual propaganda for the rampart, taken on August 14, 1961, showed "Kampfgruppen der Arbeiterklasse" (Combat Groups of the Working Class) lined up in front of the Brandenburg Gate to protect the GDR (Figs. 3.6 and 3.7). These groups had been organized in the 1950s as paramilitary reserves for the army; they embodied the tradition of "proletarian self-defense."[20]

East German photographs of the Anti-Fascist Protective Rampart consistently avoided showing any details of the border barriers; all obstacles of the death strip were omitted from the East German visual vocabulary. Nonetheless, the architects of the separation barrier still carefully designed every item of the death strip in such a way as to avoid fueling Western propaganda. In designing the elements of the Berlin border area, they especially tried to avoid any visual resemblance to the concentration camps. For instance, the first-generation watchtowers, which were made out of wood and resembled concentration camp watchtowers, were quickly

FIGURE 3.7 Symbolic reenactment of the iconic image of the "Combat Groups of the Working Class" in East Berlin on July 4, 1987, the 750th anniversary of the city of Berlin. Bundesarchiv, 183-1987-0704-057, photo: Rainer Mittelstädt.

replaced by brick and plaster towers with a very different design.[21] Seeking international acceptance and recognition, the GDR even tried to make the wall look increasingly "humane" as time went by.

The West responded to the Anti-Fascist Protective Rampart with a counter-propaganda campaign. West Berlin Mayor Willy Brandt coined the poignant, if less innovative, name "Schandmauer" (Wall of Shame).[22] The West German press framed the wall's construction in the context of the Nazi past. For instance, just eight days after the initial erection of the Wall, *Der Telegraf* presented a photo series with the caption: "In the East: concentration camp, in the West: free" (Im Osten: KZ, Im Westen: Frei).[23]

The West's Wall narrative was also enforced by American presidential and vice-presidential visits to the Wall. Anxiety about seclusion had already been part of the West Berlin psyche prior to 1961, especially since the 1948–1949 Berlin Airlift, when Western allies supplied the people of West Berlin during an entire year of Soviet blockade. Diplomatic visits from the "outside," and most importantly from the United States, helped ease this anxiety. The American presidential and vice-presidential visits also revitalized the memory of the Berlin Airlift, and strengthened the feeling that the West "belonged together" against all odds—and walls. The most notable visits were those of Vice President Lyndon Johnson

(1961) and Presidents John F. Kennedy (1963) and Ronald Reagan (1987). Kennedy and Reagan also offered some of "the" Berlin Wall's more memorable one-liners: "Ich bin ein Berliner" and "Mr. Gorbachev, tear down this wall!," respectively. Paradoxically, Kennedy's sentence was both universal and particular. He used himself as a symbol, turning himself as an icon of American presidency and culture into a local, a "Berliner," speaking German. But he also *universalized* the wall by identifying himself with Berliners, signaling that "we are all Berliners now, all living under the shadow of this wall." Reagan's universalization was more strictly geopolitical: he told the Soviet (not the East German) leader, to tear down the "wall," reasserting the Berlin Wall's role as the central symbol of the Cold War. He used the second-person imperative, rarely employed by U.S. presidents in delicate diplomatic contexts, which rendered the line particularly memorable. Reagan made his announcement right in front of the Brandenburg Gate and the Berlin Wall, offering a clear visual contrast between the existing reality of division and the desired future of openness. In fact, the Secret Service had to erect a glass partition between him and the Brandenburg Gate to protect the president from potential snipers on the Eastern side. A physical, nontransparent wall of protection was not an option; the West did not want to erect a second wall, not even temporarily.[24] Overall both Presidents Kennedy and Reagan offered powerful rhetorical statements that highlighted the symbolic power of the Berlin Wall and engraved its image in international memory.

In its visual imagery, the West focused on divided families and communities: children separated from their parents or their extended families, weddings where essential guests were absent, and friends who could wave at each other only from a distance.[25] Another set of images showed high-level foreign politicians as they observed the horrors of the death strip. The West also stressed the undesirability of the Berlin Wall with the help of escape and victim stories. Through these narratives and images, the various generations and versions of the wall were unified. The exact shape and material of the Wall did not matter to the West. What mattered that the Wall separated communities that belonged together.

Highly publicized incidents included, for example, the first successful escape by an East German border guard (Conrad Schumann, August 15, 1961); the first deadly shot fired at the Berlin border (Günter Litfin, August 24, 1961); a visually well-documented case in which border guards from both sides let an escapee bleed to death on the death strip (Peter Fechter, August 17, 1962; Fig. 3.8); and the story of the last escapee to be shot dead at the Berlin Wall—he had thought that the order to shoot was no longer

FIGURE 3.8 Peter Fechter (1944–1962) was a bricklayer from East Berlin who was shot by an East German border patrol while attempting to scale the Berlin Wall on August 17, 1962. Border guards did not respond to his cries for help and carried away his body an hour after he had been shot. Ullstein Bild/The Granger Collection, New York.

in effect (Chris Gueffroy, February 6, 1989). Escape stories included descriptions of the elaborate tricks necessary to overcome the Wall, like the use of tunnels, air balloons, and bulldozers.[26]

Similarly to escape stories, Western lists of Berlin Wall victims helped fortify the concept of "the" Berlin Wall as well—even if the development of an adequate definition of the "victims of the Berlin Wall" was particularly challenging.[27] Most cases—apart from the obvious one of being shot at the death strip—were difficult to classify: some escapees died from injuries after arriving on the Western side, others suffered heart attacks during their escapes, and the Berlin Wall's psychological effects also shortened many lives. The recently established Berlin Wall Memorial's photo collection of the victims, the "Window of Remembrance," leaves some of the windows blank, signaling that there are likely more victims of the Berlin Wall who have not been identified yet (Fig. 3.9). Despite challenges of identification and classification, Western narratives of victims and escapes fortified the concept of "the" Berlin Wall—a wall that people desperately wanted to overcome.

Multiple narratives and circumstances, then, helped shape the mental image of "the" Berlin Wall. At the same time, neither the East nor the West visualized the realities of the death strip. On both sides, *people* embodied the propaganda message. On the Eastern side, the working class, fighting back fascism with its very own body, dominated the visual image of the Wall; on the Western side, freedom-loving individuals played this role. In each case the imagery focused on persons and hid the *objects* of the border area. In this sense, the visual practices of the East and the West were surprisingly similar. Both contributed to an image of "the" Berlin Wall and an idealized image of the "people;" both veiled the actual details of the death strip. At the same time, there was also an important difference between the two sides: while East German propaganda revolved around one central image of the Anti-Fascist Protective Rampart focusing on the Brandenburg Gate, the West had many photographs depicting the Berlin Wall in circulation—although all of them dealt exclusively with the Wall's Western side.[28]

FIGURE 3.9 "Window of Remembrance" at the Berlin Wall Memorial. Photo: Julia Sonnevend, 2015.

If the lack of visual representations of the death strip is more or less understandable in the case of the East, it is harder to explain what motivated the West: surely, showing the real brutalities of the death strip would have been an influential tool for Western propaganda. Besides, every year millions of visitors actually *saw* the death strip with their own eyes from platforms on the Western side (Fig. 3.10). Most of these platforms were erected for West Berlin police, but were available for everyone interested in a peek to the other side. At central locations, like Bernauer Strasse/Eberswalder Strasse, the Brandenburg Gate, Potsdamer Platz, Checkpoint Charlie, and the Oberbaum Bridge, special viewing platforms were built directly for tourists. Why did the visual representations not build on such personal visual experiences of the death strip? Perhaps stories of escape, victimhood, and personal trauma seemed better vehicles for the message of freedom and humanity. The mental image of "the" Berlin Wall, eclipsing the horrors of the death strip, constituted a quick and easy reference to *all* omitted details.

Another explanation for the West's omission of the death strip from visual representations may be the fact that the West simply got used to the existence of the Wall. While the Wall initially seemed both outrageous and impermeable to West Germans, it became relatively normal and

FIGURE 3.10 U.S. President Jimmy Carter on a viewing platform at Potsdamer Platz, looking over from West Berlin to East Berlin on July 15, 1978. Bundesarchiv, 00005671, photo: Engelbert Reineke.

relatively permeable over time. Writing about the West German image of the Wall, German historian Hermann Wentker described the period between 1971 and 1989 as "the normalization of the abnormal."[29] In the sixties the Berlin Wall was a slap in the face for West Germans, and they protested against it intensely; by 1976, however, only forty-five percent of them knew the correct answer to the simple survey question: "What happened on August 13, 1961?"[30] Parks and private gardens at the Berlin Wall became—or remained—acceptable sites for enjoying freshly grilled wurst with friends and family, and nearby gunshots only occasionally disturbed the peaceful harmony.[31] In other words, for the West "the" Berlin Wall turned mostly into a symbol—detached from the realities of the border area, and elevated above historical facts. Or as Peter Schneider put it quite bluntly in his famous book *The Wall Jumper*, "[o]nce the initial panic died, the massive structure faded increasingly to a metaphor in the West German consciousness. [...] Whether there was life beyond the death strip soon mattered only to pigeons and cats."[32]

There was the increasingly efficient Berlin border-separation barrier that prevented East German mass exodus—and whoever tried to cross the Berlin border from the East faced the actual realities of the death strip. And there was also "the" Berlin Wall, a symbol of separation and difference for *both* sides. As a symbol, the Berlin Wall is not susceptible to the tools of accuracy and objectivity: it requires us to think in abstract terms. The Berlin Wall represents *separation* between East Germans and West Germans; it also stands for the *difference* between communism and capitalism. Even for a symbol, though, the Berlin Wall is quite puzzling: we would assume a central symbol of the Cold War to be something initiated by the Soviets and deemed unacceptable by the Americans—or the other way around, some American project that the Soviets hoped to eliminate. The Berlin Wall was neither really. As American historian Hope M. Harrison has shown, throughout the fifties the hardline East German leadership insisted on building the Berlin Wall, while post-Stalinist Soviet leader Nikita Khrushchev held off on the idea until 1961. Khrushchev suggested, instead, that the underlying problems that triggered the mass emigration should be solved.[33] And although Western politicians often condemned the Berlin Wall with words and certainly did not initiate its construction, they did not actually *act* much against the separation. As President John F. Kennedy summarized the Western position right after the Berlin border was sealed: "not a very nice solution, but ... a hell of a lot better than a war."[34]

Nonetheless, the Berlin Wall as a symbol prevails in spite of all these facts. It influenced the entire discourse of the Cold War, and it remains with us today. Moreover, the story of the Berlin Wall offered a readily available vocabulary in which the story of the *fall* of the Berlin Wall could be told: a vocabulary dedicated to feelings and imagination, not to facts and reality. This preexisting language made the story of the fall of the Berlin Wall an especially strong and compelling one. As British historian Timothy Garton Ash pointed out: "[i]n German, all nouns take an initial capital letter, so even a bungalow wall is a *Mauer* with a capital M. In English, there are many walls, but only one Wall. It's the one that 'fell' on the night of Thursday 9 November 1989, giving us history's new rhyme: the fall of the Wall."[35]

Foundation II: The Forgotten Sociopolitical Context of the Fall of the Berlin Wall

As the first part of this chapter explained, the Berlin Wall as symbol rose above historical details and facts. It began to live a life somewhat independent from its material context. Something similar happened to the story of the fall of the Berlin Wall as it became a global iconic event. Just as we tend to forget the numerous iterations and obstacles of the Berlin separation barrier when we recall the Berlin Wall, we also tend to *forget* the East German political and bureaucratic struggles of 1989, recalling the fall of the Berlin Wall instead. But no matter how miraculous or sudden it may now appear, the Berlin Wall did not fall in a vacuum. Instead, the fall of the Berlin Wall was embedded in a long, dispersed, contradictory transitional and revolutionary process. To understand the narration of the fall of the Berlin Wall as global iconic event, we must first refresh our memory of its social, political, and cultural context. For, in order to construct a simple and transportable myth of a miraculously "falling wall," this dense and confusing past would have to be forgotten.

The story of the "East German 1989" consists of at least six separate strands or puzzle pieces: the Soviet Union's changing relations with East and West Germany; East Germany's economic deterioration; growing East German public discontent expressed through mass exodus and mass demonstrations; the weakening and split of the East German leadership; the influence of West German electronic media on the East German society; and the decision process surrounding the new East German travel law that was the most direct trigger for the fall of the Berlin Wall. What follows is a short narrative regarding each of these pieces of the puzzle. Again, recalling these details helps us see how a global iconic event comes into being by leaving its confusing context behind.

The GDR was never politically independent from the Soviet Union. The GDR was established on October 7, 1949, on the territory of the Soviet occupation zone, as a state with the unique mission to show the superiority of communism. In line with this mission, the GDR received political, financial, and military support from the Soviet Union throughout its existence. In return, the GDR, as a postfascist and socialist country, oriented itself toward the Soviet Union.[36]

By the 1980s, however, the economic crisis forced the Soviet Union to rethink its relations to the Eastern bloc. In November 1986 Soviet Communist Party General Secretary Mikhail Gorbachev announced major changes regarding the Soviet relationship to socialist countries. Gorbachev declared "the independence of each party, its right to make sovereign decisions about the problems of development in its country"; he also emphasized each country's "responsibility to its own people."[37] By providing this level of independence and autonomy, Gorbachev hoped to stabilize the region; he did not intend to put an end to the alliance.[38]

At the end of October 1989, the ever-increasing debt brought East German economists to consider negotiating with West Germany about substantial financial assistance.[39] The alternative option was a major change in economic and social policy, along with a radical reduction in the standard of living. This seemed impossible in a country that obtained its legitimacy from the promise of social welfare. When Erich Honecker came to power in 1971, he had promised to maintain the unity of social and economic policy. Basic services and goods were heavily subsidized in East Germany, while price hikes were unimaginable from a political standpoint. To cover the high state subventions the country put itself in debt; the many inefficiencies of the state-controlled economy caused major supply shortfalls, even in basic food products.[40] The Soviet Union had frequently rescued East Germany financially before, but Mikhail Gorbachev clearly signaled that this time, the Soviet Union would not be able to provide East Germany with its much-needed financial assistance. On November 6, 1989, just three days before the fall of the Berlin Wall, East and West Germany began to negotiate a credit, and West Germany conditioned its financial support upon East German political reforms.

By this time widespread social dissatisfaction was palpable all over East Germany. Signaling the levels of public discontent with the regime, more and more East Germans voted with their feet—and tried to leave the country. On May 2, 1989, Hungary began dismantling its fortified border with Austria. Even after this symbolic act, however, Hungary did not allow East German citizens to cross the border to the West. Still, many East Germans used the summer break to visit Hungary in the hope of leaving the East German state behind. The situation began to escalate: approximately two thousand East Germans had crossed the Austro-Hungarian border illegally by August 20, 1989, and several thousands more were residing in Hungarian refugee camps. Other would-be East German emigrants stormed the West German embassies in Prague, Warsaw, and Budapest. Finally, on the night of September 10, 1989, Hungary opened the border to Austria for East German citizens, resulting in eighteen thousand border crossings over the next three days.[41]

Around this time, Czechoslovakia tightened the control of its border with Hungary, trying to create a new, invisible wall for East Germans. As a result, more than ten thousand East German citizens were occupying the West German embassy in Prague at the end of September 1989, demanding the right to leave for West Germany. This conflict provided one of the most dramatic scenes of the East German crisis. On September 30, 1989, Honecker gave in and permitted the embassy occupiers to emigrate to West Germany. To get to West Germany, the Prague embassy emigrants traveled through East Germany in sealed trains (Fig. 3.11). They were stripped of their citizenship and their identity documents were confiscated. The East German leadership wanted to humiliate the emigrants by branding them as traitors, but this "performance" had the opposite effect: fellow East Germans saluted the refugees as the trains traveled through the country. On the train, the simultaneously frightened and cheerful refugees, who lacked any form of trust toward their political leaders, could not believe that they were free until they actually crossed the border, where they were greeted by West German crowds. West German television captured and transmitted the moving, once-in-a-lifetime visuals to the East.[42] In a context in which the use of sealed trains to transport people had strong historical connotations, the Prague embassy incident delivered a major blow to the image of an "antifascist" East Germany.

The mass exodus fueled the protests that were taking place on East German soil.[43] There had been active opposition groups well before the start of the mass exodus. Most of these started out as human rights,

FIGURE 3.11 Children at the windows of the German Reichsbahn's special train on October 5, 1989. The train carried East German refugees who had waited for emigration in the German Embassy in Prague. Bundesarchiv, 00021378, photo: Arne Schambeck.

environmental protection, or pro-peace initiatives during the late seventies and early eighties. Many initiatives were supported and protected by the Lutheran church. But the levels of public support for, and the visibility of, their opposition activities increased substantially after the start of the emigration wave in the summer of 1989. Independent political groups were founded as well, most notably *Neues Forum, Demokratie Jetzt,* and *Demokratischer Aufbruch.*[44]

During 1989, demonstrations and other forms of political resistance were taking place in approximately five hundred locations in East Germany, including Dresden, Plauen, and Karl-Marx-Stadt (currently Chemnitz). The center of opposition activity was Leipzig, where demonstrations began each Monday with a prayer for peace in the Church of St. Nicholas. On October 9, 1989, seventy thousand demonstrators occupied the streets of Leipzig. And the number of demonstrators kept growing by the week. On November 6, 1989, three days before the fall of the Berlin Wall, more than two hundred thousand protesters in Leipzig chanted: "We are the people!" and "We need no laws, the Wall must go!" On the very same day, one hundred thousand protesters took to the streets of Dresden, and sixty thousand stormed the marketplace of Halle.[45] The protest wave seemed unstoppable.

In the midst of this social crisis, the East German political leadership was starting to fall apart. In East Germany's centralized structure, everybody expected solutions to come from the Central Committee and the Politburo. However, the leader, Erich Honecker, was increasingly ill and seemed to have lost touch with the pulse of the times. The highest ranks of party leadership seemed oblivious to the level of public discontent in the country.[46] Finally, on October 17 and 18, 1989, Honecker was forced out. The fifty-two-year-old Egon Krenz became the new General Secretary of the SED Central Committee, who immediately promised the introduction of a new, more permissive travel law. Further changes in leadership included the firing of the Central Committee Secretaries of Economics and of Agitation and Propaganda (the latter meant a serious weakening of media control). On November 7, 1989, the Council of Ministers also resigned. Ultimately, on November 8, just one day before the fall of the Berlin Wall, the entire Politburo tendered its resignation.[47]

The West German electronic media made sure to keep the East German population well informed about the collapse of the GDR's political and economic systems. On average, "only" ten percent of the East German population actually participated in the protest activities. The overwhelming majority of East Germans followed their own revolution on television.[48] There are few reliable data from this period, but researchers estimate that up to ninety percent of East Germans had access to West German television in the late eighties.[49] A 1988 study, based on interviews with emigrants who left East Germany for West Germany, found major differences in their engagement with, and appreciation of, East versus West German television. These interviewees were of course exceptionally critical of the country they had left behind, but the results still offer some insights. Eighty-two percent of the interviewees claimed to watch West German television "almost daily"; another twelve percent watched it "frequently"; five percent "sometimes"; and only one percent "rarely" viewed West German television programs.[50] The researcher who conducted the study concluded in 1988 that each night an "electronic reunification" was taking place between the two German societies.[51] Nothing really explains why East Germany allowed this virtual reunification to happen despite the fact that it gave ample opportunity to compare the different living standards, and different levels of freedom, on the two sides of the Wall. Some Western specialists speculate that it was an attempt to quiet protests against travel restrictions. For the GDR government, nightly "virtual emigration" was always better than real emigration. Many also point out the immense technological challenges of jamming specific content at this time.[52]

When everything seemed to collapse, the East German leadership tried to calm things down by easing the restrictions on travel. Back in October 1989, during the Prague Embassy incident, East Germany had withdrawn the right of its citizens to travel to Czechoslovakia without a visa. On November 1, East Germany reversed this decision, prompting additional tens of thousands of people to leave. Czech authorities were not pleased. As British historian Frederick Taylor put it, Czechoslovakia had little intention of turning into an East German refugee camp.[53] Therefore, on November 4, 1989, under pressure from Czechoslovakia, the East German leadership finally permitted its citizens to cross Czechoslovakia *and* leave for West Germany. Over the next three days, thirty thousand East Germans used this opportunity to flee to the West.[54]

This situation again put enormous pressure on Czechoslovakia: it had now become a crowded highway to West Germany. Instead of crossing directly from East to West Germany, refugees traveled through Czechoslovakia to the desired West. East Germany had to find a way to release this pressure. The East German leadership had been preparing new travel legislation for a while, but the Politburo thought it premature to implement the entire new travel regulation when negotiations with West Germany about the much-needed financial assistance were still ongoing.[55] As a compromise, the party leadership decided, on November 6, 1989, to at least publish a draft of the new travel legislation. The draft included plenty of opportunity for the authorities to deny permission to travel and allowed for only thirty days of travel a year. Again, party leaders did not fully grasp the level of frustration among its citizens. Instead of calming the waters, the new draft inspired passionate demonstrations. It appeared that all the reforms came too late, or in the wrong shape.

Next, the Politburo, trying to find at least a temporary solution for the crisis in Czechoslovakia, decided on an early promulgation of that portion of the travel legislation that regulated permanent emigration.[56] The draft regulation did not introduce complete and immediate freedom to travel; it required the possession of a passport and a visa. At the time, four million East German citizens had passports (the total population of East Germany was 16.7 million). Other East Germans would have to apply for one, and then wait as the document traveled through bureaucratic labyrinths. With this tactic, the East German leadership sought to avoid a

stampede and to slow down the mass exodus. The bureaucrats who prepared the draft also wanted to make sure that the border guards and other
relevant authorities would have enough time to prepare for the crowds
of applicants. Therefore, they decided *not* to release information regarding the new travel regulation through the party-controlled East German
media until the next day, at 4 a.m. on November 10, 1989.[57]

On November 9, 1989, given the dramatic situation at home as well
as abroad, the draft went through the bureaucratic stages with the speed
of light, in the hope that it could be passed by 6 p.m.—thus leaving an
entire night for preparations by the passport and registration authorities.
Egon Krenz received the draft at 3 p.m. and quickly got it approved by
both the Central Committee and the Politburo. The travel regulation was
meant to be announced by the spokesman of the government, who knew
of the plans to release the information only on the next day. However,
between 5 and 5:30 p.m. November 9, for reasons still unknown, Krenz
gave the draft and the related press release to Politburo member Günther
Schabowski, who was about to serve as a party spokesman at a live international press conference.

Schabowski had not been present at the meetings of the Central
Committee and the Politburo where the new travel regulation and its
launch had been discussed. He claims to have been with journalists, but
no journalist has ever confirmed his claims. His whereabouts on the fateful afternoon of November 9, 1989, remain a "mystery." Due to his absence
from the Central Committee discussion, he did *not* know that the regulation would not go into effect until the next morning.[58] He was also uninformed about the exact details of the draft. However, Krenz claims that he
told Schabowski either that "[t]his will be a sensation for us" (according
to Schabowski's memory), or that "this news will affect the whole world"
(according to Krenz's memory).[59] But even if Krenz indeed said this, lots
of events in East Germany made for sensational world news in those days;
so when at 6 p.m. on November 9, 1989 an exhausted Schabowski entered
a large press conference room filled with bored journalists, he was quite
unprepared to make history. He did not even read the draft until he had to
announce it in front of the cameras of the world.[60]

When we take all these pieces of the GDR puzzle into account—the
changing Soviet relations; the collapsing economy; the growing social
dissatisfaction manifested in mass exodus and mass demonstrations; a
weakening political leadership; influential Western media; and a hastily
prepared new travel regulation—the fall of the Berlin Wall seems less of

a magical event. In fact, it comes to look more like the inevitable eruption of an old volcano; but that is not how we remember it.

This chapter aimed to show that each global iconic event, including the fall of the Berlin Wall, is part of a complex process, a series of interconnected moments with historic significance. When we narrate an event, we push these contextual details to the background and focus on "surprise," "magic," and "unexpectedness." This chapter also showed that the story of the Berlin Wall was narrated with an elevated mythical language, centering on feelings rather than facts. This language would greatly enforce the narrative of the fall of the Berlin Wall as a global iconic event.

4

Mythologization

GERMAN HISTORIAN HANS-HERMANN Hertle, author of the most comprehensive book on the "fall of the Berlin Wall," once remarked that "[i]n relation to the intention behind it, Schabowski's announcement is the world's greatest disaster in the history of the press conference."[1] That claim seems hard to prove: is there anyone who has knowledge of *all* the disastrous press conferences that took place in world history? But the East German press conference did show that even the most awkward press conference can go down in history, and may even be turned into a global icon of freedom.

In this chapter I track this miraculous transformation. I show how the elevated language and mythical message of the fall of the Berlin Wall was gradually developed. I describe the press conference, where an uninformed East German party official, Günter Schabowski, announced the new regulation on freedom of travel and, as he did so, made crucial mistakes. Then I look at how West German and American news agencies and television covered this press conference and its aftermath on November 9, 1989, turning an awkward occurrence into a memorable "event." I will show how confusing the developments of November 9, 1989 were—much more confusing than our simplified image of the fall of the Berlin Wall lets on. I will also suggest that in our story of the event, we tend to rule out the possibility that the media did not just *cover* the fall; it may, through its imaginations and interpretations, have helped to precipitate it.

An Awkward and Boring Occurrence: The International Press Conference on November 9, 1989, in East Berlin

When I mention the "fall of the Berlin Wall," my reader is likely to imagine something spectacular; images of joyful people opening bottles of champagne on top of the wall that divided them for almost three decades. But in reality, the beginning of the "fall of the Berlin Wall" looked like this:

FIGURE 4.1 Press conference at the International Press Center at Mohrenstrasse, East Berlin, November 9, 1989. On the podium from left to right: Central Committee members Helga Labs, Manfred Banaschak, Günther Schabowski, and Gerhard Beil. Bundesarchiv, 183-1989-1109-030, photo: Thomas Lehmann.

The image of the historic press conference did not make a very likely candidate for iconicity (Fig. 4.1). The press conference room had a drab seventies feel to it, with socialist shades of red and brown. The room was packed, but it was not buzzing with excitement. Journalists representing East and West both attended the conference. Ideologically different, they were all equally exhausted from an ever-escalating political crisis that needed continuous coverage. Journalists were still grappling with the news they had heard the day before at a similar press conference—that the entire Politburo had tendered its resignation. *Frankfurter Rundschau* correspondent Karl-Heinz Baum's feelings probably mirrored those of many other journalists that day. Baum told his colleagues at the headquarters: "I attend the press conference of the Central Committee of the SED (Socialist Unity Party of Germany), listen to what Schabowski says; then I go to sleep. If he says something important, I will write a lead article tomorrow."[2]

Thanks to East Germany's radical media reforms, East German state television offered *live* coverage of the event. But for the better part of an hour, the press conference was far from fascinating. Schabowski began the conference at 6 p.m. and spoke for fifty-three minutes before the topic of travel even came up. He presented his free-floating thoughts on a party conference to be organized in December—"Parteitagsscheiße" (party conference shit) was how West German journalists referred to this part of the information package.[3] Schabowski also offered lengthy thoughts on free elections and his party's various desperate plans for reform. Finally, at 6:53 p.m., came the decisive, if poorly formulated, question from Italian journalist Riccardo Ehrman:

QUESTION: My name is Riccardo Ehrman, representing the Italian press agency ANSA. Mr. Schabowski, you spoke about mistakes. Don't you believe that it was a big mistake to introduce this travel law several days ago?

SCHABOWSKI: No, I don't believe so. (Um) We know about this tendency in the population, this need of the population, to travel or to leave the GDR [German Democratic Republic]. And (um) we have ideas about what we have to bring about, (such as) all the things I mentioned before, or sought to mention in my response to the question from the TASS correspondent, namely a complex renewal of the society (um) and thereby achieve that many of these elements . . . (um) that people do not feel compelled to solve their personal problems in this way.

Those are quite a number of steps, as I said, and (um) we can't start them all at once. There are series of steps, and the chance, through expanding travel possibilities . . . the chance, through legalizing exit and making it easier to leave, to free the people from a (um) let us say psychological pressure . . . Many of these steps took place without adequate consideration. We know that through conversations, through the need to return to the GDR, (um) through conversations with people who find themselves in an unbelievably complicated situation in the FRG [Federal Republic of Germany] because the FRG is having a great deal of trouble providing shelter for these refugees.

So, the absorptive capacity of the FRG is essentially exhausted. There are already more than, or less than provisional (um), that these people have to count on, if they are put up there. (um). Shelter is the minimum for constructing an existence. Finding work is decisive, essential . . .

[Central Committee Member] Beil: (softly) . . . integration . . .

SCHABOWSKI: . . . yes, and the necessary integration into the society, which cannot happen when one is living in a tent or an emergency shelter, or is hanging around unemployed.

So, we want . . . through a number of changes, including the travel law, to [create] the chance, the sovereign decision of the citizens to travel wherever they want. (um) We are naturally (um) concerned that the possibilities of this travel regulation—it is still not in effect, it's only a draft.

A decision was made today, as far as I know (looking toward Central Committee members Labs and Banaschak in hope of confirmation). A recommendation from the politburo was taken up that we take a passage from the [draft of] travel regulation and put it into effect, that, (um)—as it is called, for better or worse—that regulates permanent exit, leaving the Republic. Since we find it (um) unacceptable that this movement is taking place (um) across the territory of an allied state, (um) which is not an easy burden for that country to bear. Therefore (um), we have decided today (um) to implement a regulation that allows every citizen of the German Democratic Republic (um) to (um) leave the GDR through any of the border crossings.

QUESTION: (many voices) When does that go into effect?

RICCARDO EHRMAN, REPORTER, ANSA: Without a passport? Without a passport? (no, no)

KRZYSZTOF JANOWSKI, REPORTER, VOICE OF AMERICA: When is that in effect? . . . (confusion, voices . . .) At what point does the regulation take effect?

SCHABOWSKI: What?

PETER BRINKMANN, REPORTER, *BILD ZEITUNG*: At once? When . . . ?

SCHABOWSKI: (. . . scratches his head) You see, comrades, I was informed today (puts on his glasses as he speaks further), that such an announcement had been (um) distributed earlier today. You should actually have it already. So, (reading very quickly from the paper):

1) "Applications for travel abroad by private individuals can now be made without the previously existing requirements (of demonstrating a need to travel or proving familial relationships). The travel authorizations will be issued within a short time. Grounds for denial will only be applied in particular exceptional cases. The responsible departments of passport and registration control in the People's Police district offices in the

GDR are instructed to issue visas for permanent exit without delays and without presentation of the existing requirements for permanent exit."

RICCARDO EHRMAN, REPORTER, ANSA: With a passport?

SCHABOWSKI: (um ...) (reads:) "Permanent exit is possible via all GDR border crossings to the FRG. These changes replace the temporary practice of issuing [travel] authorizations through GDR consulates and permanent exit with a GDR personal identity card via third countries."

(Looks up) (um) I cannot answer the question about passports at this point. (Looks questioningly at Labs and Banaschak.) That is also a technical question. I don't know, the passports have to ... so that everyone has a passport, they first have to be distributed. But we want to ...

BANASCHAK: The substance of the announcement is decisive ...

SCHABOWSKI: ... is the ...

QUESTION: When does it go into effect?

SCHABOWSKI: (Looks through his papers ...) That goes into effect, according to my information, immediately, without delay (looking through his papers further).

LABS: (quietly) ... without delay.

BEIL: (quietly) That has to be decided by the Council of Ministers.

KRZYSZTOF JANOWSKI, REPORTER, VOICE OF AMERICA: In Berlin also? (... Many voices ...)

PETER BRINKMANN, REPORTER, *BILD ZEITUNG*: You only said the FRG, is the regulation also valid for West Berlin?

SCHABOWSKI: (reading aloud quickly) "As the Press Office of the Ministry ... the Council of Ministers decided that until the *Volkskammer* implements a corresponding law, this transition regulation will be in effect."

PETER BRINKMANN, REPORTER, *BILD ZEITUNG*: Does this also apply to West Berlin? You only mentioned the FRG.

SCHABOWSKI: (shrugs his shoulders, frowns, looks at his papers) So ... (pause), um hmmm (reads aloud): "Permanent exit can take place via all border crossings from the GDR to the FRG and West Berlin, respectively."

KRZYSZTOF JANOWSKI, REPORTER, VOICE OF AMERICA: Another question also: does that mean that effective immediately, GDR citizens— Krzysztof Janowski, Voice of America—does that mean that effective immediately, all GDR citizens cannot emigrate via Czechoslovakia or Poland?

SCHABOWSKI: No, that is not addressed at all. We hope instead that the movement will (um) regulate itself in this manner, as we are trying to.

QUESTION: (many voices, incomprehensible question)

SCHABOWSKI: I haven't heard anything to the contrary.

QUESTION: (many voices, incomprehensible)

SCHABOWSKI: I haven't heard anything to the contrary.

QUESTION: (many voices, incomprehensible)

SCHABOWSKI: I haven't heard anything to the contrary.

I'm expressing myself so carefully because I'm not up to date on this question, but just before I came over here I was given this information. (Several journalists hurry from the room.)

QUESTION: Mr. Schabowski, what is going to happen to the Berlin Wall now?

SCHABOWSKI: It has been brought to my attention that it is 7:00 p.m. That has to be the last question. Thank you for your understanding.

(um ...) What will happen to the Berlin Wall? Information has already been provided in connection with travel activities. (um) The issue of travel, (um) the ability to cross the Wall from our side, ... hasn't been answered yet and exclusively the question in the sense ... , so this, I'll put it this way, fortified state border of the GDR ... (um) We have always said that there have to be several other factors (um) taken into consideration. And they deal with the complex of questions that Comrade Krenz, in his talk in the—addressed in view of the relations between the GDR and the FRG, in ditto light of the (um) necessity of continuing the process of assuring peace with new initiatives.

And (um) surely the debate about these questions (um) will be positively influenced if the FRG and NATO also agree to and implement disarmament measures in a similar manner to that of the GDR and other socialist countries. Thank you very much.[4]

The scene did not sparkle. It was not golden; rather, it was gray—or a worn-out socialist red. Schabowski's announcement was awkward, boring, and painfully drawn out. Nevertheless, the press conference constituted a decisive moment in history. The exhausted and under-informed Schabowski was bound to make mistakes, and he did make two crucial ones (Fig. 4.2). First, he did not emphasize the requirement of passport and visa, which was meant to slow down the *process* of border opening. Second, he mistakenly announced the regulation's *immediate* effect, moving the border opening from November 10, 1989, to a day earlier,

FIGURE 4.2 East German politician Günther Schabowski (1929–2015) during the infamous press conference in East Berlin on November 9, 1989. Mehner—Ullstein Bild/The Granger Collection, New York.

November 9, 1989. How did this happen? In such a banal way that it is almost hard to believe. Schabowski got confused by the question "[w]hen does it go into effect?" He looked through his documents and found two seemingly useful words: "immediately" and "without delay." These words were in the documents, but were *not* about the regulation's day of effect. At the same time, Schabowski overlooked the end of the document, where the last sentence clearly indicated the delayed effect (from November 9 to November 10). His confused announcement may seem amusing now, but it had drastic consequences. The border control no longer had time to prepare for the crowds. The border guards had to face a potential storming of the border without sufficient planning. By calling the Berlin Wall "a fortified state border of the GDR," Schabowski tried to soften the symbolic force of his announcement. But it was too late. Although his announcement in itself did not immediately open the borders, it provided "space" for interpretation.

Who deserves the credit for this confusing yet liberating final scene of the Schabowski press conference? Should it go to Riccardo Ehrman, for asking the first question and some of the follow-up questions? Or should the credit go to the successful albeit unorganized team effort of a small group of journalists who asked a sequence of crucial questions? Or is it Günter Schabowski to whom recognition is due, as he did not shy away from answering journalists' questions even though his knowledge of the draft legislation was so limited? In what follows, I will offer sketches of the key protagonists and their roles in the press conference. Examining the dynamics of the journalistic questioning at the press conference is key if we want to understand how and why the fall of the Berlin Wall came to be narrated as it did.

Colleagues describe Italian correspondent Riccardo Ehrman as a lovable person, who is somewhat careless with details. Facts and myths are often mixed up in his accounts of events.[5] Ehrman enjoys talking about his role in the fall of the Berlin Wall, and he does so in a playful manner. Some of his story's building blocks have remained the same throughout its various versions. He claims to have arrived late at the conference because he could not find a parking spot. Therefore he was seated to the right of the podium, close to Schabowski.[6] Displaying a mixture of pride and modesty, he believes that he gave history a slight push with his first question about the travel law;[7] in a somewhat different version of his narrative, he believes to have given history a "cue."[8]

There are also elements in his narrative that are changing. Over the last two decades, Ehrman has been trying more and more to shift his legacy away from being the person who asked the first question, and toward being the person who understood the answer instantaneously. Emphasizing how quickly he understood the stakes involved, Ehrman frequently points out that he, together with a West German diplomat, left the conference hall right after Schabowski's statement, before the conference was over. The West German diplomat ran out of the room to inform Chancellor Kohl, while Ehrman informed the Italian news agency ANSA. Ehrman believes he deserves special credit for *decoding* the Communist German language of the scene and immediately offering the ultimate interpretation and universal phrase for his news agency: "La caduta del Muro di Berlino" (the fall of the Berlin Wall).[9]

Ehrman's account also keeps changing in one key respect. For twenty years, he framed his first question about the travel law as an entirely spontaneous one.[10] But in April 2009, annoyed by an article in *Die Welt* that claimed that whatever the Italian journalist had contributed had been by chance, Ehrman presented a substantially updated version. According to this new version, Ehrman got a "tip" to raise the issue of travel at the press conference—his question, in other words, was prompted. The tip came from one of his long-term sources, Günter Pötschke, director of the East German press agency ADN. According to Ehrman, Pötschke had phoned him right before the press conference and had urged him to ask a question about the freedom to travel.[11] Ehrman justified his belated release of this information with the journalistic ethic of source protection[12]—even though the director of ADN had died three years before Ehrman's update. Ehrman upheld this version of the story for only five years. In 2014, at the twenty-fifth anniversary of the fall of the Berlin Wall, he again threw in a new narrative bomb, taking back the claim that his question at the press conference was prompted.[13] Who knows? Maybe he will again soon revise the narrative, adding another layer of confusion to the story.

Ehrman also believes that he was the one to ask the two crucial follow-up questions, about the regulation's day of effect and its application to West Berlin, but former *Bild Zeitung* journalist Peter Brinkmann claims these questions as his own.[14] In September 2009, Brinkmann even acquired a signed note from Schabowski that was meant to end the confusion regarding the ownership of the famous follow-up questions once and for all.[15] In the note, Schabowski tried to solve the ownership question with a soccer metaphor: Ehrman gave the ball the first kick, moving it into the area of the goalpost; and then it was Brinkmann who finally scored the goal. "Both deserve recognition"—Schabowski concluded, sounding like a good preschool teacher. As the *Wall Street Journal* summarized the dispute twenty years after the fall of the Berlin Wall: "The world believes Ronald Reagan, Mikhail Gorbachev or peaceful protests brought down the Berlin Wall 20 years ago next month. But for those who had front-row seats, the argument boils down to Ehrman vs. Brinkmann."[16]

The dispute's intensity and perseverance belie the actual quality of the questions at stake. These questions did not require investigative work from the journalists, nor were they posed in a uniquely eloquent way. The questions in dispute are: "At once? When … ?" and two questions about West Berlin: "You only said the FRG, is the regulation also valid for West Berlin?" and: "Does this also apply for West Berlin? You only mentioned the FRG." Still, due perhaps to their immediacy and directness, these questions have become central to the narrative of the fall of the Berlin Wall.

Actually, Ehrman and Brinkmann are not the only ones claiming credit for the earth-shattering press conference; Günter Schabowski also competed in this strange battle for prestige. So how do we interpret Schabowski's role in the unfolding of the event? One thing is clear: he had little understanding of the dangers of a Western press conference, especially one with *live* television coverage. The East German regime's inexperience with this media format may explain why he was willing to present a new regulation that he had never read and that was accepted at a meeting he did not even attend.[17]

Throughout the conference, he received multiple questions that constituted appropriate occasions to present the new regulation. As the former editor-in-chief of the central party organ *Neues Deutschland*, Schabowski could have stirred up the scene much earlier, had he wanted to. For instance, just before Ehrman asked his question, Schabowski was asked what would happen if none of the party's reform plans succeeded and the refugee wave continued. Schabowski went off on a lengthy answer about the importance of trusting one's ability to control the crisis. Why did he not combine this statement of faith with an announcement of the travel law? If anything, the new travel law was meant to stem the tide of refugees. From the roadmap Schabowski wrote for himself on a piece of paper right before the conference, it is clear that he planned to present the travel law at the end of the conference; and no amount of journalistic prompting led him to waver from this original plan.

Why did Schabowski want to announce the regulation at the end? There are at least three possible explanations. First, he may have wanted to do so in order to express that the new law was a decision of the Council of Ministers, not of the Politburo.[18] In fact, he marked this information about the law in his notes for the press conference.[19] Second, if Krenz did indeed suggest to Schabowski that the announcement would make world news, Schabowski probably wanted it to be the sensation of the conference. From the video recording of the press conference, it would seem that Schabowski enjoyed the excitement that was running in the air at the end of the "show": the crowd of journalists surrounding him, the feeling of shaping history, even if in a somewhat unprofessional way. Third, although Schabowski denied this, he might have been tipped to single Ehrman out for questions at the end. This surmise is supported by the observation that he interrupted the question of another journalist in order to let Ehrman speak at the crucial time: seven minutes before the end of the press conference.

Perhaps, the discussion about who deserves recognition for the event—Ehrman, Brinkmann, or Schabowski—would be a better informed one if we first asked a series of questions. First: did Schabowski actually need a specific journalistic question in order to *start* speaking about the new regulation? This is not likely: he could have used almost any of the previous questions to move on to the announcement. With a direct request from Egon Krenz to announce the regulation, he probably would not have left the topic out of the conference regardless. Moreover, as evidenced by his note, he planned to announce the regulation at the end of the conference.

Was he then pushed by journalists to *continue* speaking about the regulation? Yes: he was pushed by journalists to specify the regulation's day of effect and its application to West Berlin, and to comment on the passport requirement. Without these specific questions, presumably he would not have gotten himself into this level of confusion. Day of effect and areas of application—are these not obvious questions to ask about any new legislation? They are. But in the written and oral history of the fall of the Berlin Wall, likely due to the prestige of aggressive journalistic questioning of high-level "enemy" officials, these questions would come to play a uniquely strong role.

From an Awkward Occurrence to a Mythical "Event": Media Constructions of the Fall of the Berlin Wall

A focus on the importance of the press conference questions, however, provides a deeply misleading account of the fall of the Berlin Wall. This account overestimates the power of journalistic questioning and underestimates the influence of another crucial journalistic practice: *interpretation*. While the journalists' questions caused confusion at the press conference, they did not yet construct an "event." The fall of the Berlin Wall was gradually born, over many hours of intense and often confusing meaning-making in media.

After the press conference most journalists remained confused. Some of them stormed the podium and tried to extract further information from Schabowski. The most urgent case was that of the press agencies. They had to unpack the conference's meaning within minutes. The first two news agency reports, from Reuters at 7:03 p.m. and the West German news agency Deutsche Presseagentur (DPA) at 7:04 p.m., featured the somewhat confusing formulation that "from now on" any GDR citizen was entitled to leave the country "via all border crossing points."[20] While Reuters mentioned that the appropriate police offices would immediately provide visas for emigration, DPA omitted any technical details of the border crossing process. These news agency reports, while leaving out some important aspects, did not yet provide an interpretation of the event.

The real interpretative push came from the Associated Press (AP). At 7:05 p.m., AP announced that "according to information supplied by SED Politburo member Günter Schabowski," the GDR was "opening its borders."[21] The headline was "GDR opens borders." AP's announcement moved beyond the realm of strict accuracy and *interpreted* the Schabowski announcement. It also indirectly connected the event to the mythical message of "end of division," in a new world with fewer impermeable borders.

The author of the AP announcement, Frieder Reimold of the West Berlin office of AP, was very conscious of this interpretative step of simplification and universalization. After considering the inclusion of passport and visa requirements into the news agency report, he decided to emphasize the opening of the border instead: "It does not matter how many bureaucratic steps they will introduce, like permissions from the People's police or regulations on passports: all that is no longer relevant. That is only a technical step: What do they do actually? The most important is that: [they] open the wall."[22] A decade after the historic night of November 9, 1989, Reimold said that he would now formulate the AP announcement in a more careful or cautious way. But his actions cannot be adjusted in retrospect.

It took some time until AP's interpretation became prominent in the West German television coverage. On the first major West German evening television news show after the press conference, *Heute* (Today), from West German Zweites Deutsches Fernsehen (ZDF) (Second German Television) at 7 p.m., news about the press conference was the eighth item, and it did not feature AP's strong words. The news nearly failed to make it to *Heute* at all: the ZDF reporter left the Schabowski conference before its crucial final scene and the chief editor in the headquarters in Mainz was uncertain about the meaning of the announcement.[23] Reflecting the reigning confusion, at 7:35 p.m. in the evening news show of Sender Freies Berlin (SFB)—the most watched news show in Berlin, West Berlin Mayor Walter Momper said that "everything begins tomorrow." But, contradicting himself somewhat, he also claimed that this day, November 9, 1989, was the day people have all longed for.[24]

By 7:41 p.m., the West German news agency DPA had turned AP's hopeful prediction ("GDR opens borders") into an existing reality: "The GDR border to the FRG and to West Berlin *is* open."[25] At 7:41 p.m., and again at 7:56 p.m., DPA also called Schabowski's announcement a "sensation." The various news agency reports influenced the headline of the very popular West German evening news *Tagesschau* (Day Show) at 8 p.m.

Tagesschau opened its bulletin with the news of the border opening, using a clear and resonant headline: "GDR opens borders."[26]

Tagesschau's headline was direct and sensational, but its coverage also conveyed some confusion. The related report started by explaining that the topic of the "refugee wave" had come up only at the end of Schabowski's conference. Then, without further interpretation, the report showed a one-minute excerpt of the press conference, including the question about the regulation's application to West Berlin. At the end of the excerpt, *Tagesschau* offered an accessible summary: "so overnight even the Wall is supposed to become permeable."[27] After this defining sentence, the rest of the news broadcast moved on to other topics. The fall of the Berlin Wall did not dominate the scene. The other covered topics included a meeting of the Central Committee about the ongoing crisis; the refugee wave through Czechoslovakia; the living standards of the refugees in West Germany; and an extensive interview with Chancellor Kohl in Poland. *Tagesschau* featured detailed coverage on West German pension reforms, new poverty statistics, and train ticket price hikes. In its foreign reporting, *Tagesschau* had some even more banal topics, in addition to Turkish and Chinese politics, it also spent time on a scandal around the diet of cows in the Netherlands and the U.K., and a ship collision in Bremerhaven. The Schabowski announcement had been ranked top news, but *Tagesschau* was not preoccupied with it. However, at the very end of *Tagesschau*, a visibly enthusiastic news anchor announced that the late evening news, *Tagesthemen* at 10:30 p.m., would provide further reporting on the GDR's "border opening."

Despite the promise made in *Tagesschau*, the late evening news did not start at 10:30 p.m. This was not because of the historic fall of the Berlin Wall; there was a longer-than-expected VfB Stuttgart–FC Bayern München soccer game that needed coverage. Only a nine-minute-long news broadcast in the halftime break referred to the potentially global "event." Finally, after soccer received sufficient coverage, history got its turn and *Tagesthemen* aired at 10:42 p.m. *Tagesthemen* began with an image of the Brandenburg Gate along with the commentary:

The Brandenburg Gate tonight. As symbol of Berlin's division it has served its time. Likewise the Berlin Wall, which has divided East and West for 28 years. The GDR gave way to people's pressure: travel in the direction of the West *is* free.[28]

Anchorman Hanns Joachim Friedrichs, often referred to as the German Walter Cronkite, opened the late evening news with the statement that many Germans recall to this day:

> Good evening, ladies and gentlemen. One should always be care-
> ful when it comes to the use of superlatives. They are scuffed very
> quickly; but tonight we might dare to use one: this November 9 is
> a historical day. The GDR announced that from now on the borders
> are open for anyone. *The gates of the Wall are wide open.*[29]

Were the gates of the wall wide open at that time? No, certainly not. In the hours before *Tagesthemen*'s belated airing, much had happened at the borders—but the gates of the Wall were *not* "wide open." Friedrich's announcement was wishful thinking—or a self-fulfilling prophecy. Substantial crowds began to gather at border crossing points after the 8 p.m. *Tagesschau*. At this time, the GDR border patrols at the border crossing points were without orders from their superiors. The Central Committee had a meeting that ran until 8:45 p.m., and its members were unavailable for questions. The patrol guards therefore advised East German citizens to *leave* the border crossing points and wait until the next day.

The Bornholmer Strasse border crossing point was the most popular one, due to its proximity to the lively artistic neighborhoods of Prenzlauer Berg, rich with cafés and intellectuals. By 9:20 p.m., around five hundred to one thousand East Germans had gathered at this border crossing point. Under pressure from the ever-growing crowds, the border guards permit-ted the "most provocative" citizens to cross the border. Many of these early border crossers got a stamp in their passport that stripped them of their citizenship.[30] By 11:30 p.m., about an hour after Friedrich's announcement, the border guards could no longer resist the pressure from the crowds. The chief officer of passport control at Bornholmer Strasse announced the "opening of the floodgates." With this decision, the *first* gate was finally opened. In making this radical and independent decision, the chief offi-cer hoped to save the lives of the border guards under his command.[31] But even this gate opening did not yet mean that all gates were "wide open." The gates opened gradually, one after the other.

When Hanns Joachim Friedrichs announced around 10:42 p.m. that "the gates of the wall are wide open," he knew from phone calls that the border had already become permeable to *some* East Germans.[32] However,

Friedrichs must also have known that most border crossing points were still *completely sealed*. Even at Bornholmer Strasse, only a few were permitted to leave East Germany at the time of his announcement. However, his mythical announcement envisioned, and very likely influenced, the real opening of the border about an hour later. Friedrichs' historic sentence was a kind of performative utterance.[33] It changed the social and visual reality it was describing. The image of wide-open gates he presented drew on the readily transportable metaphor for freedom and inspired viewers to act.

In his last interview, in 1995, the cancer-stricken Friedrichs mentioned the sentence "the gates in the wall are wide open" as the most important sentence of his life. But then he also said in the *exact same* interview: "that's what I had learned during my five years at the BBC: keeping distance, not associating yourself with anything, not even with a good one." [34] Friedrichs somehow did not see the contradiction between his most important professional ideal (objectivity) and his most important sentence. Embracing his own interpretive power seemed too much for this veteran journalist, even at his deathbed.[35]

Right after Friedrichs' elevated introduction, *Tagesthemen* gave *live* coverage from Berlin. Unfortunately, the satellite-broadcast visual scene, provided from the border crossing point at Invalidenstrasse by reporter Robin Lautenbach, could not have offered a stronger contrast to Friedrichs' words: the imagery featured *closed* gates, calm border guards, impatient journalists, and not a single border crossing. The few East German citizens who showed up at that border crossing point were advised by the border guards to wait until tomorrow morning. (Lautenbach had no choice in the selection of the border crossing point; satellite technology at the time did not permit him to move to a more appropriate location.) *Tagesthemen* also showed a recorded video from half an hour earlier, which made the contrast between words and images even more evident. In this video, Lautenbach announced *right in front of the heavily guarded* Brandenburg Gate that the Berlin Wall, a "symbol of German division and the Cold War," was now "merely a monument."

But even after these debacles Lautenbach's struggles were not yet over. After a short item on closed border crossing points that emphasized the visa requirement, *Tagesthemen* switched again back to him. This time he got a little lucky. He encountered a few witnesses who had at least *seen* some East Germans crossing the Berlin Wall.[36] The visual scene of this interview was slightly more hopeful than the first visual impression provided by *Tagesthemen* had been, but it still lacked all the visual markers we now identify with the fall of the Berlin Wall. It certainly did not show wide-open gates. A West German interviewee in blue sweatpants reported seeing a crying East German couple cross the border around 9:25 p.m. at Bornholmer Strasse. According to the witness, when the East German couple arrived on the Western side, they all cried together. Another two witnesses interviewed by Lautenbach confirmed that East Germans, in cars and on foot, in fact crossed the border and had no troubles with returning. These people must have belonged to the *few* who were permitted to leave in order to relieve pressure. But the gates at Bornholmer Strasse were closed to most East German citizens. And at Invalidenstrasse, where Lautenbach stood, border guards were still sending everybody back.

However, in his reporting Lautenbach named the border crossing points where some crossings had already occurred: Bornholmer Strasse, Wedding, Sonnenallee, and Checkpoint Charlie. He and his interviewees also emphasized that the border crossings took place "without any complications." These two pieces of information, offered in a very popular evening newscast, must have inspired many more East Germans to test the borders. After these interviews, with visible relief at having at last delivered "something" to *Tagesthemen*, Lautenbach turned the broadcast back to the studio in Hamburg.

Both Friedrichs' and Lautenbach's announcements were rhetorically charged, but they did not set the tone for the entire *Tagesthemen*. *Tagesthemen* was rather a patchwork of distinct styles. Occasionally, the elevated tone with regard to the "border opening" made way for irony. For example, *Tagesthemen* mentioned that SFB was receiving many phone calls from American television channels asking "whether it was true that the Wall was torn down." SFB reporter Erhard Thomas responded: "it is not that far yet." The press conference was also covered with some irony: the related reporting included the conference's final question about the future of the Berlin Wall, and the news anchor sounded ironic when he repeated Schabowski's careful phrase for the Berlin Wall: "the question about the role of this *fortified state border of the GDR* will become even more pressing in the coming days and weeks."[37]

Tagesthemen also featured modest and cautious tones. It aired a recorded interview with Chancellor Kohl that still reflected confusion about the press conference's possible outcomes. Answering the first journalistic question regarding the border opening, Kohl gave an exceptionally careful answer: "What will emerge from this decision, I do not know."[38]

But following the interview, a clip covering the Bundestag's reaction to the news spoke of "a historic moment" and "an unbelievable announcement," and showed the Bundestag's sudden (and, in post–World War II Germany, unusual) eruption into singing the national anthem. In the Bundestag Green Party Representative Helmut Lippelt even said: "We are joyful and we all welcome that the Wall fell."[39]

After that clip, *Tagesthemen* moved on to a commentary by the director of the television station SFB.[40] The commentary employed the same elevated, metaphorical style as Friedrichs had done in his announcement, and started with a sentence that was centered around powerful symbols: "The building 'GDR' has been dilapidated for a while. Now even walls fall."[41] But this commentary was not followed by news on Berlin; instead, viewers were offered a detailed report on the West German state Nordrhein-Westfalen's cultural week in the East German city of Leipzig, and a lengthy interview with the Nordrhein-Westfalen governor. At the beginning of the interview, which had been recorded two hours before it aired, Friedrichs had formulated his line about the gates in the wall in a more careful and open-ended way, in present continuous: "the gates in the wall are opening to everyone." At the same time, Friedrichs also emphasized that the events of the day were "German history at first hand."

Tagesthemen did not switch to Berlin after the interview, either. Without any images from Berlin, another lengthy interview came from Leipzig, covering the chronic lack of physicians in East Germany caused by the emigration wave. Thereafter, the rest of *Tagesthemen* was dedicated to the West German chancellor's visit to Poland, the Soviet Union's reaction to East German "developments," shifts in Chinese communist politics, elections in Jordan, a U.S.–Philippines presidential meeting in Washington, West German pension reforms, the ship collision in Bremerhaven, and the recent soccer game. Finally, at the very end, a short report provided news from a border crossing point in Niedersachsen. A visibly frustrated reporter almost apologized for the fact that the border had not yet been stormed. But he did interview two East German citizens who had miraculously been let through with only a government-issued identity card. The reporter emphasized that the border guards were prepared for the storming of the border that night. He also suggested that things would most likely not kick off until the next day. Then *Tagesthemen*, the most important late evening news of West Germany, ended its coverage for the day.

In sum, West German television coverage on the historic night of November 9, 1989, was incoherent and perhaps even messy. Much of the newscast was not even about the Berlin Wall. Moreover, in the Berlin coverage, the news anchor's words pictured open gates, but the actual pictures showed gates that were all but closed. Words were speaking louder than pictures and imposing a meaning on pictures that simply did not illustrate, or worse contradicted, what the words were saying. Nonetheless, with its imagination of "wide-open gates," West German television provided a simple and readily transportable interpretation of the press conference: a contemporary myth. Germans from both sides went to the border crossing points to form ever-growing crowds. At around 11:30 p.m., Bornholmer Strasse was the first bastion to fall. This first victory was followed by victories at other border crossing points, culminating in a feast of happiness of historic proportions at the Brandenburg Gate in the early morning of November 10, 1989 (Figs. 4.3 and 4.4).

Media coverage in itself does not make history. The border opening required curious and brave citizens, an impotent East German political leadership, and independent decisions made by border-control guards. Conversation in pubs, on the streets, and over the phone also inspired people to test the "new" borders. That said, according to leading historians, media scholars, and journalists, West German broadcast media were without doubt a crucial factor in the unfolding of the fall of the Berlin

0073365   BERLIN WALL, 1989.
Credit: ullstein bild / The Granger Collection, New York

FIGURE 4.3 The Brandenburg Gate during the night of November 9–10, 1989. Peewee—Ullstein Bild/The Granger Collection, New York.

FIGURE 4.4 East Germans are greeted on Kurfürstendamm in West Berlin on November 9, 1989. Bundesarchiv—Bundesregierung, 00059615, photo: Klaus Lehnarzt.

Wall on November 9, 1989.[42] German historian Hans-Hermann Hertle, in the afterword of the eleventh edition of his monograph about the fall of Berlin Wall, offered in fact a radical statement on media's role in the event's unfolding:

> [a]s this event's protagonists, Schabowski and Krenz, Jäger [the chief officer who opened the Bornholmer Strasse crossing point] and Ehrman, emigrants and protesters, Hungarians and Czechs, Kohl and Gorbachev are all "openers of the Berlin Wall"—at the same time, they are not "the" opener. The storming of the border crossing points and the Brandenburg Gate by tens of thousands of East and West Berliners, that made the Berlin Wall fall in the night from November 9 to November 10, 1989, was not triggered by them, but *by the media*—and first and foremost, by ARD's "Tagesthemen" with Hanns Joachim Friedrichs' commentary.[43]

There were more than *four and a half hours* between Schabowski's live-covered announcement and the breakthrough at the very first border crossing point. It is hard to explain this lengthy gap without the power of a mythical journalistic language in West German broadcast media about "end of division" and "wide-open gates" that used the archaic mental images of a "falling wall." This language most likely provided inspiration to test the borders.

During these historic hours, West German broadcast media were able to influence actions on the ground with their capability to directly communicate with the East. But the construction of a myth on this historic night was not confined to West Germany. International media had the task of spreading the mythical message overseas. I will focus on NBC, because its coverage became the most acclaimed international coverage of the fall of the Berlin Wall. Of the leading television-news organizations of the world, only NBC was able to provide *live* visual coverage of the event from the beginning, having installed multi-camera capabilities at the Brandenburg Gate with a direct link to New York.[44] According to former NBC news anchor Tom Brokaw, they were in Berlin to cover the general crisis, but they did not anticipate "the" global iconic event. As Brokaw summarized the decision to visit Berlin:

> Press access to the East was limited, but since we knew that the chaos was growing, NBC News's foreign editor, Jerry Lamprecht, suggested I spend a couple of days in Berlin anchoring *Nightly News*, particularly because there was so little going on at home at the time. I thought it was a good idea and so did Bill Wheatley, *Nightly*'s executive producer, as well as Michael Gartner and Don Browne, the top two NBC News executives at the time. I left for Berlin on a late flight Monday, Nov. 7 and began reporting from the Eastern sector the next day.[45]

In the age of immobile media, setting up in Berlin a day earlier provided NBC with a crucial advantage. Moreover, Tom Brokaw also had a prearranged interview with Schabowski scheduled right after the press conference, so NBC had the exclusive chance to extract information from the confused party official. The American broadcasters also had—generally—the advantage of time difference: when Schabowski's press conference ended at 7 p.m. in Berlin, it was only 1 p.m. in New York and 10 a.m. in Los Angeles. The American live coverage thus had time to build up an event in front of substantial audiences.

But meaning-making and mythmaking around an event is not an easy matter, even for experienced NBC journalists. When Brokaw sat down with Schabowski right after the press conference, the American reporter was working within a news format, the one-on-one interview, that he was very comfortable with. But instead of a regular interview, his conversation turned into an episode of surreal comedy. Brokaw, behaving like a nice but forceful therapist, tried to get clear answers from a sleep-deprived East German party official who simply did not have clear answers. The result was a strange "dance" between the two, where Brokaw asked focused questions *very* slowly, while Schabowski tried to avoid direct answers. In the interview, Schabowski also resisted the discourse around a mythical "wall" altogether. Even at the very end of his energy, in an English conversation where he was at a linguistic disadvantage, he did not give up this rhetorical (and political) fight:

BROKAW: Mr. Schabowski, do I understand correctly? Citizens of the GDR can leave through any checkpoint that they choose for personal reasons. They no longer have to go through a third country?

SCHABOWSKI: They are not further forced to leave GDR by transit through another country.

BROKAW: It is possible for them to go through the *Wall* at some point? [emphasis added]

SCHABOWSKI: It is possible from them to go through the *border*. [Schabowski gave a big smile after his response, emphasis added][46]

It was crucial for Schabowski to resist the Western framing of the "wall," and to present the separation barrier as a regular "border." He could have just repeated Brokaw's sentence, but he wanted to correct the international symbol of division ("wall") to a technical term ("border").

The meaning of the event was far from decided at this point. Showing that neither of them thought the "Berlin Wall" would "fall" very soon, in the interview Brokaw even spent time inquiring about Schabowski's identity, whether he was still a communist amidst the massive crisis. What Brokaw hoped to achieve is unclear: it was quite unlikely that a top East German official would confess communism's sins to him in a Western television interview. As expected, Schabowski emphasized that he was a devoted communist, signaling to the viewers that this press conference was part of an ongoing reform process, not an "event," let alone a global iconic event.

After the interview, Brokaw thought it was certain that the border crossing points would be opened—but only a day later.[47] So he made his announcement in front of the Brandenburg Gate a little later accordingly: "Tom Brokaw at the Berlin Wall. This is a historic night. The

East German government has just declared that East German citizens will be able to cross the Wall from *tomorrow morning forward*—without restrictions."[48]

Brokaw accurately informed the American audience about the regulation's day of effect. His announcement in front of the Brandenburg Gate was not confusing: he spoke about a *future* reality to come. In the evening news, Brokaw even tried to place the announcement of the new travel law in its broader context, emphasizing the larger importance of the promise of free elections next year. But, perhaps fortunately, the German audience had access to the more imaginative and mythologized West German coverage that inspired *immediate* action. The actions on the ground thus did not follow Brokaw's careful and accurate prediction and narrowly factual commentary.

As the night continued, Brokaw found himself happily covering a different reality: emotional and arresting scenes traveled from Berlin to New York on his direct line, changing the course of history. NBC's visuals, aired in special editions, showed ever-growing crowds and a cheerful atmosphere at the Berlin Wall. A new transnational event was born; a miraculously peaceful border opening presented itself on the screen, capturing the American imagination on a faraway continent. It is not surprising that Brokaw still kept a piece of the Berlin Wall on his office desk twenty years after the "fall of the Berlin Wall," he said as "an enduring reminder of that night: an NBC News triumph, but most of all, a symbol of the power of people determined not to live as political prisoners forever."[49]

Building an "Event": Memorable Myths and Forgettable Facts

There are two popular beliefs about media's role in November 9, 1989, that I have tried to deconstruct in this chapter. The first belief is that the fall of the Berlin Wall received immediate and visually spectacular media coverage due to the historic significance of the event. As I have shown, this belief does not represent the reality of West German television coverage that night. A few dedicated West German broadcast journalists produced memorable coverage, often with words rather than images, while much of the media content, even in newscasts, was dedicated to other topics. Similarly, the most acclaimed American coverage had also built up the event *gradually*, step by step turning an awkward occurrence into an international symbol.

The second belief is that the fall of the Berlin Wall was a spontaneous event—covered, but not triggered, by the media. Or, more precisely, that the media were a trigger only to the extent that journalists' questions led to the unprepared announcement of the new travel regulation. In this chapter, I have shown that the power of journalistic questioning has been overestimated in connection with the fall of the Berlin Wall, and at the expense of the power of journalistic mythmaking and interpretation. Again, the real storming of the border crossing points did not begin immediately after the live covered press conference at which Schabowski, responding to journalists' repeated questions, "announced" the new travel regulation. The storming of the border happened over time, after hours of intense interpretation, imagination, and confusion.

The media triggering of the fall of the Berlin Wall was not an orchestrated journalistic effort. The event's television coverage was diverse. Dealing with an event that was still open-ended, the coverage was sometimes even contradictory. But those who listened received something stronger than mere information: a story. This story was delivered in a disjointed way, but its foundations were established. During the night of November 9, 1989, a mythical journalistic language represented and made history—not objective and narrowly factual reporting. Careful claims, while accurate at the moment, proved forgettable over time. In contrast, bold claims about wide-open gates memorably reflected the shape of history to come.

5

Condensation

HOW DOES AN event start to travel through time? What packaging does it need in order to overcome cultural and geographical barriers and distances? Here I track the steps by which the complex and confusing developments of November 9, 1989, were condensed into simple phrases ("fall of the Berlin Wall"/"opening of the border"), a short narrative ("freedom," "end of division"), and a recognizable visual scene. I analyze the coverage of the fall of the Berlin Wall in American and West German media with a focus on textual and visual condensation. The communist East German and Soviet coverage, as examples of counter-narration, will be the topic of the next chapter.

The time difference between East Germany and the United States enabled the American print media to cover the fall of the Berlin Wall extensively as soon as the next day, on November 10, 1989. The first American headlines were symbolically crowded: "Fallen Symbol: The Berlin Wall No Longer Will Hold Germans Behind Iron Curtain" (*Wall Street Journal*), "The Wall is Gone: Thousands Rejoice as Border is Opened" (*Seattle Times*), " 'The Wall No Longer Divides Berliners'/Germans Celebrate As Borders Are Opened" (*St. Petersburg Times*, Florida), "The Berlin Wall is Crumbling, Bush, Leaders Hail Decision" (*St. Louis Post-Dispatch*, Missouri).

The *Washington Post* featured the powerful headline: "East Germany Opens Berlin Wall and Borders, Allowing Citizens to Travel Freely to the West."[1] Its front page already displayed the ultimate visual condensation of the event: the image of the Brandenburg Gate, with crowds standing on the top of the Berlin Wall (Fig. 5.1). The lead article did not speak of the awkwardness of the press conference, the multiplicity of early interpretations, the confusion on the ground. It started with a strongly worded paragraph: "Communist East Germany today opened its borders to the

FIGURE 5.1 Front page of the *Washington Post* on November 10, 1989.

West, including the Berlin Wall, announcing that its citizens could travel or emigrate freely, in the most stunning step since World War II toward ending the East-West division of Europe." The article did not highlight the importance of West German broadcast media in the making of the event, either; the quick border opening's immediate causes were left remarkably blurred: *"As word spread,* hundreds of jubilant East Berliners poured into West Berlin, on their first visits ever to the western half of the city, divided for 28 years by the 13-foot-high concrete wall that is the best-known landmark along the Iron Curtain."[2]

A day later, the *Washington Post* covered the Soviet perception of the event with verbal images of a falling wall: "[t]he Soviet Union welcomed what it called the 'virtual destruction of the Berlin Wall,' but warned that it would not tolerate the reunification of the two German states or an East German departure from the Warsaw Pact military alliance."[3] And in a different formulation, "Soviets Accept Wall's Fall, Not Reunification."[4] The *Washington Post* thus needed only a day to condense the event into its ultimate simple phrases, a short narrative of freedom, and a recognizable visual scene.

On November 10, 1989, the *Los Angeles Times* summarized the event in the headline "Berlin Wall Crumbling."[5] The two related images showed an East German making "a point by slamming at Berlin Wall with a hammer" and youth climbing the Berlin Wall at Checkpoint Charlie. The lead article started with the condensed narrative of the event: "East German border guards began dismantling sections of the Berlin Wall today, just a day after Communist authorities *threw open* the nation's prison-like frontiers, and more than 100,000 citizens poured across to the West." The tedious international press conference of the day before, in which most journalists almost fell asleep, was quickly replaced by the memorable mental image of "throwing open" a mythical frontier. A day later a front-page article's title celebrated the "fall of the wall."[6] In the central image, "youths scrambled up the Berlin Wall to join hundreds of their countrymen in celebration."[7] The *Los Angeles Times* had spent a maximum of two days (arguably only one) to condense the event into a readily transportable format.

On November 10, 1989, the *New York Times'* headline read "East Germany Opens Frontier to the West for Emigration or Visits; Thousands Cross" (Fig. 5.2). The central visual scene was "East Berliners dancing atop the Berlin Wall near the Brandenburg Gate." The newspaper's lead article mentioned the power of media coverage, but assigned no interpretative power to journalists: "Once Schabowski's announcement was *read on radio and television,* a tentative trickle of East Germans testing the new regulations quickly turned into a jubilant horde, which joined at the border crossings with crowds of flag-waving, cheering West Germans."[8] *Reading* Schabowski's announcement clearly would not have been enough, especially because the press conference received live coverage anyway. What

FIGURE 5.2 Front page of the *New York Times* on November 10, 1989.

viewers and listeners needed was *interpretation* that provided inspiration on both sides to test the borders.

The *Chicago Tribune* announced the event in a headline filled with symbols: "East Germans Open Wall: Citizens on both sides dance atop barrier."[9] The lead article provided a quick, accessible summary of an iconic event of freedom, without mentioning any confusion at the press conference. The role of West German broadcast media in triggering the event received no mention here either.

A short day after the border opening, *USA Today* announced "The Wall Is Gone." Its central article presented a magical surprise-event of freedom:

> AT THE BERLIN WALL—East Germans—told they were free to travel anywhere—wept, hugged, danced and kissed in both halves of divided Berlin today after East Germany opened its borders for the first time since 1961. The joyous scene occurred at the world's monument to communism, symbol for 28 years of the Cold War and testament to the 191 East Germans who've perished trying to crawl, climb or even fly over it. Berliners celebrated into the early hours, climbing atop the concrete barrier and chipping away with hammers. Others danced at Checkpoint Charlie and the Brandenburg Gate. But also near the Gate, candles flickered in front of simple wooden crosses that stand in memory of the people killed trying to escape. Strangers embraced strangers as cars packed with East Germans and others paraded through West Berlin.[10]

The story was framed as a fairy tale of the power of ordinary people to overcome a crippling division. The event was quickly removed from its context, distanced from its initial awkwardness. The event's "makers," especially politicians and journalists, were not part of the mythical story. Everything just "happened," like a miracle, without elaborate construction. The event's media narration was all but omitted.

The Brandenburg Gate became the central image of the event with remarkable speed: its role was established within one short day. Of course the coverage built on the already existing symbolic power of the Brandenburg Gate in German and international imagination. The neo-classical triumphal arch was commissioned by Prussian King Frederick William II and completed in 1791. It was modeled after the gate to the Acropolis in Athens. On the top of the Brandenburg Gate is the Quadriga: a chariot driven by a goddess of victory and pulled by four horses. While originally a monument dedicated to victory and peace, the Brandenburg Gate has come to embody not only German pride but also defeat. When Napoleon occupied Berlin in 1806, he marched through the Brandenburg Gate and ordered the Quadriga to be shipped to Paris (it was only returned after Napoleon's own defeat in 1814–1815). The Brandenburg

Gate's striking appearance and multilayered history have made it one of the central symbols of German national identity. After the magical night of November 9, 1989, the Brandenburg Gate again gained a new meaning: "symbol of openness."

This newly attached meaning was somewhat ironic and contradictory. On the one hand, the imagery of crowds occupying the Brandenburg Gate area on the night of November 9, 1989, provided the fall of the Berlin Wall with a uniquely memorable visual scene. On the other hand, the Brandenburg Gate, unlike other points at which people were crossing the border, remained *closed* for six weeks after that exceptional, uncontrolled night of November 9, 1989. It was the last weapon of the GDR, the ultimate symbol the regime kept in its "hands" as long as possible. If anything, the Brandenburg Gate was a symbol of contrasts, or even an inaccurate symbol: open in imagination and imagery, but still (or again) closed in reality (Figs. 5.3 and 5.4).

The tendency to focus on the Brandenburg Gate while speaking of a magical event also characterized NBC's historic coverage on November 10, 1989. In the *Evening News*, Tom Brokaw, standing in front of the massive Berlin Wall, declared that "this wall has been converted now from a symbol of oppression to a monument to liberty and freedom."[11] NBC

0073366   BRANDENBURG GATE, 1989.
Credit: ullstein bild / The Granger Collection, New York

FIGURE 5.3 Berliners celebrate at the Brandenburg Gate, November 12, 1989. Peters—Ullstein Bild/The Granger Collection, New York.

FIGURE 5.4 East German soldiers on the Berlin Wall in front of the Brandenburg Gate, November 12, 1989. AGIP—Rue des Archives/The Granger Collection, New York.

also showed crowds on both sides of the wall chanting, "The wall must go." Brokaw spoke of a sudden, peaceful change, happily celebrated in Berlin:

> And back here at the Brandenburg Gate, it is the 4th of July and Armistice Day all rolled into one tonight. It happened so suddenly— the wall finally opened. The journey made countless times in the mind could be made at last in person.[12]

While conveying the celebratory atmosphere of the town, Brokaw completely left out the agents responsible for the opening. Broadcast media's role received no mention at all. The wall "suddenly" opened—by whom and how seemed a topic no longer worth considering.

If the decontextualization of the event seems inevitable, the removal of journalistic influence is more puzzling. Why did media interpretations of the event not receive acknowledgment by American media? Why did American journalists not take pride in their Western colleagues' shaping of the event just a day before? Somehow, they chose to delete their own role, leaving their power as members of a key interpretive community unacknowledged. It seems as if not only politicians but also journalists had to be edited out from the narrative to make the event "magical" and "revolutionary." Their inclusion would have threatened the message that *ordinary* people can make radical change happen.

One possible answer is that journalists may not have been fully aware of their interpretative role in the event. But even in this case, they could have reflected more on the accidental nature of both the Schabowski press conference and its aftermath. Understanding the power of interpretation may need time, but not representing awkwardness, boredom, and happenstance was a matter of choice.

Some readers might have a different, more critical view of these characteristics of the media coverage of the fall of the Berlin Wall. These readers might say that all these media representations are global media distortions at their finest; strategic Western misrepresentations of a distant event, clear cases of what media scholar Barbie Zelizer called "cannibalization of memory."[13] But how did the *local* West German media cover the fall of the Berlin Wall, on the ground, fully aware of the contexts and contradictions? Was its narration significantly different from the "distant" American coverage?

On November 10, 1989, the West German press was still searching for the right kind of language for the event of November 9, 1989. Since the event took place so late in the night, most newspapers needed a day to find the appropriate words and tone—but no more than that. By November 11, West German print coverage and television coverage were remarkably similar in terms of their words and their visuals. On November 10, 1989 *Die Welt* chose a careful headline—"The SED Opens Borders to the West: Nobody Will Be Prevented from Departure"[14]—and displayed an image of Krenz and Schabowski in front of the Central Committee headquarters. The next day, by contrast, the newspaper used West Berlin Mayor Walter Momper's quote as a headline—"The German People Are the Happiest in the World"[15]—and it covered the entire front page with characteristic imagery of the fall of the Berlin Wall. Not a single politician made it to the November 11 front-page imagery.

The *Frankfurter Allgemeine Zeitung* (*FAZ*) went through a similar shift in language between November 10 and November 11, 1989. The headline on November 10, 1989, used the complex formulation "The GDR Opens Its Borders to the Federal Republic."[16] In contrast, on November 11 the *FAZ* made a condensed and universalized announcement about freedom: "Wall and Barbed Wire Do Not Divide Anymore."[17] The headline on November 10, 1989, still applied the language of the early news agency announcements and tied the event to its local context ("GDR," "Federal Republic").

On November 11, 1989, the headline employed a strongly elevated language, speaking about the common human experience of division. The emotional claim that "wall and barbed wire do not divide anymore" presented the event as an international event of freedom, the meaning and resonance of which carried well beyond the borders of Berlin.[18]

On November 10, 1989, the front page of the *Süddeutsche Zeitung* did not have any information on the historic occasion at all. On November 11, however, the newspaper led with strong symbolic language and imagery (Fig. 5.5). The headline was "The GDR Cracks the Wall," a sentence taken from an AP announcement drafted by Frieder Reimold (the author of the

FIGURE 5.5 "The GDR Cracks the Wall," front page of *Süddeutsche Zeitung* on November 11, 1989.

famous "GDR opens borders" announcement from November 9, 1989). This time Reimold referred to the East German leadership's decision to open further border crossing points. As a front-page image, the *Süddeutsche Zeitung* printed a photograph of the Berlin Wall conquered by a jubilant crowd. The subtitle read "The Wall no longer divides: Berliners from both sides celebrated until early Friday in front of the Brandenburg Gate." The front page also printed Willy Brandt's commentary in bold: "Berlin will live and the Wall will fall." Again, the language emphasized the internationally resonant experience of overcoming physical division.

The West German tabloid *Bild Zeitung*, with its general sympathy for bold claims and bombastic headlines, was quicker to find its condensed pitch. Already on November 10, 1989, it simply announced: "Done! The Wall Is Open."[19] The front page did not feature any distinctive imagery that day, but by November 11, 1989, *Bild Zeitung* had also settled on the image of the Brandenburg Gate as the central symbolic scene of the event.

On November 10, 1989, West German newspapers did not praise, or even allude to, the power of the mythical language provided by West German television. Journalists were only praised for their assertive questions at the press conference. The *Berliner Morgenpost*, for example, wrote that "it was three minutes before the planned end of the conference, when Schabowski—in response to a journalist's question—almost casually announced the sensation: the GDR opens the borders for its citizens to the West."[20] The fact that West German television may have played a role in inspiring people to test the new travel law was mentioned nowhere either. Even a day later, the same *Berliner Morgenpost* reporter still believed that the West German television coverage had only helped to make Berlin "a topic in the world"; its potential role in precipitating the Berlin Wall's fall was not mentioned in his article.[21]

Overcoming their original slowness and incoherence, West German television channels provided frequent live coverage in special editions on November 10, 1989. The *Tagesschau*, which had been a patchwork of distinct styles on November 9, found its voice by November 10, 1989. "Open borders," its yellow caption declared—and the smiling news anchor announced the latest developments in front of an image of the "feast" at Brandenburg Gate. *Tagesschau* provided enthusiastic and detailed reporting about the short-term visits and the permanent emigrations that had been taking place since the borders had opened. However, it lacked any reporting on the exact unfolding of the event just a day before.

The event appeared as a sudden, miraculous eruption—heroic, and in no way media-triggered. The coverage told a story of ever-increasing numbers of citizens succeeding in crossing the border in the evening, first with state-issued identification in hand, later without any documentation at all. The coverage focused on citizens and their hugs, smiles, and tears. Politicians were given attention only insofar as they commented on the event that had already unfolded. For instance, Walter Momper's claim about the German people being the happiest in the world was presented as central—it was in fact aired twice. In contrast, his prediction, made a day before, that "everything would begin tomorrow" had already faded from memory. On November 10, 1989, in front of a cheering crowd, Willy Brandt—who, as mayor of West Berlin in 1961, embodied all the memories of the Berlin Wall—declared his belief that "separation through barbed wire and a death strip was against the stream of history." He did not detail exactly how the Berlin Wall "fell" just a day before.

The elevated language featured simple and readily transportable symbols of oppression and liberation. All the awkwardness, confusion, and open-endedness of the day before vanished from the coverage. Accident, misunderstanding, and "failure" did not fit the grand narrative—and were omitted. Nor was the event placed in context; it appeared in isolation, not as one moment in an ongoing reform process. *Tagesschau* did not remind the viewers that East Germany had been working on new travel legislation for a while, nor did its coverage show how this particular piece of legislature fit into the larger East German plans for renewal.[22] Facts, processes, and contradictions were put aside to highlight the historic "event." One of the few exceptions was President Richard von Weizsäcker's appeal for "prudence and a feeling of responsibility." He reminded both sides of the need for a step-by-step process to freedom. However, Weizsäcker also employed some of the symbolic language in his commentary when he said that "freedom cannot be walled in." Another example of cautious communication was Chancellor Helmut Kohl's speech in front of the Schöneberg town hall, in which he delivered the message of "calmness" and "restraint." Showing that the West German audience was far from coherent in its opinions, the Christian Democrat Kohl's speech received plenty of whistles and boos by his opposition in the crowd.

Tagesthemen adopted the same vocabulary as *Tagesschau*. It focused on interviews with visitors to West Berlin. The word of the day was "Wahnsinn!" (Crazy! or Awesome!), which was repeated in almost every interview. *Tagesthemen* showed crowds celebrating the fall of the Berlin

Wall, and hitting the walls with their hammers. The event was presented as an event of "the people" overcoming a boundary that had separated them for almost three decades.

The background image for news anchor Hanns Joachim Friedrichs showed crowds standing on and surrounding the Berlin Wall in front of the Brandenburg Gate. *Tagesthemen* also reported that East German border troops had restored the order on the east side of Brandenburg Gate by the morning of November 10, 1989. While crowds were still celebrating on the West side, on the East side friendly but firm border guards reminded everyone of the limitations of the newly won freedom to travel. ZDF's evening news show, *Heute*, also used the Brandenburg Gate as a key visual marker. News anchor Volker Jelaffle spoke in front of an image of the Brandenburg Gate occupied by a euphoric crowd.

While the Brandenburg Gate served as a central symbol for abstract concepts like "division" and "freedom," the coverage also focused on more materialistic aspects of the event. Both television and print news highlighted that most visits to West Berlin were short-term visits with a commercial component. East Germans received 100 German marks as welcoming money, to be picked up at visitor centers and at designated banks. After they picked up this very modest sum, their first trips were often to consumer areas of Kurfürstendamm (Ku'damm), where they admired the variety of goods. Some purchased the small souvenirs they were able to afford; others saved the amount for an uncertain future. While coverage about the Brandenburg Gate area centered on the common, celebratory experience of both East and West Germans, the reporting on these brief shopping trips indicated difference—both between communism and capitalism and between East and West Germans.

The Brandenburg Gate and Ku'damm became the most important symbolic places, representing two key components of the fall of the Berlin Wall's message: "end of German division" and "universal defeat of the economic order of communism." However, the two were in immediate contradiction: the communal joy of having overcome the tight control at the Brandenburg Gate for a miraculous night was not followed by a similarly communal experience at Ku'damm. Here, economic inequality structured the experience, thus revealing a stronger division between East and West than any physical wall could provide. West German newspapers often published this contrasting imagery on a single page. For instance, *Bild Zeitung* on November 15, 1989, juxtaposed a photograph of the impromptu performance of cellist Mstislav Rostropovich at the Berlin Wall with an article about East Germans who stood in long lines for the modest welcoming money. But even stories on the visits to the shopping district sometimes captured "events." For instance, four days after the fall of the Berlin Wall *Bild Zeitung* reported on the arrival of the "Open Wall Baby."[23] The East German baby had been born unexpectedly under a maple tree in West Berlin after her unassuming parents paid a brief visit to Ku'damm.

Two symbolic objects embodied the economic message of the "fall of communism" more than any other: the "capitalist" banana and the "communist" Trabant, nicknamed "Trabi" (Fig. 5.6)[24] The objects, very different in nature to begin with, stood for a balanced opposition: the banana, available in the West but almost unavailable in the East, stood for Western abundance; the car Trabi, with its basic design and long waiting lists, represented the state-controlled economy and limited access to goods.

FIGURE 5.6 Entrepreneur Günther Fielmann distributes bananas to East German visitors on November 15, 1989. Ullstein Bild/The Granger Collection, New York.

While the Brandenburg Gate and Ku'damm served as symbolic places, and the banana and the Trabant as symbolic objects, Willy Brandt became the symbolic figure in media representations—embodying, as he did, the entire history of the Berlin Wall. His symbolic power was enhanced by a visit from Senator Ted Kennedy, evoking the famous imagery of President John F. Kennedy's visit to Berlin, which also featured Willy Brandt.

After ten enthusiastic days, around November 19, 1989, the West German press coverage started to focus on how life would return to some degree of normality. The journalistic language returned to its regular

objective and factual style. Frequently discussed topics included the problem of parking thousands of East German cars in West Berlin, potential
ways to control the black market, and negotiations between East and West
German politicians. However, use of the mythical language persisted in
connection with one topic: the much-anticipated opening of the central
symbolic place of the event, the Brandenburg Gate.

Hundreds of international journalists camped at the Brandenburg
Gate area to push for the Brandenburg Gate's permanent opening. Their
camping in the area was also likely inspired by the ultimate fear of every
journalist: "what if they open the Brandenburg Gate without me?" This
fear was probably enhanced by the "frustrating" experience of having
missed the announcement of the fall of the Berlin Wall. This time, journalists desired a media event in the traditional sense: a preplanned, well-
designed funeral for the Berlin Wall.

Journalists pushed for the opening of the Brandenburg Gate not just by
being physically present in the area, but also by printing large headlines and
powerful imagery from the fall of the Berlin Wall onward. They frequently
gave coverage about themselves. On November 17, 1989, for instance, *Bild
Zeitung* reported that seven hundred international journalists were camping in the Brandenburg Gate area despite severe weather conditions. The
tabloid interviewed multiple American journalists about their experience
of "waiting."[25] Interviews with international journalists were also a frequent item in West German news. On November 15, 1989, the late-evening
news show *Tagesthemen* even made the ironic comment that these days,
journalists simply waited, and then they "reported on waiting."

Finally, after almost six weeks of waiting, on December 22, 1989, the
Brandenburg Gate was opened. It was a media event in the traditional
sense, co-organized by East and West Germany, providing the international media with plenty of opportunities for reverent narration (Fig. 5.7).
Ironically, today it is the confusing and accidental fall of the Berlin Wall
that is remembered as the symbolic closure of the social trauma of the
Berlin Wall—much more so than its well-organized international funeral.

Overall, in both the "local" West German and the "global" American
media, the confusing and contradictory developments of November 9,
1989, were condensed with breathtaking speed into a simple phrase ("fall
of the Berlin Wall"/"opening of the Berlin Wall"), a short narrative of
"freedom" and "end of division," and a recognizable visual scene (celebratory crowds at the Brandenburg Gate, at other areas of the Berlin Wall,
and in various parts of West Berlin). The story of the fall of the Berlin

FIGURE 5.7 "Berlin's Nicest Gift. The Brandenburg Gate on the East Side Just Before 3PM Yesterday Afternoon: Thousands Awaited the Moment of Opening," *Berliner Morgenpost*, December 23, 1989, 3.

Wall was stripped of its accidental nature and initial awkwardness. The potential influence of West German television coverage was pushed to the background in order to highlight the power of ordinary citizens. The East German leadership's three weeks of work on the new travel regulation did not become a core element of the story. The "event" got embodied in symbolic persons, objects, and places. The fall of the Berlin Wall was elevated above its local contextual details, thus becoming readily transportable. The event's simplified package of phrase(s), narrative, and imagery was ready to travel through time, space, and media.

6

Counter-narration

COULD THE STORY of the fall of the Berlin Wall have been told in a distinctively different way? In theory, the East German leadership had a choice between counter-narration and under-narration. In the case of the fall of the Berlin Wall, counter-narration would have involved crafting a powerful counter-story that deconstructed the Western mythical, elevated story of the fall of the Berlin Wall. This counter-story would have constrained the event's Western condensation into a simple phrase, a short narrative, and a recognizable scene. And ultimately, it could have prevented the original tale of the fall of the Berlin Wall from traveling through time, space, and media.

The other, somewhat less ambitious, option was what I call under-narration: telling a story about the "ordinary" rather than the "exceptional." As Daniel Dayan's and Elihu Katz's *Media Events* described this narrative strategy, albeit without naming it:

> The same public event may be treated as a media event by networks or channels in one country and as news by those of other countries. The same public occasion is thus submitted to two different textual treatments, an ordinary treatment (news) and an extraordinary one (media event). Opting for the news treatment flatly rejects the event's aim of being experienced as an occasion. News broadcasts distance the event. They offer a cold look at its ideological claims, denying their spectators any possibility of "flowing with" the event.[1]

The East German media adopted the strategy of under-narration and did not attempt to spread a counter-narrative. The narrative constructed by East German media presented November 9, 1989, as merely one administrative moment that belonged to a long process of deliberate political reform. In doing this, East Germany abandoned the antifascist narrative that would have focused on the dangers of nationalism and reunification in the German context.[2] Instead of trying to revitalize the mythical narrative of the Anti-Fascist Protective Rampart, East German media employed a generally factual and objective reporting style—which proved, in the battle with the mythical Western narrative, to be the weaker one. In some ways, the weakness of the narrative reflected the weakness of the narrator.

This chapter will present a detailed analysis of the development of the narrative of the simple "news event" in *Aktuelle Kamera*, the foremost East German evening television news show, and in two particularly influential East German dailies, *Neues Deutschland* and *Berliner Zeitung* from the accidental day of November 9, 1989 (fall of the Berlin Wall), until the ceremonial day of December 22, 1989 (opening of the Brandenburg Gate). The chapter will also show that the East German coverage was highly similar to the Soviet coverage in its depiction of the event.

On November 9, 1989, Günter Pötschke, director of the East German news agency ADN, followed the Schabowski conference on television. His first reaction: "I thought I [did] not hear and see well!"[3] Before he could initiate a call, Pötschke received a call from the government's spokesman, who was equally stunned—and together they decided to change the original day and time at which the new travel regulation was supposed to go into effect and to accept Schabowski's "interpretation" of an immediate effect.[4] At 7:04 p.m., only four minutes after the Schabowski conference, ADN distributed a press release to all its East German clients (the press release was not meant to be publicized until the next day). This way, instead of correcting Schabowski's mistake, the East German media ended up communicating the regulation's immediate significance.

East Germany's most important evening news show, *Aktuelle Kamera*, began thirty minutes after the Schabowski conference, at 7:30 p.m. It opened with the news that a party conference was to be held in December. The item titled "Travels: New Regulations of the Council of Ministers" came in second; it mainly involved the news anchor reading a lengthy excerpt from the new travel regulation that was full of obscure legal language. In line with the traditions of East German media coverage, *Aktuelle Kamera* presented but did not interpret the available news items. The related clip from the Schabowski conference largely avoided the topic of new travel regulations and featured Schabowski's monotone analysis of the new election laws instead. Then the news anchor quickly moved on to the next news item. At the very end of that evening's show, well into the twenty-eighth minute, *Aktuelle Kamera* finally returned to the topic of the new travel regulation, showing a lengthy excerpt of the Schabowski conference. It aired the last question that had been asked at the international press conference: "Mr. Schabowski, what is going to happen to the Berlin Wall now?" It also showed Schabowski's answer:

> What will happen to the Berlin Wall? Information has already been provided in connection with travel activities. (um) The issue of travel, (um) the ability to cross the Wall from our side, ... hasn't been answered yet and exclusively the question in the sense ..., so this, I'll put it this way, fortified state border of the GDR.... (um) We have always said that there have to be several other factors (um) taken into consideration. And they deal with the complex of questions that Comrade Krenz, in his talk in the—addressed in view of the relations between the GDR and the FRG, in ditto light of the (um) necessity of continuing the process of assuring peace with new initiatives.
>
> And (um) surely the debate about these questions (um) will be positively influenced if the FRG and NATO also agree to and implement disarmament measures in a similar manner to that of the GDR and other socialist countries. Thank you very much.[5]

After this excerpt, viewers were left without any additional commentary on the "fortified state border of the GDR;" *Aktuelle Kamera* turned to the weather forecast, and then ended, as usual, at 8 p.m.

Between its 7:04 p.m. press release on November 9, 1989, and 2:06 a.m. on November 10, 1989, the East German news agency ADN remained silent—with the exception of a short supplemental announcement at 10:55 p.m. that detailed the offices to which citizens needed to turn for visas.[6] The reason was that, due to ongoing meetings, ADN did not receive any guidance or directions from the political leadership until 10 p.m., at which point it was advised to remain silent so as to avoid adding fuel to the fire.

East German television still did something "revolutionary" to its standards; close to 10 p.m. it interrupted the scheduled program *twice* to read the ADN announcement to its perplexed audience. These pieces of factual information were so short, however, and they came so late in the game that they were too weak to battle the already pretty strong *story* told by Western media. Finally, on November 10, at 2:06 a.m., the ADN editors, who were still unable to receive clear guidance from the political leadership, released a brief statement that was a powerful example of careful under-narration:

> Numerous GDR citizens crossed the border to Berlin (West) tonight after the announcement of the new travel regulation and after they showed their identity cards to the GDR border guards. Many declared their intention to return to the GDR after a several hour visit. Citizens of the West also paid short visits to the GDR.[7]

In the evening news of November 10, 1989, *Aktuelle Kamera* opened with the statement that "tens of thousands [had] used the new travel regulations," showing lines of Trabis at border crossing points. The headline displayed on the background to the news anchor read "Neue Reiseregelung" ["new travel regulation"]. This time the evening news also featured a long video announcement from the Interior Minister regarding the logistical details of the new regulation. Video excerpts showed the organized and friendly work that border guards at various border crossing points were doing. One excerpt even featured East German travelers who were handing out flowers to border guards as a sign of their appreciation. Through brief interviews with travelers, the show emphasized that East Germans were paying short visits to West Berlin and quickly returned to their home country afterward. It also presented international reactions to the "the new travel regulation," including a comment by the West German president. Toward the end of the newscast, the anchor returned to the "news of the day," namely "new travel regulations"; the related report covered the situation at offices responsible for visas. Finally, at the very end of *Aktuelle Kamera*, an excerpt showed crowds that had gathered at the Brandenburg Gate around 2 p.m. that day—young people, mostly, who were engaged in "a diverse dialogue" with the border guards. This friendly dialogue was the main focus of the report. Another news item, presented by the same anchor but recorded at 6 p.m., featured West German youth at the Brandenburg Gate. The reporter discussed the crowd's alcohol consumption, and the demolition of the wall with hammers. During those four hours between 2 p.m. and 6 p.m., the reporter's tone and attitude had shifted radically: the more recent scene was no longer framed as a dialogue. But a direct condemnation of the crowd could have been controversial, and the report tried to be balanced, not really opting for either positive or openly negative coverage. Besides these careful closing reports, the Berlin Wall did not come up once throughout the entire evening news show. [8]

The coverage of the news event in the central party daily *Neues Deutschland* can be summarized in a few short paragraphs as well. On November 10, 1989, the day after the news event, *Neues Deutschland* framed the story as being about "new travel regulations." Its front page included only the official press release of the new travel regulation, under the title "GDR government spokesman about the new travel regulations." The press release was introduced by a single sentence that held that, according to the government's spokesman, the regulation would go into effect immediately, and would remain in effect until an appropriate travel law was passed.

Of course the possibilities of editors were limited due to the late unfolding of the event the night before. But a day later, on November 11, 1989—when compelling photographs would have been widely available—*Neues Deutschland* still published only the transcript of the television announcement of the Interior Minister on its front page. The related photograph, showing a Trabi crossing the border, was captioned "Much traffic at border crossing points." Inside the newspaper, related articles described the quick and "non-bureaucratic" process of acquiring visas.

On Monday, November 13, after a Sunday break, *Neues Deutschland* published a front-page article titled "Hundreds of Thousands Used the New Travel Regulation of the GDR."[9] The attached photograph showed a meeting between the mayors of East and West Berlin. After four days, then, not a single emblematic photograph of the fall of the Berlin Wall had made it to the front page of East Germany's most important party daily. On November 14, 1989, only a tiny front-page article (an ADN press release) referred to the historic event, under the title "Almost a Million GDR Citizens Traveled to the FRG."[10] On November 15, 1989, *Neues Deutschland* was ready to move on to different topics.

The East German daily *Berliner Zeitung*'s coverage was similarly minimalist. On November 10, 1989, the newspaper's front page only featured the official press release, with a little section in italics that specified the requirement of travel documents (visa and passport for temporary trips, only identity card for permanent leave). A day later, *Berliner Zeitung* covered the border opening under the title "Hundreds of Thousands of GDR Citizens Went Sightseeing in West Berlin." The subtitles read "Memorable Day—Most Come Back—Trust Grows Again" (Fig. 6.1). The newspaper's related articles focused on the shortness and bureaucratic ease of the visits. One of the articles gave the following concise summary of the "news event:" "since late Thursday evening GDR citizens can cross the border to West Berlin with an un-bureaucratically issued visa—simply a stamp in the ID."[11]

FIGURE 6.1 "Hundreds of Thousands of GDR Citizens Went Sightseeing to West Berlin," front page of *Berliner Zeitung* on November 11, 1989.

On November 13, 1989, a *Berliner Zeitung* cover article titled "Demolishing the Wall in Berlin?"[12] expressed the concern that West German neo-Nazis had gone on a rampage at the Brandenburg Gate. On November 15, the front page carried an article titled "Almost Six Million Visas Issued Since November 9, 1989."[13] By November 16, 1989, one day later than in *Neues Deutschland*, the story of the "new travel regulation" had disappeared completely from the front page of *Berliner Zeitung*.

The story of the new travel regulation had a lifecycle of only a week in East German media, but it was revived somewhat around the time of the Brandenburg Gate's official opening. Here, for the first time, East German journalists started to use an elevated language in connection with the border opening, similar to that of their West German colleagues. East German journalists also began to employ the same visual vocabulary as the West, and published multiple images of the Brandenburg Gate and of celebratory crowds surrounding it. The headlines expressed enthusiasm, elevation, and emotion—all the while emphasizing that this well-planned "event" had been coproduced by East and West (Fig. 6.2).

From the East German perspective, November 9, 1989, had marked only the introduction of new travel regulations, a nonevent that had been

FIGURE 6.2 "The Brandenburg Gate is Open—Symbol of Deep Changes in the Center of Europe. It Got So Far on Friday Evening. The Brandenburg Gate Will be Opened for Visitor Traffic. Hans Modrow, Helmut Kohl, Erhard Krack, and Walter Momper Together Carry Out This Act," front page of *Neues Deutschland* on December 23–24, 1989.

misrepresented as an "event" in the West. By contrast, the opening of the Brandenburg Gate on December 22, 1989, was accepted and presented as an "event" on both sides (Fig. 6.3). Somehow, though, this well-organized and universally accepted ceremonial media event never embedded itself in international memory. Perhaps it was too organized, or too official: it certainly lacked any sense of surprise or magic. It had been arranged by political actors, and therefore could not possibly be framed as a success story of individual or collective courage. The event did not offer any new visual markers; it only reinforced the already existing symbolic power of the Brandenburg Gate. During the time of this well-organized funeral of the Berlin Wall, *other* events fascinated journalists and audiences more. These included the revolution in Romania, the demonstrations in Bulgaria, and Helmut Kohl's historic visit to the East German city of Dresden that signaled the upcoming German reunification. These reasons may help to explain why, in the end, the accidental day of November 9, 1989, has come to overshadow the perfectly planned day of December 22, 1989.

FIGURE 6.3 West German Chancellor Helmut Kohl (at the microphone) and East German Prime Minister Hans Modrow together inaugurate the border crossing point at the Brandenburg Gate on December 22, 1989. Bundesarchiv, 00000928, photo: Klaus Lehnarzt.

The Soviet media coverage was remarkably similar to its East German counterpart's representations. In November and December of the fateful year of 1989, the central Soviet party daily *Pravda* provided some piece of news on East Germany in every second issue. To put these facts in context, it is worth noting that in 1989, *Pravda* was published every day, even on Sunday, in a press run of approximately ten million copies. In October, it decided to raise its number of pages from six to eight. One would expect that the East German political drama would receive prominent coverage in the central Soviet newspaper—well, not exactly. The articles addressing East Germany were brief and placed in the second half of the paper, on the fourth, fifth, sixth, and seventh pages. Obviously, the Soviet party leadership was not proud of the ever-escalating crisis in a socialist ally country.

There were three exceptions when East German material did land on the front page. On November 2, 1989, an article addressed a meeting between Egon Krenz and Mikhail Gorbachev. On November 15 a "welcome dispatch" for the new East German Prime Minister, Hans Modrow, was published. And on December 5, *Pravda* reported on a consultation between Gorbachev and Modrow. But even in these three cases, the emphasis was on the participation and involvement of the Soviet Union, not on the significance of happenings in East Germany. The articles also signaled that high-level politicians determine events, denying the potential influence of publics and crowds.

The visual representation of the East German revolution of 1989 was even more minimalist. In the tumultuous months of November and December 1989, *Pravda* published only two images in relation to East Germany. The first, on November 2, showed Egon Krenz (as new East German party leader) and Gorbachev meeting the press. This image was the only photograph in relation to East Germany that was published on the front page in November and December 1989. The second image, on page six on November 20, 1989, was of Hans Modrow as the new prime minister of East Germany. The photograph was next to an article that described Modrow's professional trajectory and rise to party leadership.

In terms of the coverage of November 9, 1989 (the fall of the Berlin Wall), *Pravda* addressed this "nonevent" in three brief articles on page six on November 11. The first article discussed the meeting of the East German Central Committee. The second article reported in two short paragraphs that West German Chancellor Helmut Kohl had to return from Poland to Germany due to the "dramatic situation" at the German–German border.

The third article, entitled "The Gordian Knot Was Cut," was printed *under* the first article, and its author was *Pravda*'s foreign correspondent

in Berlin. This three-hundred-word article described that due to a decision by the East German Council of Ministers, East German citizens
could now cross the border both for short-term visits and for emigration to
West Germany and West Berlin, stressing that this regulation was meant
to be in effect until a new law was passed by the parliament. According to
the article, many East Germans seized the opportunity and visited West
Germany, some in their own cars, others by public transportation. Most
of these visitors returned to East Germany after only a brief trip.

The article emphasized that the decision on travel reflected the new
East German political leadership's intention to break free from old, dog-
matic thinking and confront the challenges in the relationship of the
two German states. According to the article, this shift in the leadership's
attitude was inspired by Gorbachev's "new thinking." ("New thinking"
was Gorbachev's foreign policy slogan and principle that emphasized
the need to address global issues with a new mindset.) The article highlighted that the previous rigid thinking had caused substantial losses to
East Germany, including the emigration of two hundred thousand East
German citizens. The emigration wave was then "used" for propaganda
purposes by West German politicians and West German media. So now
that the Gordian knot has been cut, the emigration wave could no longer
be used as an argument against the East German state. Just like the East
German press, *Pravda*'s article then also referred to Schabowski's confusing, blurred answer to a journalist's question at the infamous press conference: "what is going to happen to the Berlin Wall now?"

The border opening thus was presented as a *decision* by East Germany
that proved the East German party leadership's intention for renewal.
Pravda both hid the articles in relation to the East German political tur-
moil (printing them on less significant pages and in small type) and min-
imized the significance of the "fall of the Berlin Wall" (this glorious name
would have never made it through the censors if it had been proposed at
all). The newspaper aimed to imply that the East German leadership in
fact "led" the reform process in the country. The leadership was by no
means just a bystander, let alone a "victim" of history.

Overall the East German and Soviet party-controlled media framed
November 9, 1989, as a moment in a complex, deliberate, and continuous
reform process. Instead of an event, a standalone item, the "new travel
regulation" was presented as part of a chain of occurrences. This representation was no less accurate than the Western coverage; it may in fact
have been *more* accurate. The East German and Soviet coverage did not

strip the border opening of its larger social, political, and cultural context. Instead, the coverage kept the border opening embedded in a broader web of social actions and circumstances. At the same time, the coverage also presented the happenings of November 9, 1989, in a more favorable light from the East German leadership's perspective, arguing that what seemed haphazard was in fact deliberate and planned.

There were also similarities between East and West in their representation of November 9, 1989. For different reasons, they both chose not to make the awkwardness and accidental character of the Schabowski conference a central component of their narratives. The West German media probably did so for narrative reasons—to turn the day into a coherent event. Their East German and Soviet counterparts employed the same strategy for political reasons—in their journalistic practice, a new travel regulation's immediate effect simply could not have been framed as the outcome of a politburo spokesman's mistake.

Beyond these similarities, the most important difference between the Western and Eastern narrative was memorability. The objective and narrowly factual East German and Soviet coverage of the new travel regulations offered little substance for social remembrance. The East German and Soviet media's practice of under-narration also provided less material for analysis for event researchers—hence the relative brevity of this chapter. In contrast, the Western narrative, with its condensed story of a simple phrase ("fall of the Berlin Wall"), short narrative ("freedom," "end of division"), and recognizable visual scene (crowds around the Berlin Wall and the Brandenburg Gate), presented a resonant social myth that has become readily transportable through time, space, and media.

7

Remediation

A QUARTER OF a century has passed since November 9, 1989. East Germany and the Soviet Union have disappeared from the world map, contemporary societies are grappling with new global conflicts, and the Berlin Wall exists only in our memories. This chapter is dedicated to the question of how powerful news stories can survive while almost everything around them changes radically. It examines how the name, narrative, and visual scene of a global iconic event travel through time, space, and media as a myth in ever-shifting social, political, and cultural settings.

Present-day visitors to Berlin often go for a walk on Potsdamer Platz. The history of the square functions as a quick summary of Berlin's history of hope and tragedy: once a vibrant, modern town square, it found itself suddenly flat and empty after World War II bombardments and was then cut in two by the Berlin Wall. After the German reunification, it was first a void and then a site for experimentation by global investors and star architects. Today, Potsdamer Platz is home to a variety of skyscrapers, a commercial and cultural center with its history hiding in plain sight. Below Potsdamer Platz, on the basement level of the entertainment complex Sony Center, the visitor finds Legoland Discovery Centre Berlin. Legoland Berlin offers all the regular features of a children's amusement park. In addition, however, it devotes one room to the history of Berlin through a display of miniatures of famous landmarks of the city. One of these landmarks is the fall of the Berlin Wall (Fig. 7.1).

The Lego scene consists of a single wall and a crowd of tiny figures with hammers in hand. The crowd is diverse; women and men, blond and dark-haired, dressed in various styles. In the background we see the Brandenburg Gate. The figures are shouting, "Die Mauer muss weg" ("The Wall must go!"), and they are waiting for a miracle to happen. When

(a)

(b)

FIGURE 7.1 Close-up of the "Fall of the Berlin Wall" in Legoland Discovery Centre Berlin. Photo: Dóra Diseri, 2015.

the visitor pushes a button, the Berlin Wall, this singular wall dividing a nation, simply falls. As it falls, *Baywatch* star David Hasselhoff begins to sing in English: "I've been looking for freedom / I've been looking so long / I've been looking for freedom / still the search goes on."

The scene includes everything that makes the fall of the Berlin Wall such a memorable event for a global audience. There is *a* wall that separates a community. The scene shows courage and strength on the part of the crowds. It also displays a sudden, split-second moment in which everything changes, followed by euphoria. The figures are too tiny for individual features; they are "the" people. It is obvious who their enemy is: "the" wall. Politicians, dealmakers, and other confusing types are simply absent. Only the Brandenburg Gate lets you know that this is Berlin; apart from that, the scene could be taking place almost anywhere, and anytime, in the world.

The Lego miniature displays the three elements of the "package" that make the fall of the Berlin Wall a global iconic event. The simple phrase "fall of the Berlin Wall" is the title of the scene. The short narrative of freedom is expressed both by the Hasselhoff song and the graffiti on the wall. The Lego landmark reproduces the recognizable visual scene of the event: the Berlin Wall, the crowds, and the Brandenburg Gate. The scene is simple and readily transportable. Even—or perhaps especially— without prior knowledge of the Berlin Wall's multifaceted history and East Germany's troubled year of 1989, the "global" visitor can immediately grasp the excitement of overcoming separation. When we look at the Lego "Fall of the Berlin Wall," what we see is a powerful effort of promotion, a visible act of social remembrance, and a strong interest from the visitors—who even stand in line to push the button.

The Lego "Fall of the Berlin Wall," while seemingly a toy, a "banal commemoration," is in fact an essential representation of the global memory of the event.[1] It conveys the popular image of the Berlin Wall as one wall that can collapse on a single day. And although this representation is particularly powerful, it is but one example of how the universal myth of the fall of the Berlin Wall can sometimes miraculously travel through time, space, and media. In this chapter, I will examine four distinct ways in which a global iconic event moves globally: through recycling, reenactment, possession, and memorialization.

Recycling: The Fall of the Berlin Wall as Analogy

Recycling happens when the phrase, narrative, and visual scene of the event are recalled, either separately or combined, in connection with seemingly similar events. On the occasion of the twentieth anniversary of the fall of the Berlin Wall, the German state-funded nonprofit Kulturprojekte Berlin GmbH initiated "The Berlin Twitter Wall," a project that ran from October 20 until November 15, 2009 (Fig. 7.2). The project addressed users of the microblogging service Twitter with the following request: "[s]hare your thoughts on the fall of the Berlin

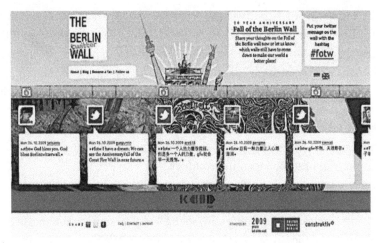

FIGURE 7.2 Online monument for the "Berlin Twitter Wall" (2009).

Wall now or let us know which walls still have to come down to make our world a better place." The arriving tweets were displayed on a website.

Let's consider, for a moment, the language of the announcement. It did not say: "Join us in celebration of this pivotal event of contemporary German history!" Instead, the announcement made the event as readily transportable as possible. The project employed the simple phrase "fall of the Berlin Wall," and it even declared the online memorial to be a site for condemning *all* of the world's walls ("let us know which walls still have to come down to make our world a better place"). The announcement opened the space up for abstraction, but Twitter users pushed the universalization of the fall of the Berlin Wall even further. The Berlin Twitter Wall quickly became a surface of protest against all sorts of walls—physical as well as virtual, and from Mexico to Israel to India.

According to the organizers, the project reached 1.4 million users. Of the approximately 7,500 tweets, a stunning forty percent were written in Chinese and thirty-one percent in English; only thirteen percent were written in German.[2] Many tweets demanded the fall of the Great Firewall of China. One tweet even alluded to the famous 1987 Berlin speech by Ronald Reagan: "Mr. Hu Jintao, please tear down this Great Firewall." The popularity of the Berlin Twitter Wall as a public sphere in which to advocate freedom of expression triggered China to block the Berlin Twitter Wall website after only six days, which gave the anniversary project an ironic contemporary political twist.

Of course, not all the tweets concerned the Great Firewall of China. Some tweets recalled the event's short narrative of freedom: "Free Facebook, free Google, free my life!" Others transported the message of freedom to seemingly distinct areas and topics of social life, like education—"Für bessere Bildungschancen! Die Herkunft darf nicht über die Zukunft entscheiden!" ("For better chances in education! Social background must not determine one's future")—or climate change: "Still many walls left to be torn down! E.g. some companies' ignorance regarding climate change & social misconduct."

Twitter users also recycled famous sentences from the history of the Berlin Wall: "No one has the intention of constructing a Twitterwall," one tweet went, echoing the words of Walter Ulbricht. Some users recalled the moment when they first heard about the Berlin Wall's fall: "I remember watching Tom Brokaw choke up as students brought down the wall and thinking there would be no nuclear war in my lifetime." Others placed this memory in a larger media context: "I was 9yo when the Berlin Wall fell. Also the same time I got my first short wave radio. The World got large quick."

The Berlin Twitter Wall highlights the way in which the fall of the Berlin Wall as social myth gets stripped of and elevated above its local context. This project shows how the fall of the Berlin Wall can be used as a reference point in radically different contexts. Through recycling, the event's phrase, narrative, and visual image become readily transportable to many parts of the world.[3]

Reenactment: Demolishing Walls From Los Angeles to Qalandiya to Berlin

When we commemorate the fall of the Berlin Wall, we recall the destruction of an object. In doing so, we aim to commemorate both the object and its fall. How can we commemorate the destruction of the object? Paradoxically, by rebuilding it. There is very little left of the material "Berlin Wall," and what there is has become precious. So to reenact the fall of the Berlin Wall, actors involved in the business of memorialization first have to reconstruct it. It may seem awkward to build and demolish fake Berlin Walls, but this peculiar miracle happens over and over again, embodying and revitalizing the myth of the fall of the Berlin Wall. Incentives for building and destroying these fake Berlin Walls can be commercial, political, or historical; some projects are outcomes of a blend of very diverse motivations.

In 2009, the Wende Museum, a small private museum in Los Angeles, decided that Los Angeles needed a Berlin Wall. More precisely, it decided that Los Angeles needed a Berlin Wall that would be cherished and a second wall that would be demolished. The Wende Museum grew out of the private collection of modern history scholar Justinian Jampol and is dedicated to the preservation and display of Cold War material culture from Eastern Europe and the Soviet Union. The museum's website defines the Wende Museum through its *distance* from Berlin: "[t]he Museum's location in Los Angeles provides independence and critical distance from current political debates in Europe, and also facilitates the questioning of preconceived ideas about our past and present."[4]

With its substantial geographical distance from the event's "place of origin," the Wende Museum seems like an unusual site at which to shape the global memory of the fall of the Berlin Wall. Still, at the twentieth anniversary of the fall of the Berlin Wall, the Wende Museum launched a large-scale, multifaceted media and public art initiative called "The Wall Project." Note the title: this was not "The *Berlin* Wall Project." Wende Museum founder Jampol was consciously encouraging the story of the fall of the Berlin Wall to travel through time, space, and media:

> So when we started *The Wall Project* then we said, listen, this is going to be a project that is not a commemoration or a memorial, but engages Los Angeles, and is about trying to visualize what it would be like if L.A. would be divided between East and West.[5]

The Wall Project consisted of two parts: the "Wall Along Wilshire" and the "Wall Across Wilshire." The Wall Along Wilshire involved the transport of ten segments of the original Berlin Wall to Los Angeles, creating "the longest stretch of the Berlin Wall in the world outside of Berlin."[6] With this project the Wende Museum triumphed over the Newseum in Washington, which had claimed to have the longest segment until then. Moving ten sections of the Berlin Wall from Berlin to Los Angeles seems like a daunting logistical task on its own, but the Wende Museum did more than mere transportation: the museum invited Los Angeles–based artists Marie Astrid Gonzalez, Farrah Karapetian, and Kent Twitchell and legendary Berlin-based French "muralist" Thierry Noir to decorate four of the ten segments, while Berlin street artist Bimer stylized a fifth segment. The remaining five segments were left in their original condition. Connecting Los Angeles-based emerging artists with renowned international Berlin Wall artists was meant to make the event both local and universal. The combination of altered and unaltered segments signaled continuity and renewal (Fig. 7.3).

The second part of the Wende Museum's commemoration was "The Wall Across Wilshire," a three-hour event in which an 80-foot "fake," stylized separation barrier was ritually demolished by a huge cheerful crowd. The barrier blocked the busy Wilshire Boulevard for a day until midnight on November 8, 2009, when it spectacularly came tumbling down. Some of the event's participants even ran away with pieces of the fake Berlin Wall, connecting to the myth on a level that the organizers did not even dream of, and certainly could not prevent. Further audiences joined the event as German television covered the event live. The international press discussed the event in many parts of the world, from Estonia to Costa Rica to Malaysia, communicating a simplified and universalized message of hope.

The involvement of renowned "wall artists" Shepard Fairey and Thierry Noir added to the event's spectacle. While Fairey's painting on the fake barrier drew parallels between the Berlin Wall and Israel's West Bank separation barrier, Noir's artwork made an analogy between the United States–Mexico separation barrier and the Berlin Wall. In an interview with the *Los Angeles Times* before the anniversary event, Fairey said

FIGURE 7.3 "The Wall Along Wilshire:" Ten segments of the Berlin Wall in Los Angeles. Photo: Julia Sonnevend, 2014.

his painting would be an "antiwar, anti-containment piece," while Noir suggested that his artwork would send the message that "every wall is not built forever."[7] The Wende Museum's project thus framed the anniversary celebration of the fall of the Berlin Wall as a celebration of the event's international social meaning ("end of division," "no more walls"). The Wall Project centered on the message of unity and freedom and pushed the complex East German historical context into the background.

Like Los Angeles, Berlin also celebrated the twentieth anniversary of the fall of the Berlin Wall by rebuilding and then demolishing the Berlin Wall. Berlin has only a few segments of the authentic Berlin Wall available for performing the event, so a fake wall was needed. Approximately one thousand oversized dominos covered a route a mile in length, from the Reichstagufer, through the Brandenburg Gate, to Potsdamer Platz. Most of the dominos had been decorated by those belonging to generations born after 1989, including children from five hundred school classes. Politicians from all over the world signed dominoes, for instance South African freedom icon Nelson Mandela, former West German foreign minister Hans-Dietrich Genscher, and former Soviet statesman Mikhail Gorbachev.

As part of the "Mauerreise—the wall in the world" project, the Goethe Institute also sent several dominos out to be decorated by students, intellectuals, and artists in seven countries that still have separation barriers: Korea, Cyprus, Yemen, Mexico, Israel, the Palestinian territories, and China. In Cyprus, the Greek and Turkish graffiti artists in fact met right at the border to co-paint their dominoes. In a series of events called "MUR|MURS|MAUER|ECHO," organized by the Institut Français, German and French students were also brought together to co-design dominoes in a cooperative workshop, signifying the newly found political harmony between Germany and France.

With approximately 15,000 contributors, the twentieth-anniversary celebration of the fall of the Berlin Wall was a megaproject of nation branding.[8] The domino project culminated in a gigantic Festival of Freedom on the evening of November 9, 2009—the exact twentieth anniversary of the fall of the Berlin Wall. The event's packed schedule offered a variety of attractions, including, at the end, the *fall* of the domino wall. Ironically, while we tend to associate the "domino theory" with U.S. Cold War narrative about the *spread* of communism from one country to another (if one country "falls" to communism, the neighboring countries would fall as dominoes too), here the metaphor was being used to commemorate the fall of *communist* regimes.

Program of the Festival of Freedom

7:00 p.m. Concert of the Berlin State's Orchestra under the direction of Daniel Barenboim (music from Wagner, Schönberg, Beethoven, and Goldmann)

7:30 p.m. International politicians and former GDR civil rights activists walk through the Brandenburg Gate and give speeches

7:45–8:30 p.m.

   The first domino falls
   Performance of Jon Bon Jovi at the Brandenburg Gate
   Interview with Mikhail Gorbachev and former German foreign minis-
   ter Hans Dietrich Genscher

8:30 p.m. The last domino falls, kicking off a fireworks display over the Brandenburg Gate

During the weekend of November 9, 2014, at the twenty-fifth anniversary of the fall of the Berlin Wall, Berlin again erected a fake Berlin Wall, this time as a light installation (Fig. 7.4). As part of the project LICHTGRENZE (border of light), thousands of illuminated, helium-filled balloons signified the Berlin Wall and embodied the project's readily transportable message: "symbol of hope for a world without walls." Visitors were able to walk along the original path of the wall and "feel" the destructive power of separation.

Each balloon had a patron. Patrons came from all segments of German society and included pastors, company employees, schoolchildren, foundation representatives, and people who were simply born on the day when the Berlin Wall was built. Each patron attached a message to his or her balloon. Many of these messages placed the story of the fall of the Berlin Wall into an internationalized narrative of hope, freedom, and liberation. For instance, representatives of various church communities wrote:

Miracles play the most beautiful part in human history. The fall of the Berlin Wall is one of them. It is not crazy to hope for more: the fall of the wall between Israel and Palestine, the fall of the wall surrounding Europe.

Jürgen Kaiser

FIGURE 7.4 A few balloons of the LICHTGRENZE at the twenty-fifth anniversary of the fall of the Berlin Wall. Photo: Julia Sonnevend, 2014.

I wish that over the next 25 years many more walls will come down inside the minds of people. What would a world without homophobia be like!

Astrid Kuhna

Belfast, Nicosia, Jerusalem, Mostar, Mitrovica—look at these places: the forced division of cities and countries can be overcome! Berlin has proved it.

Petra Kahlfeldt[9]

The illuminated balloons and the related stories and messages mesmerized the global visitors of Berlin for the weekend of the twenty-fifth anniversary of the fall of the Berlin Wall. With the help of the balloons, people were able to trace the former course of the Berlin Wall and imagine what it felt like to live in a city cruelly divided by an arbitrary wall.

Finally, on the actual day of the anniversary, November 9, 2014, a spectacular festival at the Brandenburg Gate closed the commemorative weekend. At the end of the event, the Staatskapelle Berlin and the State Opera Chorus celebrated the fall of the Berlin Wall with a performance of the fourth movement of Beethoven's Ninth Symphony ("Ode to Joy"), under the direction of Daniel Barenboim. The balloons with their patrons' messages then were released and their disappearance into the sky symbolized liberation. The organizers asked the large crowd of participants to tell the world about their experiences using the hashtags #fallofthewall25 or #fotw25 on Facebook, Twitter, and Instagram. All the messages appeared on a website, stylized as "messages" attached to virtual balloons. In the words of the organizers, the balloon project was meant to communicate that "the fall of the Berlin Wall is an enduring, *global symbol of hope* for a more peaceful world and for overcoming injustice and dictatorships."[10] This reconstructed, fake Berlin Wall, built from the ephemeral material of light, "talked" in a readily transportable language to global and local audiences. Its designers made the story of the fall of the Berlin Wall travel through at least some cultural and geographical boundaries.

Not everyone was satisfied with the official anniversary celebrations. Just days before the ceremonies dedicated to the twenty-fifth anniversary, a performance art group removed several white crosses from the heart of Berlin that commemorated the victims of the Berlin Wall. The "White Crosses" memorial was established in 1971, on the tenth anniversary of the construction of the Berlin Wall, by a group of private citizens who called themselves the Berliner Bürger-Verein. The Berliner Bürger-Verein erected crosses in remembrance of East Germans who tried to cross the Berlin Wall and were shot by border guards. Originally, the crosses marked the locations where the victims died, but the memorial was relocated multiple times due to ongoing construction work in reunified Berlin.

Beginning of November 2014, the white crosses suddenly disappeared from Berlin and resurfaced on the fences of Europe, where many contemporary refugees lose their lives. Crosses were placed at the tall border fence between Morocco and the Spanish enclave of Melilla on the North African coast; this fence is meant to block illegal immigration and smuggling from Morocco to the European Union. White crosses were also erected at the barbed-wire fence of Bulgaria, which was built in 2014, exactly twenty-five years after the fall of the Berlin Wall. The fence limits the influx of Syrian refugees from Turkey to Bulgaria that caused a humanitarian crisis in Bulgaria, the poorest member state of the European Union. Human rights organizations have strongly condemned both fences for putting the lives of refugees at dire risk.

The organizer of the white cross performance was the Center for Political Beauty, which defines itself as "an assault team exploring moral beauty and human greatness in politics." It is an association of performance artists under the direction of philosopher and theater director Philipp Ruch. In their online statement the group argued that "[w]hile in Berlin balloons will rise into the air and nostalgic, sedative speeches will be held, German civil society will in an act of political beauty bring down the European external walls." They also added that the "European Curtain" must fall.[11] In Berlin, at the site where the white crosses once stood, a note awaited the visitors: "There's no thinking going on here."

The director of the official Berlin Wall Memorial, Axel Klausmeier, reacted harshly: "Each of the crosses is in memory of a wall victim with their own fate, their own motives for the attempted escape with their own lives. Those who demand more respect for the dignity of human individuals—which we supported wholeheartedly—should also respect the dignity of the individual victims of the wall."[12] For him, using a memorial of the Berlin Wall to protest against contemporary walls was too radical a step in the universalization of the event. His response reflects the inevitable clash between individualized and universalized forms of commemoration.

In the absence of the real Berlin Wall, the division's horrors are increasingly distant, especially for new generations and international audiences. Fake Berlin Walls, whether official or countercultural, thus imitate the "real" experience, and their staged falls send the message of (at least some) hope. These projects offer the possibility of reenacting the event, while key tourist sites in Berlin are still marked by confusion about how to recall the fall of the Berlin Wall. This confusion is particularly visible in front of the Brandenburg Gate, where, as a tourist attraction, performers are dressed like Lenin, Darth Vader, and a Soviet soldier but have a hard time performing the memory of the fall of the Berlin Wall. Both the story of the Berlin Wall and stories from global visual culture seem to win over the visual power of the fall of the Berlin Wall, at least in street performances.

FIGURE 7.5 Original segment of the Berlin Wall in front of Westin Grand Berlin; the sign warns that "damages to the wall are not permitted." Photo: Dóra Diseri, 2015.

Some commemorative events in Berlin thus use original pieces of the Berlin Wall to reenact the event. In 2009, the Westin Grand Berlin, a hotel in the heart of the German capital, offered a "Fall of the Berlin Wall" package that included participating in the demolition of an *original* segment of the Berlin Wall (Fig. 7.5). The package consisted of two nights in the hotel, breakfast, and a hammer and chisel to chip out a piece of souvenir. The package also included a map of the Berlin Wall, a Berlin curried sausage, and a glass of champagne. In a country so dedicated to the preservation of cultural heritage and so sensitive about historical memory, tourists paying a mere 200 euros were invited to destroy a key historical object—and to toast the destruction with champagne. Signaling the exceptional power of the fall of the Berlin Wall as a global social myth, the 1989 visual scenes of destruction and "freedom" repeatedly triumph over the traditions of landmark protection.

While Los Angeles and Berlin first needed to *build* separation barriers in order to reenact the fall of the Berlin Wall, other places in the world have more recent separation barriers that people sometimes try to tear down performatively. Israel's separation barrier on the West Bank provides an especially rich case study in this respect. Graffiti on the separation barrier directly recall the Berlin Wall. Anti–separation barrier protesters also tend to perform some of the recognizable visual scenes. On the twentieth anniversary of the fall of the Berlin Wall, around 150 Palestinian activists

FIGURE 7.6 "THE WALL MUST FALL"—Mosaic in the Aida Palestinian refugee camp on the West Bank. Photo: Julia Sonnevend, 2014.

and foreign supporters pulled down segments of the Israeli separation barrier near the Qalandiya refugee camp, outside Ramallah. They also stood on the top of the "wall," thus reenacting the original visual scenes. Their campaign statement, "Stop the Wall," made a direct link between the Berlin Wall and Israel's barrier: "Today is the 20th anniversary of the fall of the Berlin Wall and marks the first day of a week of resistance to the apartheid wall in Palestine and around the globe."[13] Connecting the story of the anti-emigration wall of East Germany to that of the antiterrorism wall of Israel, protesters blocked out substantial contextual differences and implied a universal social meaning of *all* separation barriers, regardless of purpose or location (Fig. 7.6).

Possession: Touching the Berlin Wall

In addition to recycling and reenacting the fall of the Berlin Wall, possessing a piece or a segment of the Berlin Wall is also a common way in which people commemorate both the Berlin Wall and its fall.[14] Small pieces of the Berlin Wall are available for purchase in most souvenir stores in Berlin, and they are popular items in many international online stores. Pieces of the Berlin Wall often come with a certificate that verifies their authenticity. Frequently, such Berlin Wall pieces are also decorated with famous lines from the wall's history, like former East German General

FIGURE 7.7 Postcard with a piece of the Berlin Wall. Photo: Julia Sonnevend, 2015.

Secretary Erich Honecker's one-liner from January 1989: "[t]he wall will remain here for another hundred years."

The fall of the Berlin Wall is also commemorated on postcards that have included a piece of the Berlin Wall in some characteristic image from the Wall's history. The tiny chipped fragment in the plastic container (Fig. 7.7) indirectly refers to the historic day of November 9, 1989. These postcards also suggest that the Berlin Wall's distinctive imagery can overshadow the imagery of the fall of the Berlin Wall. The fall of the Berlin Wall is present, as symbolized by the piece of the wall, but the event does not constitute the central visual scene of the postcard.

Large segments of the Berlin Wall can also be found all over the world, from Hawaii Community College in Honolulu to the Nemacolin Woodland Resort in Pennsylvania to the European Parliament in Brussels.[15] Berlin Wall remnants find homes in commercial centers, embassies, museums, parks, parliaments, presidential libraries, and schools. Often displayed in publicly accessible places without surveillance, these powerful mementos are at the mercy of visitors, whose attitudes toward them vary. Sometimes the segments are subject to further destruction, or to artistic acts of reinterpretation. For instance, after falling prey to souvenir hunters, two segments of the Berlin Wall placed in a public park in Budapest (Hungary) were subsequently painted completely red by an anonymous artist (Fig. 7.8). As a consequence, on the fifteenth anniversary of the fall of the Berlin Wall, the segments were

FIGURE 7.8 Repainted Berlin Wall segments in the Maltese Charity Service's garden in Budapest, Hungary. The Service gave shelter to thousands of East Germans in 1989. One of the refugees left her Trabi there on her way to the West. Photo: Peter Sonnevend, 2013.

moved to a safer location. The segments are owned by the no-longer-active Hungarian Alliance of Free Democrats, which used to be a long-term coalition partner of the postcommunist Hungarian Socialist Party. The red paint may have been in reference to this fact, although the exact motives remain unknown. This case highlights the clash between the desire to preserve the Berlin Wall and the wish to playfully remember the *fall* of the Berlin Wall.

Touching or possessing a piece or segment of the Berlin Wall is thus a type of secular ritual, but these practices also resemble our interaction with religious icons. The displayed Berlin Wall segments act as bridges between the present and the "historic" past in simultaneously corporeal and metaphysical ways. These sacred objects seem to be consubstantial with what they represent, much like worshipped religious objects. The Berlin Wall gained not only a religious but also an artistic "aura" in Walter Benjamin's sense, marked off from everyday use through its new purpose of being on display, while bearing and conveying in its own material form the visible and tangible marks of history. When we touch or possess a piece of the Berlin Wall, we enter its sacred space and hope to feel both its magic and its trauma.

However, touching is also a problematic form of connecting to the myth of the fall of the Berlin Wall. The fall of the Berlin Wall is a global iconic event about overcoming division, about *demolishing* walls and scattering their pieces as far from each other as possible. At the same time, we also wish to *preserve* the original Berlin Wall for commemorative practices. But the more we "touch" the wall, the less likely it will remain with us for a long period of time. This clash of expectations is particularly salient in exhibitions dedicated to the Berlin Wall. A vivid example is the Berlin Wall Gallery of the Newseum in Washington, DC, that aims to tell the influence of news and information on the demise of East Germany. Many years after the fall of the Berlin Wall, the Newseum's Wall Gallery exhibition presents a magical, "unexpected" event that was celebrated with champagne, hammers, and chisels:

> Unexpectedly, on November 9, 1989, East German authorities lifted travel restrictions to the West. The news spread quickly. Berliners from both sides of the city climbed over the wall and danced on top of it, sharing songs and champagne in a joyful reunion. With hammers and chisels, many pounded away at the once-fearsome barrier. After a little more than 28 years, the wall had fallen.

According to the Newseum website, its Berlin Wall Gallery features "eight 12-foot-high concrete sections of the original wall—the largest display of unaltered portions of the wall outside of Germany." Note that the Newseum distinguishes itself from the Wende Museum by presenting the longest "unaltered" section of the Berlin Wall. In the exhibition space, next to the "unaltered portions" of the wall, a large sign instructs visitors: "do not touch—please help us preserve the condition of the Berlin Wall" (Fig. 7.9). While the exhibit tells the story of a *fall* of a wall, it sets firm limits to the wall's further destruction. More precisely, it tells the destruction myth in words, presenting a condensed, magical story for imagination, not for action.

Memorialization: Media Memory, Memorials, and Exhibitions

Finally, the fourth way in which an event can travel internationally is through memorialization: the global iconic event's direct commemoration in journalism, memorials, and exhibitions. While it is relatively easy to

FIGURE 7.9 The Berlin Wall Gallery in the Newseum in Washington, DC. Photo: Julia Sonnevend, 2014.

marginalize the context of the event during practices of recycling, reenacting, and possessing, for direct commemoration such practices of internationalization are more challenging. Direct commemorative practices often have to deal with hard facts, strong personal memories, and actual places— all of which can get in the way of playful mythmaking. This clash, between simplified memory and contested memory, is visible in the German print and television coverage of the event as it evolved over time.

German newspapers gave only limited coverage to the first anniversary of the fall of the Berlin Wall; it came just after the spectacular coverage of German reunification. At this first anniversary, German media also struggled with the weight of the fall of the Berlin Wall relative to that of the Nazi pogrom of Kristallnacht in 1938. Both events took place on November 9, but their remembrance required distinctively different journalistic tones. Moreover, November 9 also marked the proclamation of the German Republic in 1918, and the defeat of Adolf Hitler's Beer Hall Putsch in Munich in 1923. The coincidence of these dates was repeatedly recognized by German media in their coverage of the first anniversary of the fall of the Berlin Wall.

The competition from the other events became less substantial with each successive anniversary: in the coverage of the tenth anniversary they were barely mentioned, and at the twentieth anniversary they became

FIGURE 7.10 "Heute vor einem Jahr: Das Ende der Mauer" ["Today a Year Ago: The End of the Wall"], front page of *Berliner Morgenpost* on November 9, 1990.

even less prominent. Meanwhile, the remembrance of the fall of the Berlin Wall grew substantially in size. This growth is visible even in the amount of front-page space dedicated to the event's commemoration— see, for example, the *Berliner Morgenpost*'s front pages of November 9, 1990, 1999, and 2009 (Figs. 7.10, 7.11, and 7.12,)

Nonetheless, the competition among multiple historic events pre-vented the fall of the Berlin Wall from becoming a national holiday in Germany. Chancellor Kohl's advisers found the clash with Kristallnacht impossible to overcome.[16] Instead, October 3 was named the new national holiday, "The Day of German Unity"—signifying the day of German reunification in the legal, not in the symbolic, sense. But November 9 as a potential national holiday is still debated, especially in newspapers at anniversaries. Some argue that a "national day of remembrance" could

FIGURE 7.11 "Berlin feiert den Jahrestag des Mauerfalls" ["Berlin Celebrates the Anniversary of the Wall's Fall"], front page of *Berliner Morgenpost* on November 9, 1999.

reflect on the diversity of events that happened on this fateful day in German history and would force Germany to remember *all* the colors of its past. Others, however, find it impossible to set the right tone for the remembrance of events ranging from a nationalistic pogrom to a euphoric symbolic moment of national unity. Currently, the "fall of the Berlin Wall" thus has to be remembered without one of the most typical forms of commemorating an event: a well-designed national holiday.

The event found expression in other commemorative practices, however. In addition to journalistic commemoration, exhibitions and

FIGURE 7.12 "Revolution für die Freiheit" ["Revolution for Freedom"], front page of *Berliner Morgenpost* on November 9, 2009.

memorials also try to summarize the story of the event in a concise way for international and local audiences. These memorials confront one of the city's central paradoxes; "[Berlin] became a top tourist destination the very moment it tore down its most famous landmark."[17] The Berlin Wall did not have any foundations; demolished sites therefore do not leave archeological traces behind. In other words, when the Berlin Wall "goes, it is gone forever."[18]

While establishing sites of memory, historians, archivists, curators, and museum directors, among others, also often find themselves confronted with the power of "place" as it blocks practices of universalization.[19]

Every attempt to give shape to the "void" of the Berlin Wall inevitably runs up against the strong personal memories of those who had experienced the wall as a massive border-separation barrier, not only as a symbol.[20] The clash between the need to construct an official cultural memory and the presence of deeply traumatic personal communicative memories is still acutely visible in the newly established Berlin Wall Memorial.[21] The memorial makes explicit the broad range of tensions, frustrations, and beauties faced by a new site of memory in a historically "loaded" place.

The Berlin Wall Memorial is situated on Bernauer Strasse, a street on which photographs of some of the most tragic Berlin Wall scenes were taken in the early sixties. The photographs showed escapees jumping from soon-to-be-walled-in windows, parents waving at the weddings of their children, and the digging of elaborate tunnels of hope below the Berlin border-control regime. This historically charged location is the locus for the Berlin Wall Memorial that was, eventually, extended along almost a mile of the original Berlin Wall border strip. The memorial's construction began on the eighth anniversary of the fall of the Berlin Wall, November 9, 1997. Its first part was opened on the thirty-seventh anniversary of the construction of the Berlin Wall, August 13, 1998. Since 2003, the Berlin Wall Memorial also features a viewing platform from which visitors can

FIGURE 7.13 Viewing platform at the Berlin Wall Memorial overlooking a reconstructed "death strip." Photo: Julia Sonnevend, 2015.

observe a long stretch of border installations (Fig. 7.13) and since 2014 a new exhibition that tells the story of the Berlin Wall and the East German process of political transition. Each element of the memorial is the outcome of exceptionally heated debates.

While confusing and seemingly endless, the debate revolved around a clear core conflict. One group of individuals and communities wanted to demolish the wall once and for all (this was the dominant voice after the fall of the Berlin Wall), while the other desired its historical preservation for social remembrance (this is the leading view now). One of the strongest anti–Berlin Wall voices came from the nearby East German Protestant Sophien Parish. Its assertive pastor demanded that the parish's cemetery ground, which originally ran alongside the wall and was confiscated by East Germany, be returned. Without any consultation, in 1997 he even arranged the removal of thirty-two segments of the Berlin Wall from a previously intact long stretch of the wall (Fig. 7.14). The pastor meant to "protect" the World War II mass graves that purportedly lay below the Berlin Wall, but as it turned out, excavation revealed no graves at all.[22] The parish's controversial actions led many to switch sides and ultimately

FIGURE 7.14 Original segments of the Berlin Wall, moved by Pastor Hildebrandt of the Sophien Parish in his hunt for imaginary mass graves of World War II bombing victims. Now these segments are part of the Berlin Wall Memorial. They are mementos of passionate debates about the Berlin Wall's complex legacy. Photo: Julia Sonnevend, 2015.

support the establishment of a Berlin Wall Memorial. Over time, the Sophien Parish's anti–Berlin Wall Memorial voices also softened.

In contrast to the Sophien Parish's position, another nearby religious institution, the Reconciliation Parish, unexpectedly became one of the most dedicated advocates for Berlin Wall preservation. Their stand is particularly stunning in light of the fact that the parish's church, which was on the "death strip," had been blown up by East Germany as recently as 1985: the images of the church tower in collapse had traveled around the world, causing immense outrage. Yet after this massive trauma, the pastor of the parish, Manfred Fischer, became one of the strongest supporters of Berlin Wall preservation—he even stood in front of the bulldozers that came to demolish the Berlin Wall. With the preservation of segments of the Berlin Wall, Fisher wanted to commemorate the victims and educate new generations who may not have accurate mental images of the Berlin Wall's horrors. When he passed away in 2013, German newspapers mourned the "Mauerpfarrer" ("Pastor of the Wall.")[23]

In addition to the Berlin Wall Memorial as the central site of commemoration, many other memorials, museums, and artistic projects in Berlin communicate the memory of the Berlin Wall. In 2006, the Berlin Senate passed an extensive "Masterplan to Preserve the Memory of the Berlin Wall."[24] A particular trigger for systematic planning came from a random project in 2004 by Alexandra Hildebrandt, the director of the Mauer (Wall) Museum at Checkpoint Charlie. The Mauer Museum was founded by her husband, human rights activist Rainer Hildebrandt, in 1962. The museum was originally a small apartment-sized exhibition dedicated to the newly built Berlin Wall, but the somewhat chaotically arranged private exhibition over time became one of the central memorial sites of the Berlin Wall. In 2004, at the fifteenth anniversary of the fall of the Berlin Wall, Alexandra Hildebrandt decided to erect a "Freedom Memorial" in close proximity to the museum. The memorial consisted of 120 original segments of the Berlin Wall (at a site where the Berlin Wall never stood in this form) and 1,067 crosses dedicated to the victims of the German–German border-control regime. The memorial was designed to be a temporary "art installation," lasting until the end of 2004, but it quickly became a huge success, with demands for its permanent stay. Finally, after much controversy it was removed on July 5, 2005. Many supporters chained themselves to the crosses; others organized demonstrations. Clearly, the city of Berlin had to come up with new, adequate commemorative sites for citizens and visitors of Berlin, who demanded this in ever-greater numbers.

As solution, the Senate's "Masterplan to Preserve the Memory of the Berlin Wall" listed numerous "decentralized sites" of memory that deserve protection, including the remaining two command posts, the East Side Gallery, the wall remnants on Potsdamer Platz, the Palace of Tears, and many others.[25] The Berlin Wall's memory is thus communicated through a *network* of commemorative places. The visitors grasp or at least sense the size and significance of the Berlin Wall by visiting these distant and quite diverse sites of memory.

A particularly moving example of a decentralized site of memory is the "The Watchtower at Kieler Eck—Memorial for Günter Litfin" (Fig. 7.15). When visitors to Berlin take a short stroll from the central train station, they can stumble into a former East German command post now turned into a harrowing private memorial, dedicated to Günter Litfin and the victims of the Berlin Wall. Günter Litfin was the first escapee to be shot dead at the sealed border on August 24, 1961. He was a young tailor who supported his family by taking a job in West Berlin. A short ten days after the erection of the border fence, Litfin hoped to quickly swim to the West in a narrow canal, almost making to safety when pointed shots from East German border guards took his life. His brother, Jürgen Litfin, now runs the memorial site close to the Humboldt harbor where his brother took the lethal bullets.

The command post—a tall, massive gray tower—is a lonely reminder of history, surrounded by newly built pink and white residential buildings. Command posts were used to monitor and direct the watchtowers at the death strip. There were originally thirty-one of them in Berlin, but only two survived. Jürgen Litfin, "an outspoken eyewitness of history" as *Lonely Planet* recently called him, opened the memorial on August 24, 2003, exactly forty-two years after his brother's death. He gives daily tours of the tower and the small exhibition, not sparing on curse words while describing the former GDR. After the downfall of the East German regime, with the help of East German opposition leader and civil rights activist Joachim Gauck, Jürgen Liftin also researched the files of the border guards who murdered his brother. The outcome was a trial in 1997, which—as in other Berlin Wall proceedings—led to only minor sentences. But when Joachim Gauck recently became German president, Jürgen Litfin received one of the highest German federal prizes from him on the twenty-fifth anniversary of the fall of the Berlin Wall. The prize was a small recognition of a never-to-be healed trauma.

FIGURE 7.15 "The Watchtower at Kieler Eck—Memorial for Günter Litfin." In the picture, in front of the command post, is Jürgen Litfin, brother of the first victim of the Berlin Wall. Photo: Julia Sonnevend, 2015.

Some memorials were not part of strategic city planning but still serve as very popular sites of memory for the Berlin Wall. A powerful example is "The Wall" panorama by Yadegar Asisi that was unveiled in 2012. The 60-meter-long and 14-meter-high circular panorama is placed at Checkpoint Charlie, a particularly popular site for tourists. It invites the viewer to look at the massive border-control regime from an imaginary scaffolding on a house on a typical day in the 1980s. Asisi lived in Berlin during this time, but the panorama is not an exact representation of any particular day or even place, but a condensation of different moments of time and various sites of memory. Just like most visual representations of the Berlin Wall, this panorama also provides a Western perspective. Visitors look from Kreuzberg in the western part of the city to the eastern Mitte.

Perhaps shockingly to many, Asisi's panorama shows everyday life; people are fixing cars, punks hang out with friends, and families carry pieces of furniture to their new apartments. Everybody lives around this border as if the division were *normal*. Visitors to the panorama might find this normalcy particularly perplexing, since before entering the space of the panorama they can look at original videos from 1961, when people desperately protested the newly built fences and walls. While in the entrance hall visitors see crying families and angry crowds, on the panorama nothing remains from these moments of desperation. Perhaps only the touristic aspects of the scene, visitors on a viewing platform and a group of tourists taking pictures of the Berlin Wall, hint at something "unique." As Asisi summarized his feelings about the project in the panorama's brochure: "I am alarmed by the answer to the question of what life was like by the Wall, namely it was normal. We have to understand this normality." Asisi's panorama was also meant to be temporary, but it has become so much part of the city's fabric that it may stay for a longer period of time. This spectacular and tragic panorama even found an unexpected fan in the famous Berlin Wall author Peter Schneider, who in his newest book offers—from him, rare—high praise: "[the panorama] presents the drama of the former border system so well that all other memorials created after the fall of the Wall pale in comparison."[26]

There are also private memorials to the Berlin Wall that can range from arbitrary to downright bizarre. The most characteristic example is the activity of the huge Axel Springer media company in Berlin. Axel Springer, the company's founder, had been a dedicated champion of reunification throughout Germany's division; in 1959 he even commissioned an exceptionally tall golden headquarters for his publishing house right at the border of the Soviet-occupied sector—in order, he said, to create a lighthouse of the Free West. His top-floor office overlooked the "death strip." Decades after Springer's death, Axel Springer AG, which controls newspapers, magazines, online publications, and broadcast stations in thirty-six countries, remains invested in the memorialization of the fall of the Berlin Wall. While it has the financial means to fund new memorials, it does not necessarily have the expertise to make delicate decisions about aesthetic design (Fig. 7.16). These private memorials sometimes stir controversy by not following official aesthetic and historical expectations, but they nonetheless contribute to the long-term remembrance of the fall of the Berlin Wall.

Overall these various decentralized sites of memory invite visitors to Berlin to "track" the traces of the Berlin Wall, to connect the dots, and to imagine the barrier's impact on lives and souls in the city. By being a web of official and private memorials, these sites also show the various vested interests in preserving (and demolishing) the Berlin Wall. Decentralization as an organizing principle highlights that events related to the Berlin Wall are too recent to have a single, unified culture of commemoration. Differences of opinion and conflicts in feelings are represented in these scattered sites of memory.

Remediation: The Travel of Events Through Time, Space, and Media

In this chapter I have shown four main ways in which the story of the "fall of the Berlin Wall" remains alive today: recycling, reenactment, possession, and memorialization. I also emphasized that although the story of the fall of the Berlin Wall is a remarkably successful "traveler," some conditions, especially local ones, may still block its universalization. These conditions include personal memories; individual and group frustrations; intellectual property issues; ideological contestations; competing historical events; and conflicting commercial interests, among others. Acts of mythologization, universalization, and simplification inevitably disappoint many of those who experienced the process of political transition in all of its confusing, contradictory, and deeply personal fullness.

At the same time, through practices of recycling, reenactment, possession, and memorialization, the event's simplified and universalized story becomes accessible to an international and/or young audience, who arrive in Berlin in large numbers on budget flights every Friday. In fact, around sixty percent of visitors to the Berlin Wall Memorial are under twenty-five, and they are predominantly international.[27] These young

FIGURE 7.16 "Balancing act" by Stephan Balkenhol (2009) commemorates the fiftieth anniversary of the laying of the foundation stone of the Axel Springer building. The sculpture is framed by original pieces of the Berlin Wall. In the aesthetic interpretation of Dr. Mathias Döpfner, the chief executive of Axel Springer AG, "[t]he balancing man on the wall is on the one hand a sign of triumph over this architectural structure of division; climbing the Wall was deadly in the days of the shoot-to-kill order. At the same time the sculpture reminds us that dealing responsibly with freedom gained remains something invisible, varying—a balancing act" (Axel Springer, "50 Years"). Photo: Julia Sonnevend, 2014.

explorers, after a night of heavy partying, want to see the "Berlin Wall," dead or alive, so Berlin has to provide "some Berlin Wall" for them. Many locals also take comfort, reassurance, and pride in the sacralization provided by the event's mythologized format. A global iconic event is a bit like a framed wedding photograph or a eulogy at a funeral: an enhanced version of the past. Myth can become memory over time, representing a history and a life we wish or long for. Mythical stories remain with us in condensed and simplified forms, sneaking into our understanding of the world today.

8

Stories Without Borders

THINKING WITH GLOBAL ICONIC EVENTS

... at its most elementary, event is not something that occurs within the world, but is a change of the very frame through which we perceive the world and engage in it.

—SLAVOJ ŽIŽEK, *Event*[1]

AT THE BEGINNING of my book, theoretical chapters provided a new concept of global iconic events. Then, one global iconic event unfolded in front of the eyes of the reader. I showed that since 1989, from the "mess" on the ground a holy "mass" has been born: a spectacular global iconic event, the "fall of the Berlin Wall," has asked for admission into our international memory. In a demonstration of the story's unique portability, the fall of the Berlin Wall is often used as a reference point for contemporary revolutions, social clashes, and practices of separation. The event is evoked in contexts as diverse as the conflict between North and South Korea, China's Internet policy, and the Syrian refugee crisis. People recycle the event's name, narrative, and visual scene; reenact its famous scenes; want to touch physical remains of the event; and also frequently memorialize it in anniversary journalism and museums. Throughout the diffusion and remediation of the event something is achieved—but what exactly? How do global iconic events change us enduringly? What do we gain from understanding their formation? In this chapter, I will ponder three ways in which global iconic events in general and the fall of the Berlin Wall in particular may shape individuals and societies: (1) as frames of mind, (2) as "predictive pictures" for future events, and (3) as tools to confront late modernity.

Global Iconic Events as Frames of Mind: Our New "Walls" of Division

In November 2014, the Getty Museum in Los Angeles organized a conference entitled *New Walled Order: The Aesthetics and Politics of Barriers*. The conference brought together political scientists, urban designers, photographers, architects, and media scholars to consider why contemporary societies still build separation barriers. The conference started with a panel on the Berlin Wall, then continued with two further panels about the separation barriers dividing Israel and Palestine and the United States and Mexico. Both the title of the conference and the panels' topics implied the existence of an overarching category called "barriers" or "walls" of division. The variety of reasons for erecting these walls—and the substantial difference among them—seemed less crucial to the conference organizers than the potential to bring all these "walls" together under *one* conceptual umbrella.

This desire to discuss contemporary "walls" reflects a social reality: even in the twenty-first century, countries often decide to build barriers of division. Separation barriers might seem archaic in a "globalizing" world, but their construction is on the rise worldwide; since the fall of the Berlin Wall, at least forty countries have built new walls. There are in fact *more* separation barriers now than there were in 1989. Contemporary separation barriers include Egypt's barrier around Sharm El-Sheikh against the infiltration of terrorists; Brunei's border fence against illegal immigrants at the Limbang border; the Kazakh–Uzbekistan barrier against drug trafficking and illegal immigration; India's fence across part of the border with Bangladesh in order to bar terrorists, illegal immigrants, and drugs; the United States' separation barrier at the Mexican border against illegal immigrants and drug trafficking; Saudi Arabia's fence against ISIS on the Iraqi border; and Hungary's antimigration fence on the Serbian border. According to French political scientist Alexandra Novosseloff, who conducted a thorough comparative analysis of recent separation walls: "[t]he novelty of today's walls is that they are built on recognized borders in response to the new challenges and fears related to globalization—and issues like terrorism, poverty, organized crime, and migration movements."[2] Her words indicate that something may indeed be achieved by the comparison of contemporary walls of division.

The conceptual link among unique separation barriers seems to have been established with the help of an international icon: the Berlin Wall.

The mythical story of the Berlin Wall clearly does *not* prevent us from building new walls, but it enables us to talk about them using a common vocabulary and a common conceptual framework. The fall of the Berlin Wall as global iconic event frames walls as controversial and communicates the possibility of their eventual "fall." The Berlin Wall's design and political message also offer direct comparisons for contemporary walls. For instance, French photographer Maurice Sherif, who meticulously recorded each segment of the U.S.–Mexican border wall from the American side over five years, from 2006 until 2011, introduced his impressive album with the following comparative remarks:

> Comparisons with the Berlin Wall, which was 96 miles long (155 kilometers), are inevitable. The American wall, still under construction, is expected to reach at least 1,952 miles in length. The average height of the Berlin Wall was 11.8 feet (3.6 meters), compared with the maximum current height of American's wall at 25 feet (8 meters). The political comparisons are explored in the essays that accompany the photographs.[3]

For Sherif, the Berlin Wall offered a way to communicate the excesses of the American Wall. In other words, the mental image of the Berlin Wall made the American Wall even less acceptable.

The loaded memory of the Berlin Wall also shapes our basic *vocabulary* when we speak about contemporary separation barriers. For instance, this global iconic event inspires contemporary political leaders to frame their countries' separation barriers as "fences": temporary and permeable. In contrast, the activists opposing those separation barriers, recalling the Berlin Wall, tend to frame them as "walls": permanent and impermeable. The Berlin Wall thus offers us a framework of thought and a related vocabulary to classify separation barriers. Walls, never; fences, maybe. Both naming practices ("wall," "fence") take history seriously. At the same time, they are also somewhat ahistorical. As this book has shown, "the" Berlin Wall went through four distinct phases of design during its twenty-eight-year existence, including the initial moment when it comprised "only" a few strands of barbed wire. Nonetheless, we still apply the term "wall" to all its four phases. Being a fence does not prevent a separation barrier from being called a "wall." The reverse is also true: you may call a massive wall a fence, but few will trust your judgment.

Moreover, the Berlin Wall was a product of a unique historical situation in which *one* community was divided in two. Contemporary separation barriers often reflect deeply felt symbolic and social boundaries. If the Israeli West Bank separation barrier suddenly came down, it would hardly result in a frenzy of Israeli–Palestinian hugs, let alone in "reunification." And even in less conflict-ridden situations, walls tend not to separate the *same* community. If the United States–Mexico wall fell on a magical day, the two countries would not be united and would certainly still consider the issue of illegal immigration.

It seems the global iconization of the fall of the Berlin Wall tells an important tale about the advantages and challenges of decontextualized stories. On the one hand, the fall of the Berlin Wall is an inspiring global social myth for freedom fighters and activists around the world: it is a *mindset to think with* about contemporary practices of division. On the other hand, its current simplified version allows it to be applied to contexts to which it has little or no relation. Practices of decontextualization make stories more transportable, but they can also render them close to banal. This delicate balance has to be found in connection with each global iconic event, and each time it will be a unique balance.

Global Iconic Events as "Predictive Pictures" for Future Events

Global iconic events can also work as what I call "predictive pictures" for future events. What does that mean? Currently, any separation wall evokes in memory not only the story of the Berlin Wall but also its *fall*. The fall of the Berlin Wall offers a predictive picture of the potential fall of separation walls, regardless of why they were built in the first place. For instance, graffiti on the Israeli West Bank separation barrier bluntly state that "all walls come down eventually," "tear down this wall," and "this wall must fall" (Fig. 8.1). Some graffiti even use specific sentences in German from the history of the Berlin Wall—for instance, Honecker's previously mentioned sentence from January 1989: "[t]he wall will remain here for another hundred years."

The global resonance of the fall of the Berlin Wall as predictive picture is supported by a relatively recent event that dominated international news for a day: Pope Francis' abrupt stop at the Israeli West Bank separation barrier during his official visits to Palestine and Israel in May 2014.

FIGURE 8.1 "All walls come down eventually"—graffiti on the Israeli West Bank separation barrier. Photo: Julia Sonnevend, 2014.

He arrived at the Palestinian territories from Jordan, not from Israel; this act in itself was regarded as quite symbolic. He then paid an *unplanned* visit to the separation barrier to pray under the massive concrete structure that has been gradually built over the past decade. The section of the wall where Pope Francis stopped his caravan was covered by graffiti, including "Free Palestine," "BDS" (referring to the "Boycott, Divestment, and Sanctions" movement against Israel), and in grammatically incorrect English "Bethlehem look like Warsaw Ghetto." The pope stood silently at the wall, put the palm of his hand on the graffiti-covered surface, rested his head on the barrier, and murmured prayers. The scene rocked old and new media alike. Pictures spread on social media with the speed of light and an army of commentators tried to grasp the meaning of the event.

Vatican spokesman Father Federico Lombardi hoped to address the media frenzy and offer some interpretation: "I was not informed [of his plans to stop]. It was planned by him the day before ... It was a very significant way to demonstrate his participation in suffering ... It was a profound spiritual moment in front of a *symbol of division*."[4] The graffiti-covered Israeli separation wall worked as a "symbol of division" because it evoked the tragic and hopeful images of the Berlin Wall. Pope Francis built on an icon that has already been established in cosmopolitan memory, and he seemed to be suggesting that every wall of division embeds its eventual fall. But he did so in a conflict zone where there is an abundance of historical walls and every wall has multiple interpretations. For Palestinians the central issue with the West Bank separation "wall" is not its "wall-ness" but its deviation from the Green Line of 1949. They regard the wall as yet another "land grab." And for many Israelis (although there is substantial disagreement internally along political and other lines), the "fence" mostly means potential protection from terrorists. Pope Francis thus entered a complex space characterized by a multiplicity of conflicting interpretations from which he meant to engrave only one: "end of division."

The symbolic event's quick spread on social media prompted Israeli Prime Minister Benjamin Netanyahu to tweet: "I explained to the pope that building the security fence prevented many more victims that Palestinian terror planned to harm." Note the prime minister's insistence on calling the barrier a "fence," by no means a "wall." The specter of the Berlin Wall had to be avoided by all means. Clearly, the pope's intervention caused great diplomatic trouble, so he ended up squeezing in another unplanned visit to a "wall" during his trip. This time it was a memorial dedicated to the civilian victims of terrorism, erected in 1998 in Israel's national cemetery, close to the grave of the founder of modern Zionism, Theodor Herzl. The memorial wall lists the names of those who fell victim to terrorism from 1851 to the present on the land of Israel (both pre-state and modern Israel). According to the head of the Israeli government's press office, "the idea to visit the site came from Israeli officials who scrambled to find symbolism to balance the visit to the separation wall."[5] Later, Pope Francis also visited one more wall, the Western Wall, a Jewish holy site in Jerusalem's Old City, which is a standard part of almost all official visits to Israel. These latter two walls together have embodied many years of history, but they failed to capture the imagination of global media. The pope's visit to *three* walls altogether was almost comical, questioning whether any of these visits had a deep, lasting meaning worth expressing or should be seen as just one public-relations event after the next.

This case illustrates that the fall of the Berlin Wall is a powerful myth because it provides opponents of contemporary separation walls with a resonant predictive image. The image's message is simple and readily transportable—namely, no matter how powerful a separation wall seems *now*, it will nonetheless "fall" in the *future*. But as some commentators on the pope's visit argued, making walls global weapons in shaping public opinion, especially in immensely complicated conflicts, comes at a price:

It's difficult to make checkpoints dramatic. But a wall is a wall. It is imposing, a colossal structure only a state could build and that insists on its existence. You can also throw things at it. It can become a canvas for expressing all that is crushing and inhumane about state power, especially when forced on unwilling citizens. [. . .] It doesn't matter that this wall shouldn't really be compared to other walls. A wall is a wall. The portion of the barrier where Francis stood to pray was covered in graffiti. And just above his head in black spray paint were scrawled the words in broken English: "Bethlehem look like Warsaw Ghetto." This is absurd and repugnant to most of us. How can anyone possible compare a wall constructed by Nazis to pen in Jews eventually headed to mass slaughter with the concrete slabs that skirt Bethlehem? And yet, it persuaded the pope to stop his car.[6]

It persuaded the Pope to stop his car because he meant to use this wall as a "symbol of division" to communicate that all separation walls, both physical and mental, must fall. He used the story of the fall of the Berlin Wall as a *predictive picture* and projected the future image of falling walls between Palestinians and Israelis under the aegis of God and prayer. He also utilized another global iconic event, the Holocaust, to further emphasize that all walls are unacceptable. These two exceptionally powerful global iconic events made the pope's visit to the separation wall globally resonant. A checkpoint indeed would not have attracted the same level of global media interest; a graffiti-covered separation wall with a reference to the Warsaw Ghetto is one of the last things the international Twitter community would like to see, let alone approve of. By using a predictive picture, however, Pope Francis also disregarded the complex Israeli–Palestinian context and presented the wall as being the central issue at stake, not just *one* embodiment of the conflicting desire by two peoples to possess the very same sacred land. His visit was at the border of meaningful and banal, enabling interpreters to pick their respective sides.

Global Iconic Events as Tools to Confront Late Modernity

Finally, in addition to offering new frames of mind for global issues and applicable predictive pictures for future events, global iconic events might also be useful tools to confront the challenges of late modernity. Many social theorists have argued that our time is characterized by a sense of insecurity. People experience widespread risk; liquid identities, histories, and conceptions; various modes of uncertainty; and disorientation from "social acceleration."[7] Many of these scholars, however, have also pointed out that in contemporary risk societies people also long for social bonding. For instance, Polish sociologist Zygmunt Bauman analyzed gated communities of the affluent and ghettos of the global poor as sites where strong communities are formed behind walls.[8] Similarly, German sociologist Ulrich Beck argued that in risk societies we frequently see the need for social connection, even if not in the traditional forms of "family" and "household."[9] It seems that a modern sense of risk creates fluid, "liquid" relations but also a desire for community.

Why are the theories of risk society, liquid modernity, uncertainty, and the resilient longing for community relevant for the question of global iconic events? One of the most influential early writings on our uncertain times, Ulrich Beck's *Risk Society: Towards a New Modernity*, was published in the year of a major international news event, the nuclear disaster in Chernobyl in the Ukrainian Soviet Socialist Republic in 1986. Chernobyl shook confidence in nuclear technology and triggered legitimate questions about the nature of modernity itself. Beck saw increased "risk" as a characteristic of a second, reflexive modernity, when old structures and long-held assumptions of modernity no longer work, and reflexive subjects are compelled to engage with continuous hazards. In 2007, Beck again published a major book, *World at Risk*, in which he examined the prevalence of risk in twenty-first-century societies, haunted by the global "specters" of terrorism, climate change, and financial crises. It seemed to him, and to many others, that risk is still a guiding feature of our age. At the same time, while experiencing continuous risk and uncertainty, people learn to navigate these challenges.

Major events that capture the attention of global audiences tend to direct our thinking about the age we live in and the chances for self-fulfillment when everything seems to be on the move. Global iconic events thus work as *social myths for late modernity*, when some traditions are dissolving and there is a search for new binding narratives. Global iconic events have archaic elements (a wall, a flood, a disaster, an attack) combined with something ultramodern ("new" media, high-tech surveillance, nuclear technology, complex border-control regime). It is precisely this combination that enables them to communicate to contemporary risk societies. By using global iconic events as tools for thinking, people can navigate collisions between the modern and the premodern. Global iconic events are stories people can turn to when they face yet another challenge locally or globally.

Consider the global interest in the videos of ISIS in 2014 and 2015. These videos coupled hypermodern digital media with ancient, mortal fears. The simplicity of the videos' scenes captured people's imagination in distinct parts of the world. Viewers saw hostages, wearing the orange color of Guantanamo, in a desert at the edge of the world, right before the hostages' beheading. Or they looked at a captured Jordanian pilot, imprisoned in a cage, looking fearfully at the ever-approaching fire that would burn him alive. These scenes are like our worst nightmares. At the same time, they are professionally designed to be simple and readily transportable. These videos are also effectively distributed on global digital networks and platforms. By being simultaneously premodern and "super-modern," they aim to disorient and reorient individuals and societies at large. Viewers seem to be at a loss as to how to interpret them. When we now ponder global challenges ranging from political extremism to climate change to inequality to surveillance, global iconic events may serve as useful stories, "guidebooks" in our mental libraries. They offer lasting cultural repertoires for our thinking about contemporary challenges. By being both ancient and contemporary, they provide continuity in liquid modernity.

This chapter discussed global iconic events' potential to shape our discourses and practices today. The three categories it has presented— global iconic events as frames of mind, as predictive pictures, and as tools to confront late modernity—can easily be considered in connection with many global iconic events. The sinking of the Titanic, D-Day, the Indian Partition, the atomic bombings of Hiroshima and Nagasaki, the Tiananmen Square massacre, 9/11: all these global iconic events provide us with frames of mind to consider the state of our globe, predictive pictures about potential future events, and tools to grapple with challenges of our time (call it late modernity, super-modernity, second modernity, reflexive modernity, or something else). All these events, on a fundamental level, ask questions about the relationship between progress and tradition, technology and nature, hope and despair. Of course global iconic events offer a multiplicity of answers to us, and in quite diverse forms. This diversity comes from the inherent uniqueness and magic of events. They allow ideas to be tested on them, but they also offer exceptions, challenges, and sometimes even large question marks. Global iconic events require thinkers to remain humble and flexible while contemplating the role of exceptional moments in social life. Global iconic events are similar and different, structured and elusive, available and unavailable for interpretation. We can think with global iconic events, we can use them as predictive pictures, and we can reach out to them as potential salves or saviors in times of uncertainty—but we may never get a strong hold of them.

Conclusion

THIS BOOK'S COVER image shows a young woman, who with her cell phone, tries to take a picture of the reconstructed "death strip" at the Berlin Wall Memorial in 2014. It looks as if she is struggling to find some kind of connection to a place that is so cruel and unwelcoming yet so prevalent at contemporary borders of conflict zones. Like her, I too had to figure out my relation to the material remains, and to the nonmaterial memories, of the Berlin Wall. Even though I grew up in Hungary, on the Eastern side of the Iron Curtain, I have no personal memories of the fall of the Berlin Wall. I suppose that, as a ten-year-old fan of rock music, I was probably watching the newly introduced Music Television on November 9, 1989, not the news.

I do not remember this event; I have learned to remember it. I wrote much of this book while living near the Berlin Wall Memorial in the center of Berlin. I took photographs frequently of people who visited or passed the site. I recorded them as they found a way to relate to this place, to the many memories attached to each stone. I also often looked at one photograph in a Berlin Wall photo album (Fig. C.1). The photograph was taken on Bernauer Strasse in 1961, and it shows, presumably, a couple on the Western side, standing on a stepladder, waving at friends trapped in the East. When the Berlin Wall "fell" in 1989, the fall's message of unity and freedom prevailed over the message conveyed by this photograph and the many photographs like it. But the fall of the Berlin Wall did not destroy or deny the many experiences and artifacts of division: they are still with us.

Often, while walking over to former West Berlin to do my grocery shopping, I would pass by the place where this couple had stood and waved at the painfully near and far East—and I would wonder: what message does

FIGURE C.I Residents of West Berlin wave to East Berlin during the construction of the Berlin Wall in 1961. Jacoby—Ullstein Bild/The Granger Collection, New York.

their photograph send us today? Is there any? The photograph implies an inherent connection between East and West, both literally and metaphorically. The image suggests that "we are family," despite artificial divisions. Who knows, there may indeed be a lasting message in the story of the Berlin Wall. But is there any lasting message of the fall of the Berlin Wall? Since the individuals in the photograph may well have passed away before the wall came down, is this event still a success for them, and for many others who suffered from political divisions? Can we find a message in the fall of the Berlin Wall that encompasses more than inviting an aging

Jon Bon Jovi, David Hasselhoff, or the Scorpions to sing some songs at the Brandenburg Gate? Or is it in fact a good thing that the global memory of the event is, in some ways, so banal and obvious?

In this book I have argued that while the East German border opening was unintentional, confusing, and messy, its global message is not about "luck" or "accident" or "happenstance" in history. Incarnated as a *global iconic event*, the fall of the Berlin Wall has come to communicate the momentary power that the otherwise hopelessly vulnerable individual can have. The event's mythical story, condensed into a brand of a simple phrase, a short narrative, and a recognizable visual scene, provides us with a contemporary social myth. Through recycling, reenactment, possession, memorialization, and other embodiments, the event continues to travel successfully through time, space, and media, inspiring people in various parts of the world.

While formulating these claims, I became increasingly convinced that the idea that there are "events" that the media "cover"—ideally in an objective and factual way—betrays a limited understanding of both media and social life. As John Durham Peters has noted, our way of thinking about the media is still constrained by a Habermasian Protestant view of the public sphere—a view that renders us somewhat inattentive to the performative character and playfulness of our subject.[1] As I worked on this book, I became interested in the *making* of events, and I hope to have shown that media coverage is constitutive of events in highly sophisticated ways. The media alone do not "produce" historic occurrences in social life, but they do strip particular occurrences from their larger contexts, and may shape them into simple and universal stories. It is certainly possible to regard this process as "media distortion"—and much work within cultural studies has focused on precisely that. But I hoped to suggest a different way of thinking, one based on a positive understanding of myth. In journalism research, facts and context are often (let me say mythically) admired, but if you want to construct an international social myth, "facts" and "context" are the *enemy*. They are particular and local rather than universal and global. Facts and context might convince a few minds; myths, on the other hand, have a chance of occupying many diverse hearts.

Some readers of this book might wonder if it is not a bit late to enter the globalization discourse. Have I not realized that we have moved forward, that globalization literature is *so* nineties? We are after all in the post-nineties today—in the post-9/11 world of disillusionment. Have I completely missed that? I do not think so. Let me illustrate what is at stake in understanding the social construction of global iconic events with the help of two recent articles in the *New York Times*. The first article looked at how certain concentration camps have come to represent the entire, widespread, and complex "killing machine" of Nazi Germany, and argued that "these sites, infamous though they are, represent only a minuscule fraction of the entire German network." As an example, the article describes the experiences of Henry Greenbaum, an 84-year-old Holocaust survivor:

> When Mr. Greenbaum, a volunteer at the Holocaust museum [Washington, DC], tells visitors today about his wartime odyssey, listeners inevitably focus on his confinement of months at Auschwitz, the most notorious of all the camps. But the images of the other camps where the Nazis imprisoned him are ingrained in his memory as deeply as the concentration camp number—A188991—tattooed on his left forearm. In an interview, he ticked off the locations in rapid fire, the details still vivid. First came the Starachowice ghetto in his hometown in Poland, where the Germans herded his family and other local Jews in 1940, when he was just 12. Next came a slave labor camp with six-foot-high fences outside the town, where he and a sister were moved while the rest of the family was sent to die at Treblinka. After his regular work shift at a factory, the Germans would force him and other prisoners to dig trenches that were used for dumping the bodies of victims. He was sent to Auschwitz, then removed to work at a chemical manufacturing plant in Poland known as Monowitz-Buna, where he and some 50 other prisoners who had been held at the main camp at Auschwitz were taken to manufacture rubber and synthetic oil. And last was another slave labor camp at Flossenbürg, near the Czech border, where food was so scarce that the weight on his 5-foot-8-inch frame fell away to less than 100 pounds. [. . .] "Nobody even knows about these places," Mr. Greenbaum said.[2]

The article showed that our knowledge and memory of the Holocaust are narrow and limited: in our fixation on a few key sites, we simplify and condense the extensive genocide we have come to call the "Holocaust." At the same time, it is precisely this simplification that helps us communicate the event through time, space, and media. A story that focuses only on Auschwitz may not fully resemble the event, but it does represent it. It also allows Mr. Greenbaum's international (and often young) visitors, for whom imagining Auschwitz is already a massive task, to connect to him relatively quickly. What if, even after the Holocaust's history has been extended, "Auschwitz" continues to function as a global narrative device for Mr. Greenbaum to tell about Starachowice, Treblinka, Monowitz-Buna, and Flossenbürg? It might help rather than hinder him to convey his experience.

The second article, an op-ed piece titled "Are There Any Europeans Left?," contemplated the future of the European Union. In particular, it asked how emotional ties to Europe could be established among Europeans. After analyzing how economic solidarity and a common fear of war had failed to function as binding forces, the author argued:

> Perhaps the answer is to conceive of a Europe in the flesh, with colors, smells, folklore, poetic force. And variety. The goal is not one formed on familiar principles—common language or history or bloodlines—but the very opposite: a supranational, fundamentally Continental cultural understanding and reference point. [...] Promote the Continent's spiritual unity, organized around its diversity.[3]

Is there a link between these articles? I believe there is. While they seem radically different, both articles deal with the issue of "mythmaking"—"myth" being understood here as a strong story that resonates over time and across space and media. The article on the Holocaust may remind us of the importance of simplification in making an event accessible, both internationally and over time. The article on the future of the European Union highlights the significance of stories in binding societies together. It also makes the case that binding myths, in this particular case "diversity," are as powerful as any economic or military alliances.

Both articles show the need for common stories that resonate internationally. In a way they both ask the same question: what makes it to international consciousness, and why? Or, to translate these questions to my project: what binds the global society together? The current European struggle makes it clear that societies cannot be built on "hard facts" alone. Societies need common stories that function as dramatic or uplifting cultural reference points. Since the international community tells and sustains these stories through media, a sophisticated understanding of how media turn—or fail to turn—events into global social myths may help us as we face contemporary global challenges. Of course, social events always enter highly fragmented interpretative spaces, meeting with contrasting interpretations and quite a lot of ignorance. But some stories still manage to enter, remain in, and influence international memory, even if they come in multiple versions.

When we examine the social construction of global iconic events, then, the stakes are high. I revised and edited this book in Jerusalem, the mythical home of eternal stories and never-ending conflicts. After a day of hard work on the manuscript, in the evening I often took a walk in the Old City, where light installations tell the incomprehensible history of Jerusalem in a simple and readily transportable form to a global audience that has less in common than the hopeful builders of the Tower of Babel. When I think of these tourists, their efforts to connect to something they possibly could not, I tend to believe that "transnational storytelling" is magic. Instead of an obscure cultural studies project, my book turned out, to my own surprise, to be about something potentially useful for international relations. I hope that it will help us understand how powerful stories of events might shape the lives of those generations who come after us. Because in the end, after common currencies, military alliances, and international courts have failed, stories may well be all we have left to bring hope and unity.

Appendix

Notes on Research Methods

MY TRAVEL THROUGH TIME, SPACE, AND MEDIA

I think of the journalistic coverage of international news events as a discursive surface on which one can track the process of their social construction. Therefore, the central method I employed in this book was textual analysis. Textual analysis deals with a given text as well as with the ways in which that text interacts with culture.[1] I have tried to situate the analyzed representations within their larger social, cultural, and political context(s). To provide a diachronic perspective to my analysis, I have examined the media coverage of the fall of the Berlin Wall in English, German, and Russian during the first two months of coverage, as well as at the first, tenth, and twentieth anniversaries. As I will specify below, the timeframe of my analysis was further shaped by significant events.

My period of analysis for the fall of the Berlin Wall's media coverage ran from November 9, 1989, to January 9, 1990. I focused especially on the period between November 9, 1989 (the fall of the Berlin Wall), and December 22, 1989 (the opening of the Brandenburg Gate). With regard to the media remembrance of the fall of the Berlin Wall, I analyzed its journalistic commemoration on November 9, 1990, 1999, and 2009.

My sources for the textual analysis were the following West German [after 1990: German] news publications: *Frankfurter Allgemeine Zeitung, Die Welt, Die Zeit, Berliner Morgenpost, Bild, Süddeutsche Zeitung,* and *Berliner Illustrierte.* I also watched all episodes of the West German [after 1990: German] evening television news shows *Tagesschau* and *Tagesthemen* between November 9, 1989, and January 9, 1990, as well as on November 9, 1990, 1999, and 2009. In addition, I examined during the same time period the American news publications the *New York Times,* the *Washington Post, USA Today, Chicago Tribune,* and the *Wall Street Journal* as well as NBC's coverage of the event from November 9, 1989, until December 23, 1989. I surveyed the German and American electronic and print media coverage of the twenty-fifth anniversary of the fall of the Berlin Wall from November 7 until November 15, 2014.

To analyze, also through textual analysis, the East German press representation of the event, I examined the leading communist newspapers *Neues Deutschland* and *Berliner Zeitung* during the first two months of coverage (November 9, 1989, through January 9, 1990) and at the first, tenth, and twentieth anniversaries (November 9, 1990, 1999, and 2009). In terms of the initial coverage, I again focused on the period between November 9, 1989 (the fall of the Berlin Wall), and December 22, 1989 (the opening of the Brandenburg Gate). Although East Germany had ceased to exist by the first anniversary of the fall of the Berlin Wall, these news publications survived those political rumblings; therefore, I was able to examine their anniversary coverage at the first, tenth, and twentieth anniversaries. With regard to the East German television coverage, I analyzed the most important evening television news program, *Aktuelle Kamera*, in the first two months of coverage (November 9, 1989, through January 9, 1990) and also at the first anniversary (November 9, 1990). For the Soviet coverage, my main source was the central party newspaper *Pravda*. I examined its coverage from November 9, 1989, until December 23, 1989, and at the first anniversary, on November 9, 1990. To situate this coverage in a broader context, I also analyzed *Pravda* from November 1, 1989, until November 9, 1989 and from December 23, 1989, until December 31, 1989. Peter Sonnevend provided translations.

Inspired by cultural sociology, I have tried to provide a Geertzian "thick description" of mythmaking in journalism.[2] Throughout the book I have used "frames" as Goffman defined them: as "schemata of interpretation" that help individuals "locate, perceive, identify and label" occurrences both within their life spaces and the world at large.[3] Beyond these standard puzzles of methodology and selection, I came across a number of unique challenges. Like the stories I have examined, I too had to travel through time, space, and media while researching and writing this book. In what follows I will offer a detailed analysis of my own "travels"—of how I tried to overcome temporal, geographical, and cultural boundaries in my research.

Travel Through Time

The challenge of time mainly involved figuring out to what extent the things I do belong to the discipline of history. How, in particular, could I write a book that is accessible to contemporary and international audiences, while also paying respect to historical analysis? In a way my writing faced the same challenges as the stories I analyze: either I produce something that can travel through time, space, and media, or my writing becomes an obscure artifact of the past.

To confront this directly, I designed and taught an undergraduate course on *Icons of Revolution* at Freie Universität in the spring term of 2012 in Berlin. The course examined the media coverage of four revolutionary events from the twentieth and twenty-first centuries: the 1956 Hungarian revolution, the 1989 Chinese protests, the fall of the Berlin Wall, and the 2011 Egyptian revolution. My students came from six countries: Spain, the United Kingdom, France, Germany, China, and Chile. Our readings and discussions were in English, which enabled us to discuss the case studies in a relatively language-neutral and cosmopolitan setting. To my delight, since almost all of my students were born after the Berlin Wall fell, they provided me with fresh insights about this event's travel through time. I repeated the course in a slightly different format in the fall terms of 2013, 2014, and 2015 at the University of Michigan. Here all of my students were born after the Berlin Wall fell and they came from the United States and China. I also co-organized with Paul Frosh a seminar for PhD students and faculty members at the Hebrew University in Jerusalem in the spring term of 2014; this seminar especially helped me gain a more non-Western perspective on my topic. Conversations in all these courses have altered my thinking about global iconic events and made me keenly aware of events' vulnerability to forgetting and counter-narration.

Travel Through Space

With regard to space, the fall of the Berlin Wall as a case study confronted me with more complexities than I expected. I assumed there must be some sort of central digital archive on the media coverage of this pivotal event of recent German history. But to my surprise (and, initially, disappointment), the archives were neither digital nor housed in a single location. I conducted the German archival research at three locations: the Zeitungsabteilung der Staatsbibliothek zu Berlin, the Deutsches Rundfunkarchiv (DRA) in Potsdam, and the NDR Archiv in Hamburg. In the Zeitungsabteilung der Staatsbibliothek zu Berlin I researched the West German and East German newspaper coverage and remembrance of the event. The DRA in Potsdam was my archival site for the East German television news show *Aktuelle Kamera*. In the NDR Archiv in Hamburg I examined the West German television news programs *Tagesschau* and *Tagesthemen*.

Experiencing, sensing, and "feeling" these archival sites of memory strongly shaped my way of thinking about the case study. The press archive of the Staatsbibliothek zu Berlin is located in a former granary in a highly industrial neighborhood: around there, even finding a hotdog stand was a major task. In contrast, the Deutsches Rundfunkarchiv in Potsdam and the NDR Archiv in Hamburg are both part of the larger building complexes of still-functioning broadcasters. Here, during breaks from my eight-hour-a-day television watching, I emerged from a dark room filled with piles of videotapes and other old media, delighted (and stunned) to meet contemporary German television and radio stars in shiny cafeterias. At all these institutions I found a professional and welcoming staff, eager to help me find my way in their archival labyrinths.

Another important aid for my travel through space was photography. I took around three thousand photographs in Germany between April 10, 2012, and August 15, 2015. In particular, I made a detailed, multiple-moment visual documentation of the Berlin Wall Memorial and the Checkpoint Charlie Museum in Berlin. I also continuously photographed the memory of the Berlin Wall as it materialized on streets and in souvenir shops, hoping to record both intentional and ad hoc memorials of the Berlin Wall and its fall.

I conducted research in Israel from January to July 2014 as a Lady Davis Fellow at the Hebrew University and at the Truman Research Institute for the Advancement of Peace. I used this extended research time to photograph the Israeli West Bank separation barrier and to understand Israeli and Palestinian discourses around this contemporary wall. The hundreds of photographs I took there and the meaningful conversations I participated in have strongly shaped this book, especially Chapters 7 and 8.

Travel through space also involved travel through language and culture. Without my command of English, German, and Hungarian, locating and navigating the archival sites would have been entirely impossible—as would the textual analysis. Before I embarked on my research I had no idea of the extent to which access to these materials would be influenced by culture. It was challenging, for example, to strike the appropriate tone with some librarians in Germany, with my complex background of a Hungarian passport and a Columbia University/University of Michigan identification card. If being an American researcher seemed to be a reliable identity, one that was often welcomed, my East European passport sometimes caused visible disappointment. In that sense, navigating culture also meant navigating identity—and developing an acute understanding of East and West.

Travel Through Media

Finally, in addition to time and space, I also traveled through media. I had to make sense of paper clippings in the Open Society Archives in Budapest, microfilmed news articles in the Staatsbibliothek zu Berlin, videotapes of television coverage in the DRA and NDR archives in Potsdam and Hamburg, respectively, and digital archives for the fall of the Berlin Wall's American press and television coverage.

While using distinctively different technologies, I had to look for the same practices of meaning-making. Although I had initially been convinced that digital archives would be my most desirable form of archives, I realized over time that I was the happiest in the Open Society Archives in Budapest, where I covered the entire floor of a large room with paper clippings. As I walked around the room trying to make sense of them, I felt as if I were part of the "space" in which journalistic meaning-making occurred. In contrast, the highly professional digital databases containing the American coverage did not enable me to see the articles' relation to each other, nor their context. Disenchanted by the digital archives, I decided to look at the print versions of the American news publications as well, in order to situate every article in its broader journalistic space. I also thoroughly enjoyed my work with the giant and "ancient" microfilm machines in the newspaper archive division of Staatsbibliothek zu Berlin, where I looked at the German press coverage as it unfolded, incoherently, over time.

In sum, while I tracked the travel of global iconic events through time, space, and media, I also traveled through temporal, geographical, and legal-cultural boundaries myself. In my search for meaning, I had to translate and communicate—most often, though, I found myself simply listening.

Acknowledgments

Academia is a lively village of people and institutions: each book owes its existence to them. I am indebted to Michael Schudson, Todd Gitlin, Hans-Hermann Hertle, Paul Frosh, John Durham Peters, Andreas Hepp, Guobin Yang, Andie Tucher, Barbie Zelizer, Aswin Punathambekar, Paddy Scannell, Susan Douglas, Géza Morcsányi, Lynn Berger, Ri Pierce-Grove, and the excellent anonymous reviewers of Oxford University Press for their insightful comments on various versions of this manuscript. I am thankful for the vibrant and warm intellectual atmosphere of Columbia University, where this book was born. I am grateful to the University of Michigan for its relentless and generous support, especially for organizing an international book workshop dedicated to this manuscript in Ann Arbor in April 2015.

I am very thankful for four fellowships that helped me complete this book: the PepsiCo Junior Fellowship of the Harriman Institute at Columbia University (mentor: Alan H. Timberlake), the Lady Davis Fellowship of the Hebrew University of Jerusalem (mentor: Paul Frosh), the Leibniz Fellowship of the Center for Contemporary History in Potsdam (mentors: Thomas Lindenberger and Hans-Hermann Hertle), and a Visiting Lecturer position at the Freie Universität in Berlin (mentor: Margreth Lüneborg). I have received further institutional support from the Center for Cultural Sociology at Yale University, the Information Society Project at Yale Law School, the Truman Institute for the Advancement of Peace at the Hebrew University of Jerusalem, the Center on Organizational Innovation at Columbia University, the 1956 Institute, and the Open Society Archives in Budapest.

Jeffrey C. Alexander's effective and elegant mentorship has been invaluable to me from the very beginning of my doctoral studies. I will never forget our dissertation sessions every Friday in New Haven, when we were just playing with ideas, and I wished the sessions had never ended. I also would like to thank Péter György and Monroe E. Price, who recommended me to pursue my postgraduate studies in the United States ten years ago and have been wonderful mentors ever since.

My editor, James Cook, deserves all praise (and beyond) for his thoughtful, kind, and prompt manners throughout the process. It has been a true pleasure to work with him and his assistant, Amy Klopfenstein. I am grateful to Richard R. John, who gave me very valuable advice on the culture of book publishing. Berlin-based journalist and scholar Dóra Diseri took some crucial last-minute photographs for the book, enabling its timely completion. University of Michigan PhD candidates Caitlin E. Lawson and Annemarie Navar-Gill and Columbia University PhD candidate Soomin Seo served as editorial assistants during the final submission process; I hope this experience will inspire them to write their own books soon. I am also very thankful to Wendy Walker for her excellent copyediting.

I have strongly benefited from the advice of the archivists in the Zeitungsabteilung der Staatsbibliothek zu Berlin, in the Deutsches Rundfunkarchiv in Potsdam, and in the NDR Archiv in Hamburg. Historian Cristina Cuevas-Wolf provided me with invaluable advice at the Wende Museum in Los Angeles. Talks and workshops in many parts of the world, including Berlin, Sofia, Jerusalem, Haifa, Tel Aviv, San Juan, London, Ann Arbor, New York, New Haven, Budapest, Potsdam, and Hong Kong, have helped me greatly in revising the book manuscript. I especially enjoyed discussions at *The New Walled Order: The Aesthetics and Politics of Barriers* symposium at the Getty Museum in Los Angeles on November 15, 2014.

Many intellectuals have helped me think about global iconic events. I had inspiring conversations with Colin Agur, C. W. Anderson, Megan Sapnar Ankerson, Jack M. Balkin, Judit Balog, Burcu Baykurt, Zsófia Bán, Csaba Békés, Valerie Belair-Gagnon, Volker Berghahn, Henrik Bodker, Frank Bösch, András Bozóki, Tilo and Ute Brandis, Zsófia Brett, Peter Brinkmann, Aimée Brown Price, Scott Campbell, Akiba Cohen, Robin Means Coleman, Nick Couldry, Jonathan Crary, Daniel Dayan, István Deák, Elena Demke, the Flautner family, Péter Fuchs, Bernhard Giesen, Ted Glasser, Lucas Graves, Ferenc Györgyey, Jeff Hancock, Muzzamil Hussain, Ron Jacobs, Richard R. John, Zohar Kampf, Tamar Katriel, Elihu Katz, Ruth Katz, Axel Klausmeier, Péter Kondor, Annamária Kossuth, Katalin Kovács, Tamar Liebes, Jürgen Litfin, Günther von Lojewski, Oren Meyers, András Metzinger, András Mink, Jessica D. Moorman, Motti Neiger, Rasmus Kleis Nielsen, Katalin Orbán, Benjamin Peters, Amit Pinchevski, János Rainer M., András Rényi, Jacques Revel, Rivka Ribak, Christian Sandvig, Leo Schmidt, the Schudson family, Katherine Sender, Limor Shifman, Balázs Sonnevend, Kamilla Sonnevend, Lőrinc Sonnevend, Panni Sonnevend, David Stark, Rüdiger Steinmetz, Dariusz Stola, Ádám Takács, Fred Turner, Derek Vaillant, Gábor Vermes, Keren Tenenboim-Weinblatt, Espen Ytreberg, Eyal Zandberg, Ivaylo Znepolski, and many others I wish I could all list. I would also like to record my gratitude to László Darvasi, whose novels and short stories taught me a great deal about the power of narratives.

This book is dedicated to my father, Péter Sonnevend, and to the memory of my mother, Márta Mária Belohorszky (1944–2005), who are the beloved icons of my life. I will always remember my mother's encouraging words: "you belong to the first generation of Hungarian women who can fulfill their professional dreams without political, social or religious constraints."

Michael Schudson's love, curiosity, and intellectual playfulness have shaped me more than any words can express. Even writing these lines makes me smile. Thank you, Michael, for happiness.

Notes

INTRODUCTION

1. Alvarez de Toledo, *Nachrichten aus einem Land.*
2. Darnton, *Berlin Journal 1989–1990,* 12.

CHAPTER 1

1. Hegel, *Vorlesungen über die Philosophie der Weltgeschichte;* Deleuze, *Logique du sens;* Derrida, "Signature, Event, Context"; Ricoeur, *Time and Narrative;* Danto, *Narration and Knowledge;* Marion, *Being Given;* Badiou, *Being and Event;* Badiou, *Logics of Worlds;* Romano, *Event and World;* Žižek, *Event.*
2. Takács, "Return of the Event."
3. Badiou, *Logics of Worlds,* 381.
4. Nora, "Le retour de l'événement."
5. For example, Bailyn, "Problem of the Working Historian"; Bailyn, "Challenge of Modern Historiography"; Bailyn, "On Teaching and Writing History"; Ben-Yehuda, *Masada Myth;* White, *Metahistory.*
6. Sewell, "Historical Events."
7. Ibid., 844.
8. Steinfels, *Neoconservatives,* 170. See also Abbott, *Time Matters;* Abbott, "Sequence of Social Events"; Abbott, "Conceptions of Time and Events"; Abrams, *Historical Sociology;* Alexander, *Remembering the Holocaust;* Alexander, "Social Construction of Moral Universals"; Alexander, Eyerman, and Breese, *Narrating Trauma;* Eyerman, *Political Assassination;* Jacobs, *Crisis of Civil Society;* Mast, *Performative Presidency;* Vinitzky-Seroussi, "Unusual Suspects"; Wagner-Pacifici, *Art of Surrender,* "Manifesto."
9. Wagner-Pacifici, "Restlessness of Events."
10. Ibid., 1362.
11. For the Eichmann trial, see Pinchevski, Liebes and Herman, "Eichmann on the Air"; Pinchevski and Liebes, "Severed Voices." For the Kennedy assassination,

see Zelizer, *Covering the Body*. For the Vietnam War, see Hallin, *Uncensored War*; Sturken, *Tangled Memories*. For Watergate, see Schudson, *Watergate in American Memory*. For the New Left protests, see Gitlin, *Whole World is Watching*. For 9/11, see Blondheim and Liebes, "Disaster Marathon"; Scannell, *Meaning of 'Live.'*

12. For more on pseudo-events, see Boorstin, *The Image*. For discursive or conflicted media events, see Fiske, *Media Matters*. For scandals, see Lull and Hinerman, *Media Scandals*. For disaster marathons, see Liebes, "Television's Disaster Marathons." For media spectacles, see Kellner, *Media Spectacle* and *Media Spectacle and Insurrection*. For dramas of apology, see Kampf, "Public (non-) Apologies"; Kampf and Löwenheim, "Rituals of Apology."

13. See Ytreberg, "South Pole Conquest" and Bösch, "Der Untergang der Titanic."

14. For example, Frosh and Pinchevski, *Media Witnessing*; Hariman and Lucaites, *No Caption Needed*; Kitch, *Pages from the Past*; Li and Lee, "Remembering Tiananmen"; Meyers, "Still Photographs, Dynamic Memories"; Meyers, Zandberg, and Neiger, "Prime Time Commemoration"; Meyers, Neiger, and Zandberg, *Communicating Awe*; Tenenboim-Weinblatt, "Fighting for the Story's Life"; Tenenboim-Weinblatt, "Management of Visibility"; Zelizer, "Cannibalizing Memory."

15. On media and memory, see Neiger, Meyers, and Zandberg, *On Media Memory*. On journalism and memory, see Zelizer and Tenenboim-Weinblatt, *Journalism & Memory*.

16. Rothenbuhler, "From Media Events to Ritual," 62. See also Couldry, Hepp, and Krotz, *Media Events in a Global Age*. The introductory chapter provides a thorough reconstruction of the intellectual milieu in which *Media Events* was born.

17. In the introduction to *Media Events*, Dayan and Katz make readers privy to the key shifts in their decade-long conversation, admitting that the contours of their book were anything but clear from the start:

> It was television's Sadat who first aroused our interest in media events. Initially, it was the specifics of this rare example of media diplomacy that seemed worthy of analysis. But the similarities between the Sadat journey in 1977 and the earlier moon journey were irresistible, and we soon found ourselves comparing Anwar el-Sadat and Menachem Begin with the astronauts. (. . .) And soon we were comparing both the moon landing and Sadat with the journeys of the Pope (25–26).

18. Boorstin, *The Image*.

19. Rothenbuhler, "From Media Events to Ritual," 62; Hepp and Couldry, "Introduction," 2; Scannell, *Meaning of 'Live.'*

20. Paddy Scannell provided the most comprehensive list of the various traditions that *Media Events* positioned itself against: "[t]hey took issue with the historians and their dismissal of what Fernand Braudel had dubbed *histoire événementielle*; with the critics of 'the society of spectacle' from Boorstin to Debord; with Cultural Studies and its hegemonic preoccupation with the 'political'; with the

social and political scientists—notably Gladys and Kurt Lang. They parted company with the Frankfurt School luminaries, including Walter Benjamin. They were at odds with all those, who one way or another, were dismissive of public life as theatre and television as its publicity agent" (*Meaning of 'Live,'* 179).

21. Dayan and Katz, *Media Events*, 9.

22. Katz and Liebes, "No More Peace," 158.

23. Dayan and Katz studied accounts and video recordings of several events, but *Media Events* describes their methodology only in a scattered and somewhat confusing way. The first chapter mentions that the sample included a dozen events: the funerals of President Kennedy and Lord Louis Mountbatten, the royal wedding of Charles and Diana, the journeys of Pope John Paul II and Anwar el-Sadat, the debates of 1960 between John Kennedy and Richard Nixon, the Watergate hearings, the revolutionary changes of 1989 in Eastern Europe, the Olympics, "and others" (4). A footnote specifies this somewhat further by mentioning that the authors and their colleagues did empirical research on five of these events: the first presidential debates, Sadat's journey to Jerusalem, the Pope's first visit to Poland, and the 1984 Olympics—the last one being a study of audiences conducted by Eric W. Rothenbuhler (236).

24. In the preface of *Media Events*, Dayan and Katz wrote: "We speak, first of all, in a neo-Durkheimian spirit that holds that 'mechanical solidarity'—a sense of membership, similarity, equality, familiarity—is at the foundation of the 'organic solidarity' of differentiated, to say nothing of postmodern, politics" (viii).

25. Hepp and Couldry, "Introduction," 3.

26. Dayan and Katz, *Media Events*, vii.

27. Ibid., ix.

28. Ibid., ix.

29. Ibid., 211.

30. Ibid., 212. However, at the end of this section of *Media Events*, Dayan and Katz did allude to the journalistic narratives of media events and these narratives' potential to upstage official history: "[t]hus media events and their narration are in competition with the writing of history in defining the contents of collective memory. Their disruptive and heroic character is indeed what is remembered, upstaging the efforts of historians and social scientists to perceive continuities and to reach beyond the personal" (213).

31. Dayan and Katz clearly stated this binary interest in either the "world" or the "nation" as audience in an article published in preparation for *Media Events*: "[t]he corpus of material we have collected—videotapes, films, research reports—relates to events that electrified a nation or the world" (Katz, Dayan, and Motyl, "In Defense of Media Events," 43).

32. Dayan and Katz, *Media Events*, 14.

33. Dayan and Katz did so, for instance, in their brief discussion of the ad hoc microwave link between the broadcasting systems of Israel and Egypt during

the Sadat visit (*Media Events*, 5). And they mentioned imaginary spaces, where an event exists only "in" broadcast—the Kennedy–Nixon debate, during which one candidate was in New York and the other in California, is a case in point (17).

34. Here Dayan's and Katz's key example was Sadat's and Begin's different interpretations of the meaning of Sadat's historic visit: "Begin was eager for the diplomatic recognition of Israel implied by the visit of the vanquished leader. (. . .) Sadat, for his part, wished to place before the world a picture of Israel's indebtedness for his heroic gesture; he wished to use the occasion to enlist American support for himself and for Egypt; he wanted the Arab states to acknowledge his leadership and to realize that the Arab cause against Israel, particularly the return of territories, would be well served by his journey" (*Media Events*, 62).

35. An important example of the authors' tendency to downplay fragmentation in the narration of media events is the following quote: "[t]here are variations: the live broadcast of Sadat's arrival in Jerusalem was treated differently by Israeli television than by the American networks, which had more explaining to do (Zelizer, 1981). While we shall have occasion to point out these differences, they are outweighed by the similarities" (*Media Events*, 8).

36. Ibid., 27.

37. Ibid., 1.

38. Katz and Dayan, "The Audience Is a Crowd."

39. Katz and Liebes, "No More Peace."

40. Ibid., 158. In their view, "media events of the ceremonial kind seem to be receding in importance, maybe even in frequency, while the live broadcasting of disruptive events such as Disaster, Terror and War are taking center stage."

41. Ibid. In this article, Katz and Liebes built on Liebes' work on "television's disaster marathons" (see Liebes, "Television's Disaster Marathons"; Hepp and Couldry, "Introduction"). Focusing on the local television coverage of the 1996 suicide attacks on Israeli buses, Tamar Liebes argued that the "non-stop, open-ended broadcasting mode" of disasters constituted a new genre of media events. In contrast to traditional media events that are planned and support the establishment, in Liebes' view these unplanned events tend to lend the center stage of media and society to oppositional, anti-establishment forces. The continuous and sensationalized coverage of these events contributes to anxiety, panic, and hysteria in societies, substantially limiting the potential for peacemaking and deliberation. Liebes' views seem to have set the tone for the Katz and Liebes article nine years later.

42. Katz and Liebes, "No More Peace," 159.

43. See Alexander, "Watergate as Democratic Ritual." In fact, in the same 2007 article Katz and Liebes mentioned this positive aspect of Watergate: "[t]he event is preplanned, even scripted, and, in spite of the ostensible conflict, there is, even here, an integrative aspect to the shared experience, as Lang and Lang (1983) and Alexander (2003) have argued" ("No More Peace," 160).

44. Katz and Liebes, "No More Peace," 161.
45. Dayan, "Beyond Media Events," 395–397.
46. Hepp and Couldry, "Introduction."
47. Rothenbuhler, "Civil Religion and Social Solidarity," "Living Room Celebration."
48. Zelizer, "Parameters of Broadcast."
49. Zelizer, *Covering the Body.* See also Hepp and Couldry, "Introduction."
50. Zelizer, *Covering the Body*, 101.
51. Scannell, "Review Essay: Media Events," *Radio, Television, and Modern Life.*
52. Scannell, *Meaning of 'Live.'*
53. Carey, "Political Ritual on Television," 46.
54. Katz and Liebes, "No More Peace," 159; Dayan, "Beyond Media Events," 393.
55. Price and Dayan, *Owning the Olympics.*
56. It is worth noting an intellectual dispute that occurred before the publication of *Media Events in a Global Age*. In 2006, Simon Cottle made an effort to incorporate "media events" into a larger category of "mediatized rituals." Under the umbrella of mediatized rituals, Cottle renamed Dayan's and Katz's media events; he called them "celebratory media events," and distinguished them from moral panics (Cohen, *Folk Devils*), conflicted media events (Fiske, *Media Matters*; Hunt, *O.J. Simpson*), media disasters (Liebes, "Television's Disaster Marathons"; Blondheim and Liebes, "Disaster Marathon"), media scandals (Lull and Hinerman, *Media Scandals*), and mediatized public crises (Alexander and Jacobs, "Ritual and Civil Society"). Simon Cottle's model received harsh criticism from Nick Couldry and Eric W. Rothenbuhler for using a "thin" concept of rituals (Couldry and Rothenbuhler, "Mediatized Rituals: a Response"; Hepp and Couldry, "Introduction").
57. Hepp and Couldry, "Introduction," 9.
58. Translocal is a central term in Andreas Hepp's work (see "Translocal Media Cultures" and "Transculturality as a Perspective"). Hepp and Couldry have also built on Jan Nederveen Pieterse's distinction between territorial and translocal culture in their introduction to *Media Events in a Global Age*: "[t]he essence of his arguments is that territorial concepts of culture are inward looking, endogenous, focused on organicity, authenticity and identity, whereas translocal concepts of culture are outward looking, exogenous, focused on hybridity, translation and identification" (9).
59. See Durkheim, *Elementary Forms* and Shils, *Centre and Periphery.*
60. Hepp and Couldry, "Introduction," 9. See also Couldry, *Media Rituals.*
61. Hepp and Couldry, "Introduction," 12.

CHAPTER 2

1. Sewell, "Historical Events," 851.
2. Levy and Sznaider, "Memory Unbound."
3. Frosh and Pinchevski, *Media Witnessing.*

4. Alexander, *Remembering the Holocaust;* Zelizer, *Remembering to Forget.*

5. Schudson, *Watergate in American Memory;* Alexander and Jacobs, "Ritual and Civil Society."

6. Schwartz, Zerubavel, and Barnett, "Recovery of Masada"; Ben-Yehuda, *Masada Myth;* Zerubavel, *Recovered Roots.*

7. Yehoshua, *Ha-kirveha-har,* 31. Quoted in Zerubavel, "Death of Memory," 72.

8. Neiger, Meyers, and Zandberg, *On Media Memory;* Zelizer and Tenenboim-Weinblatt, *Journalism & Memory.*

9. On the visual culture of 9/11 anniversaries in newspapers, see Somerstein, "Newspapers commemorate."

10. Crary, "Géricault."

11. Bösch and Schmidt, *Medialisierte Ereignisse.*

12. Ibid. See also Lenger and Nünning, *Medienereignisse der Moderne.*

13. Quoted in Cohen and Young, *Manufacture of News,* 5.

14. Katz and Liebes, "No More Peace!"

15. As global media researcher Daya Thussu recently argued:
    "[t]he time-space compression in the 24/7 digitized media economy, with its localization and multiple and multivocal flows, visible in all shapes and sizes on such networks as MySpace and YouTube, has ensured that witnessing global events is becoming a pastime for growing number of media consumers. Whether it is the closing ceremony of the 2008 Beijing Olympics, the Mumbai terrorist attacks later that year, or the inauguration of Barack Obama, these media events have become part of a global shared experience" ("Media Identities," 231).

16. Price, "Introduction," 1.

17. Deleuze, *Logique du sens;* Sewell, "Historical Events."

18. Meyers, "Memory in Journalism"; Zandberg, "Right to Tell the (Right) Story"; Zelizer, *Covering the Body.*

19. Carey, *Media, Myths, and Narratives;* Lule, *Daily News, Eternal Stories;* Dundes, *Sacred Narrative.*

20. Eliade, *Myth and Reality.*

21. As Jack Lule defined myth in relation to journalism: "this book sees myth—and news—as telling the great stories of humankind for humankind. [. . .] In this view, myth is defined, somewhat stiffly, as a sacred, societal story that draws from archetypal figures and forms to offer exemplary models for human life" (*Daily News, Eternal Stories,* 15).

22. Schudson, "What's Unusual."

23. Alexander, *Trauma: A Social Theory.*

24. Hallin, *Uncensored War,* 116

25. For Nixon, see Alexander and Jacobs, "Ritual and Civil Society." For Pol Pot, see Alvarez, *Governments, Citizens, and Genocide.* For Slobodan Milošević, see Melson, "Paradigms of Genocide."

26. Bartmanski and Eyerman, "Katyn Massacre."
27. Alvarez, *Governments, Citizens, and Genocide.*
28. Gat, "Warsaw Ghetto Myth."
29. Sonnevend, "Counterrevolutionary Icons."
30. Landsberg, *Prosthetic Memory.*
31. Alexander, *Trauma.* Alexander argues that "[c]ompression affects not only the pragmatics but also the semantics of communication, the basic meaning units, the symbolic languages upon which interactions depend. [. . .] It is by compression of space, time, *and* meaning that globalization creates a significantly more expansive field of action and organization" (156).
32. Dayan and Katz, *Media Events.*
33. Bhabha, *Location of Culture*; Kraidy, *Hybridity.*

CHAPTER 3

1. Koselleck, "Linguistic Change," 661, emphasis added.
2. Schmidt, "Architektur und Botschaft der 'Mauer,'" 54.
3. Klausmeier and Schmidt, *Wall Remnants.*
4. Walden, *Die Mauer*; Walden, *Stacheldraht.*
5. Wentker, "Der Westen und die Mauer," 198–199.
6. Klausmeier and Schmidt, *Wall Remnants*, 15–16.
7. Anthon, "Adenauer's Ostpolitik"; Garton Ash, *In Europe's Name*; Krell, "West German Ostpolitik."
8. Sälter, "Die Sperranlagen," 122.
9. Hertle, *Berlin Wall Story*; Sälter, "Die Sperranlagen"; Klausmeier and Schmidt, *Wall Remnants*; Klausmeier, *Hinter der Mauer.*
10. Baker, "The Berlin Wall"; Rühle and Holzweißig, *Die Mauer von Berlin.*
11. Schmidt, "Die universelle Ikonisierung der Mauer," 457.
12. Ibid.
13. Ibid.; Schmidt, "Architektur und Botschaft der 'Mauer,'" 59.
14. Jarausch, "East German Antifascism"; Orlow, "GDR's Failed Search."
15. For more on political myth, see Flood, *Political Myth.*
16. Zimmering, *Mythen in der Politik der DDR.*
17. Demke, "Antifaschistischer Schutzwall."
18. Zimmering, *Mythen in der Politik der DDR*, 37.
19. Demke, "Antifaschistischer Schutzwall"; Schmidt, "Die universelle Ikonisierung der Mauer."
20. Ward, "Antifascist Defense Wall," 21; Siebeneichner, *Proletarischer Mythos und realer Sozialismus.*
21. Schmidt, "Architektur und Botschaft der 'Mauer'"; Sälter, "Die Sperranlagen."
22. Schmidt, "Die universelle Ikonisierung der Mauer," 458.
23. Demke, "Antifaschistischer Schutzwall," 105.

24. Widmer, "Reagan at the Wall."

25. Schmidt, "Die universelle Ikonisierung der Mauer."

26. Nooke, "Geglückte und gescheiterte Fluchten nach dem Mauerbau."

27. Nooke, "Todesopfer an der 'Berliner Mauer.'"

28. Schmidt, "Die universelle Ikonisierung der Mauer," 459.

29. Wentker, "Der Westen und die Mauer," 203.

30. Ibid., 204.

31. Wolfrum, *Die Mauer.*

32. Schneider, *Wall Jumper,* 12.

33. Harrison, *Driving the Soviets.*

34. Smyser, *Kennedy and the Berlin Wall.*

35. Garton Ash, "Fall of the Berlin Wall."

36. Orlow, "GDR's Failed Search."

37. Hertle, *Fall of the Wall,* 4.

38. Sarotte, *Collapse,* xxi.

39. Hertle, *Fall of the Wall.*

40. Major, *Behind the Berlin Wall,* 228–230.

41. Maier, *Dissolution;* Oplatka, *Der erste Riß in der Mauer;* Schuller, *Die deutsche Revolution.*

42. Taylor, *Berlin Wall,* 408; Major, *Behind the Berlin Wall.*

43. Hirschman, "Fate of the German Democratic Republic."

44. Maier, *Dissolution;* Pfaff, "Revolutionary Mobilization."

45. Bahrmann and Links, *Chronik der Wende;* Neubert, *Unsere Revolution;* Kowalczuk, *Endspiel.*

46. Popplewell, "East German Revolution."

47. Hertle, *Fall of the Wall.*

48. Czaplicki, *Die Rolle der Westmedien in der Revolution in der DDR,* 112.

49. Hanke, "Das 'deutsche Fernsehen,'" 10; Czaplicki, *Die Rolle der Westmedien in der Revolution in der DDR,* 114.

50. Hesse, *Westmedien in der DDR,* 42.

51. Ibid., 9.

52. Sarotte, *Post-Cold War Europe,* 41; Torpey, *Intellectuals, Socialism, and Dissent,* 97; Morozov, *Net Delusion.*

53. Taylor, *Berlin Wall,* 421.

54. Süss, "Der 9. November," 231.

55. Hertle, *Fall of the Wall.*

56. Hertle, *Chronik des Mauerfalls;* Süss, "Der 9. November."

57. Hertle, *Fall of the Wall,* 12–13.

58. Ibid.; Süss, "Der 9. November," 234.

59. Steinmetz, "Opening of the Berlin Wall," 472.

60. Hertle, *Chronik des Mauerfalls,* 134.

CHAPTER 4

1. Hertle, *Berlin Wall Story*, 193; Hertle, *Chronik des Mauerfalls*.

2. Hertle and Elsner, *Mein 9. November*, 51.

3. Grimm, "Wer War's?"

4. Hertle, "Document No. 8," 157–158; Hertle, *Berlin Wall Story*.

5. König, "Die Mythen des Riccardo Ehrman"; Grimm, "Wer War's?" Riccardo Ehrman was born in 1929 in Florence. After the war, he studied law and started to work as a print journalist, first in Florence, then in Rome. Later he worked as a correspondent for the news agencies AP and ANSA, living in Canada, the United States, and, from 1976 until 1982, East Germany. In 1982, ANSA decided to send him to New Delhi and then, in 1985, back to East Berlin. According to Ehrman, the country had not changed in those three years in between: "I went back to the same apartment, I spoke with the same officials, I saw the same police officers, it was the same GDR" (Arntz, "Der Mann, dem Schabowski die entscheidende Antwort gab"). He has a story on almost each stage of his career, which he recycles in interviews. One of his favorite stories is the one in which he met the Shah of Persia in the 1950s in Rome, who had escaped from Iran. Ehrman himself conveyed the news to him: "Your Majesty, you are back in power." The Shah responded, according to Ehrman: "Ehrman makes news happen" (Arntz, "Der Mann, dem Schabowski die entscheidende Antwort gab"). As an Austrian journalist once remarked about Ehrman, "he likes telling stories, a lot of stories" (König, "Die Mythen des Riccardo Ehrman").

6. Hertle and Elsner, *Mein 9. November*, 40.

7. König, "Die Mythen des Riccardo Ehrman."

8. Wirtz, "Was macht eigentlich Riccardo Ehrman?"

9. Ibid.; Hertle and Elsner, *Mein 9. November*, 56.

10. Hertle and Elsner, *Mein 9. November*, 40; Hertle, *Chronik des Mauerfalls*, 141.

11. Hertle, *Chronik des Mauerfalls*, 141.

12. Cesario, "It Was My Question."

13. May, "Der Tag des Riccardo Ehrman."

14. Peter Brinkmann, according to his personal website, has been "a journalist since 1975 (*Welt, Bild-Zeitung, Hamburger Morgenpost, Tango, Berliner Kurier*). Television moderator since 2001 at TV Berlin. Reporter in various wars. In Baghdad severely injured. Several times in Israel and Palestine. Meeting with Saddam Hussein and Fidel Castro. The one, only, and last correspondent of BILD-Zeitung in the GDR. Since April 1, 2010 freelance journalist" (Brinkmann, "Personal Website").

15. Schabowski, "Erklärung."

16. Walker, "Brinkmann Says."

17. Großmann, *Fernsehen, Revolution, und das Ende der DDR*.

18. Hertle, *Chronik des Mauerfalls*, 134.
19. Schabowski's note for the conference included: "TIME! Close to the end & end of the discussion, reference to *MiRa [Council of Ministers] statement* [underlined in orig.]. no PB-[politburo]paper. Affirmation of MiRa!!! Reading text travel regulations." (Schabowski's note was acquired by German historian Hans-Hermann Hertle and published in 1996 in his book *Chronik des Mauerfalls*. It is also available on www.chronikderwende.de. English translation: Steinmetz, "Opening of the Berlin Wall," 472.)
20. These Reuters reports appear in Hans-Hermann Hertle's *Chronik des Mauerfalls*:

    Reuters, 7:03 p.m., November 9, 1989: "Ausreisewillige DDR-Bürger kön-nen ab sofort über alle Grenzübergänge der DDR in die Bundesrepublik Deutschland ausreisen." *DPA*, 7:04 p.m., November 9, 1989: "Von sofort an können DDR-Bürger direkt über alle Grenzstellen zwischen der DDR und der Bundesrepublik ausreisen" (308).

21. Hertle, *Chronik des Mauerfalls*, 148.
22. Hertle and Elsner, *Mein 9. November*, 54–55.
23. Steinmetz, "Opening of the Berlin Wall," 473.
24. Hertle and Elsner, *Mein 9. November*, 59.
25. Ibid., 61, emphasis added.
26. The analysis of *Tagesschau* and *Tagesthemen* is based on research conducted in the NDR Archive in Hamburg (Germany) in 2012. Former *Sender Freies Berlin* (SFB) director Günther von Lojewski has provided contextual explanations. He was the newly appointed director of the television station SFB and responsible for the state-financed ARD network's news coverage on the evening of November 9, 1989. When Lojewski arrived at the SFB studio around 7:45 p.m., he found an excited team of journalists, whom he likened to a soccer team mourning a lost game and promising to win the next one (Lojewski, *Einigkeit und Recht und Freiheit*, 164). But Lojewski had to provide the network of public service broadcast-ers with extensive footage from Berlin on a night when his best political journal-ists and broadcast technicians were out of the country. West German Chancellor Kohl was on a visit to Poland, and for the first time a team of journalists from the special unit of West Berlin had been permitted to accompany the Chancellor to an Eastern bloc country (Lojewski, "Als die Mächtigen von den Medien über-holt wurden," 9). Lojewski was proud to have a live, German-Polish "broadcast bridge" with Warsaw on the chilly night of November 9, 1989; accidentally, he ended up needing a live connection with his very own West Berlin instead.
27. In German: "Also auch die Mauer soll über Nacht durchlässig werden."
28. Hertle, *Chronik des Mauerfalls*, 287, emphasis added.
29. Steinmetz, "Opening of the Berlin Wall," 475, emphasis added.
30. Hertle, *Fall of the Wall*.

31. Ibid., 16; Hertle, *Chronik des Mauerfalls*, 166.

32. Lojewski, "Als die Mächtigen von den Medien überholt wurden," 9.

33. For more on performative utterances, see Austin, *How to Do Things with Words*.

34. Friedrichs, "Cool bleiben, nicht kalt," 113.

35. According to interviews conducted by James S. Ettema and Theodore L. Glasser, established investigative journalists also tend to deny their ability to contribute to reality. Investigative journalists often emphasize that they merely "locate," "collect," and "present" facts. See *Custodians of Conscience*.

36. Even at this time, around 11 p.m., Lautenbach started the interview with the claim that the situation at the border crossing points is "confusing and unclear."

37. Emphasis added. In German: "Die Frage nach dem Sinn dieser befestigten Staatsgrenze der DDR wird sich in den nächsten Tagen und Wochen noch wohl noch drängend erstellen."

38. In German: "Was wirklich aus dieser Entscheidung erwachsen wird, weiss ich nicht."

39. In German: "Wir freuen uns und begrüssen alle, dass die Mauer gefallen ist."

40. Lojewski's commentary became part of *Tagesthemen* only after he personally convinced the original commentator on the phone to give up his now comparatively insignificant commentary on the European Union (Lojewski, *Einigkeit und Recht und Freiheit*, 166).

41. In German: "Das Gebäude DDR war längst baufällig. Nun fallen die Mauern" (Lojewski, *Einigkeit und Recht und Freiheit*, 168).

42. Hertle, *Chronik des Mauerfalls*; Steinmetz, "Opening of the Berlin Wall"; Lojewski, "Als die Mächtigen von den Medien überholt wurden." While not covered in this chapter, West German radio coverage also contributed to the event's relatively quick unfolding. Further research is needed to clarify the extent of its influence.

43. Hertle, *Chronik des Mauerfalls*, 280, emphasis added.

44. Sarotte, *Collapse*, 130.

45. Brokaw, "Permission to Leave."

46. *NBC Evening News*, 5:30 p.m. November 9, 1989, Vanderbilt Television News Archive.

47. Hertle and Elsner, *Mein 9. November*, 61.

48. Hertle, "Fall of the Wall," 137, emphasis added.

49. Brokaw, "Permission to Leave."

CHAPTER 5

1. McCartney, "East Germany Opens," 1.

2. Ibid., emphasis added.

3. Remnick, "Soviets Accept Wall's Fall," A23.

4. Ibid.

5. Times Wire Services, "Berlin Wall Crumbling," P1B, emphasis added.

6. Fulton and O'Connor, "O.C. German Community Celebrates", OC_A1.

7. Tuohy, "East Germans Punch," A1.

8. Schmemann, "A Jubilant Horde," A1, emphasis added.

9. Mosely, "East Germans Open," 1.

10. Walte, "The Wall is Gone," 01A.

11. *Evening News*, NBC, from 5:30 p.m., Vanderbilt Television News Archive.

12. Ibid.

13. Zelizer, "Cannibalizing Memory."

14. *Die Welt*, "SED öffnet Grenze nach Westen," 1.

15. *Die Welt*, "Deutsches Volk das glücklichste der Welt," 1.

16. *Frankfurter Allgemeine Zeitung*, "Die DDR öffnet ihre Grenze zur Bundesrepublik," 1.

17. Winters, "Mauer und Stacheldraht trennen nicht mehr," 1.

18. In line with its nonvisual front-page traditions, the *FAZ* did not display any pictures on its front page on either day.

19. *Bild Zeitung*, "Geschafft! Die Mauer ist offen!," 1.

20. Waltert, "Historischer Tag," 2.

21. Waltert, "Erst der Anfang," 2.

22. *Tagesschau* covered the reform decisions of the SED's Central Committee entirely separately from the coverage of the fall of the Berlin Wall. In this separate section, a short excerpt from an address by Egon Krenz highlighted that the "new travel regulation" was part of a larger East German reform package.

23. *Bild Zeitung*, "Sarah—das Baby der offenen Mauer," 3.

24. Stein, "The Banana and the Trabant."

25. Rienhardt, "Brandenburger Tor," 3.

CHAPTER 6

1. Dayan and Katz, *Media Events*, 114.

2. Loshitzky, "Inverting Images."

3. Hertle, *Chronik des Mauerfalls*, 149.

4. Hertle and Elsner, *Mein 9. November*, 53.

5. Hertle, "Document No. 8," 158.

6. Hertle, *Chronik des Mauerfalls*.

7. Hertle and Elsner, *Mein 9. November*, 172.

8. After *Aktuelle Kamera*, a special program was inserted starting at 8 p.m. that was meant to provide "further reporting" on the new travel regulation.

9. *Neues Deutschland*, "Hunderttausende nutzen die neuen Reiseregelungen der DDR," 1.

10. ADN, "Fast eine Million DDR Bürger reiste am Wochenende in BRD," 1.

11. *Berliner Zeitung*, "Bloss mal übern Kudamm bummeln," 6.

12. Eggert, "Die Mauer in Berlin wegreißen?," 1.
13. ADN/*Berliner Zeitung*, "Fast sechs Millionen Visa seit 9. November erteilt," 1.

CHAPTER 7

1. For more on "banal commemoration" see Vinitzky-Seroussi, "Unusual Suspects."
2. Detjen, "Die Mauer als politische Metapher," 548.
3. The practice of recycling is also often controversial; I will discuss the "darker" implications of this analogous practice in my last chapter.
4. Wende Museum, "Mission and Identity."
5. Wende Museum, "The Wall Project Documentary."
6. Wiener, *How We Forgot*, 27.
7. Wiener, "Berlin, Israel, Mexico."
8. Dinnie, *Nation Branding*; Aronczyk, *Branding the Nation*.
9. van Dülmen and Sello, *Mauergeschichten*, 60, 102.
10. Ibid., 12, emphasis added.
11. Khan, "Berlin Wall Crosses Stolen."
12. Oltermann, "Art Group Removes Berlin Wall."
13. Palestine Telegraph, "Own 'Berlin' Wall."
14. Sturken, *Tangled Memories*.
15. Kaminsky, *Die Berliner Mauer in der Welt*.
16. Domansky, "Kristallnacht," 84.
17. Knischewski and Spittler, "Remembering the Berlin Wall," 293. When it comes to the complexities involved in preserving the Berlin Wall, German historian Helmut Trotnow has offered what may well be the most concise summary: "[t]he German Historical Museum had simply proposed preserving a section of the Wall along Bernauer Strasse. The initial chaotic demolitions of the Wall, however, proceeded so rapidly that officials responsible for the protection of historic monuments could not keep pace. Whenever a section of the Wall along the street was supposed to be placed under protection, it had already been torn down before the resolution could be passed" ("Understanding the Present," 11).
18. Feversham and Schmidt, *Berliner Mauer Heute*, 10.
19. On sites of memory, see Nora, "Between Memory and History."
20. As Andreas Huyssen described Berlin after reunification: "When the Wall came down, Berlin added another chapter to its narrative of voids, a chapter that brought back shadows of the past and spooky revenants. For a couple of years, this very center of Berlin, the threshold between the Eastern and the Western parts of the city, was a seventeen-acre wasteland that extended from the Brandenburg Gate down to Potsdamer and Leipziger Platz, a wide stretch of dirt, grass, and remnants of former pavement under a big sky that seemed even bigger given the absence of any high-rise skyline so characteristic of this city" (*Present Pasts*, 55–56).

21. Assmann, *Cultural Memory.*
22. Knischewski and Spittler, "Remembering the Berlin Wall."
23. Jericho, "Mauerpfarrer."
24. Senat von Berlin, "Gesamtkonzept zur Erinnerung an die Berliner Mauer."
25. Ibid.
26. Schneider, *Berlin Now,* 158.
27. Klausmeier, "Ein unbequemes Denkmal."

CHAPTER 8

1. Žižek, *Event,* 12.
2. Novosseloff, "New Wall Order?"
3. Sherif, *American Wall,* 16.
4. Beaumont, "Pope Francis Offers Prayers," emphasis added.
5. Nitzan Chen quoted in Ball, "Pope Visits Holocaust Memorial."
6. Beckerman, "Pope Francis Cements an Icon."
7. On widespread risk, see Beck, *Risk Society*; Beck, *Weltrisikogesellschaft.* On liquid identities, histories, and conceptions, see Bauman, *Liquid Modernity*; Bauman, *Liquid Life*; Bauman, *Liquid Times.* On modes of uncertainty, see Samimian-Darash and Rabinow, *Modes of Uncertainty.* On the disorientation of social acceleration, see Rosa, *Social Acceleration.*
8. Bauman, *Community.*
9. Slater and Ritzer, "Interview with Ulrich Beck."

CONCLUSION

1. Peters, "Distrust of Representation."
2. Lichtblau, "Holocaust," SR3.
3. Guez, "Are There Any Europeans?," SR4.

APPENDIX

1. Potter, *Qualitative Methods.*
2. Alexander and Smith, "Cultural Sociology."
3. Goffman, *Frame Analysis.*

Bibliography

Abbott, Andrew. "Conceptions of Time and Events in Social Science Methods: Causal and Narrative Approaches." *Historical Methods* 23 (1990): 140–150.

Abbott, Andrew. "Sequence of Social Events: Concepts and Methods for the Analysis of Order in Social Processes." *Historical Methods* 16 (1983): 129–147.

Abbott, Andrew. *Time Matters: On Theory and Method.* Chicago: University of Chicago Press, 2001.

Abrams, Philip. *Historical Sociology.* Ithaca, NY: Cornell University Press, 1982.

ADN. "Fast eine Million DDR Bürger reiste am Wochenende in BRD." *Neues Deutschland*, November 14, 1989.

ADN/Berliner Zeitung. "Fast sechs Millionen Visa seit 9. November erteilt," *Berliner Zeitung*, November 15, 1989.

AFP Footage. "CLEAN: Palestinians Tear Down Chunk of Wall, 20 Years After Berlin." *Getty Images*, November 11, 2009. Accessed September 29, 2015. http://goo.gl/o8LmuL.

Alexander, Jeffrey C. *The Civil Sphere.* Oxford, New York: Oxford University Press, 2008.

Alexander, Jeffrey C. "Iconic Consciousness: The Material Feeling of Meaning." *Environment and Planning D: Society and Space* 26 (2008): 782–794.

Alexander, Jeffrey C. "Iconic Power and Performance." In *Iconic Power: Materiality and Meaning in Social Life*, edited by Jeffrey C. Alexander, Dominik Bartmanski, and Bernhard Giesen, 25–35. London: Palgrave Macmillan, 2012.

Alexander, Jeffrey C. "On the Social Construction of Moral Universals: The 'Holocaust' from Mass Murder to Trauma Drama." *European Journal of Social Theory* 5.1 (2002): 5–86.

Alexander, Jeffrey C. *Remembering the Holocaust: A Debate.* Oxford, New York: Oxford University Press, 2009.

Alexander, Jeffrey C. *Trauma: A Social Theory.* Cambridge, UK: Polity, 2012.

Alexander, Jeffrey C. "Watergate as Democratic Ritual." In *The Meanings of Social Life: A Cultural Sociology*, edited by Jeffrey C. Alexander, 155–179. New York: Oxford University Press, 2003.

Alexander, Jeffrey C., Ronald N. Eyerman, and Elizabeth Butler Breese, eds. *Narrating Trauma: On the Impact of Collective Suffering*. Boulder, CO: Paradigm Publishers, 2011.

Alexander, Jeffrey C., Ron Eyerman, Bernard Giesen, Neil J. Smelser, and Piotr Sztompka. *Cultural Trauma and Collective Identity*. Berkeley: University of California Press, 2004.

Alexander, Jeffrey C., Bernhard Giesen, and Jason L. Mast, eds. *Social Performance: Symbolic Action, Cultural Pragmatics, and Ritual*. Cambridge, UK: Cambridge University Press, 2006.

Alexander, Jeffrey C., and Ronald N. Jacobs. "Mass Communication, Ritual and Civil Society." In *Media, Ritual and Identity*, edited by Tamar Liebes and James Curran, 23–41. London: Routledge, 1998.

Alexander, Jeffrey C., and Philip Smith. "The Strong Program in Cultural Sociology: Elements of a Structural Hermeneutics." In *The Meanings of Social Life: A Cultural Sociology*, edited by Jeffrey C. Alexander, 11–27. New York: Oxford University Press, 2003.

Alvarez, Alex. *Governments, Citizens, and Genocide: A Comparative and Interdisciplinary Approach*. Bloomington: Indiana University Press, 2001.

Alvarez de Toledo, Alonso. *Nachrichten aus einem Land, das niemals existierte*. Berlin: Volk & Welt, 1992.

Andén-Papadopoulos, Kari. "Body Horror on the Internet: US Soldiers Recording the War in Iraq and Afghanistan." *Media, Culture & Society* 31 (2009): 921–938.

Anderson, Benedict. *Imagined Communities: Reflections on the Origin and Spread of Nationalism*. New York, London: Verso, 1991.

Andrews, Molly. "Introduction: Counter-narratives and the Power to Oppose." *Narrative Inquiry* 12.1 (2006): 1–6.

Anker, Elisabeth. "Villains, Victims and Heroes: Melodrama, Media, and September 11." *Journal of Communication* 55.1 (2005): 22–37.

Anthon, Carl G. "Adenauer's Ostpolitik, 1955–1963." *World Affairs* 139.2 (1976): 112–129.

Armstrong, Elizabeth A., and Suzanna M. Crage. "Movements and Memory: The Making of the Stonewall Myth." *American Sociological Review* 71 (2006): 724–751.

Arntz, Von Jochen. "Der Mann, dem Schabowski die entscheidende Antwort gab." *Berliner Zeitung*, November 11, 1999. Accessed September 25, 2015. http://goo.gl/KEu9c.

Aronczyk, Melissa. *Branding the Nation: The Global Business of National Identity*. New York: Oxford University Press, 2013.

Assmann, Aleida, and Sebastian Conrad. *Memory in a Global Age: Discourses, Practices, and Trajectories*. New York: Palgrave Macmillan, 2010.

Assmann, Jan. *Cultural Memory and Early Civilization: Writing, Remembrance, and Political Imagination.* Cambridge, UK: Cambridge University Press, 2011.

Austin, John L. *How to Do Things with Words.* Oxford: Clarendon Press, 1962.

Axel Springer. "50 Years Axel Springer Building Berlin—Unveiling of the 'Balancing Act' Sculpture by Stephan Balkenhol." *Axel Springer,* May 25, 2009. Accessed September 29, 2015. http://goo.gl/jlpFm.

Bach, Jonathan. "Memory Landscapes and the Labor of the Negative in Berlin." *International Journal of Politics, Culture, and Society* 26.1 (2013): 31–40.

Badiou, Alain. *Being and Event.* Translated by Oliver Feltham. London, New York: Continuum, 2005.

Badiou, Alain. *Logics of Worlds: Being and Event II.* Translated by Alberto Toscano. London, New York: Continuum, 2009.

Bahrmann, Hannes, and Christoph Links. *Chronik der Wende: Die Ereignisse in der DDR zwischen 7. Oktober 1989 und 18. März 1990.* Berlin: Links, 1999.

Bailyn, Bernard. "The Challenge of Modern Historiography." *American Historical Review* 87 (1982): 1–24.

Bailyn, Bernard. *On the Teaching and Writing of History: Responses to a Series of Questions.* Hanover, NH: University Press of New England, 1994.

Bailyn, Bernard. "The Problem of the Working Historian: A Comment." In *Philosophy and History: A Symposium,* edited by Sidney Hook, 92–101. New York: New York University Press, 1963.

Baker, Frederick. "The Berlin Wall." In *Borders and Border Politics in a Globalizing World,* edited by Paul Ganster and David E. Lorey, 21–51. Oxford: SR Books, 2005.

Ball, Deborah. "Pope Visits Holocaust Memorial and Western Wall: On the Last Day of His Visit to the Middle East, Gestures of Support for Israel." *Wall Street Journal,* May 26, 2014. Accessed September 29, 2015. http://goo.gl/QvDvhX.

Bartmanksi, Dominick, and Ronald N. Eyerman. "The Worst Was the Silence: The Unfinished Drama of the Katyn Massacre." In *Narrating Trauma: On the Impact of Collective Suffering,* edited by Ronald N. Eyerman, Jeffrey C. Alexander, and Elizabeth Butler Breese, 237–266. Boulder, CO, and London: Paradigm Publishers, 2011.

Bauman, Zygmunt. *Community: Seeking Safety in an Insecure World.* Cambridge, UK: Polity, 2001.

Bauman, Zygmunt. *Liquid Life.* Cambridge, UK: Polity, 2005.

Bauman, Zygmunt. *Liquid Modernity.* Cambridge, UK: Polity, 2000.

Bauman, Zygmunt. *Liquid Times: Living in an Age of Uncertainty.* Cambridge, UK: Polity, 2006.

Beaumont, Peter. "Pope Francis Offers Prayers at Israeli Separation Wall in Bethlehem." *The Guardian,* May 25, 2014. Accessed September 29, 2015. http://goo.gl/Pz3iSo.

Beck, Ulrich. *Risk Society: Towards a New Modernity.* London: Sage, 1992.

Beck, Ulrich. *Weltrisikogesellschaft: Auf der Suche nach der verlorenen Sicherheit.* Frankfurt am Main: Suhrkamp, 2007.

Beckerman, Gal. "How is This Wall Different? Pope Francis Cements an Icon." *Jewish Daily Forward*, May 28, 2014. Accessed September 29, 2015. http://goo. gl/Iqgoti.

Bell, Daniel. "A Moralizer's Tale. (Review of *The Image; or What Happened to the American Dream* by Daniel Boorstin)." *Kenyon Review* 25.1 (1963): 156–161.

Bennett, W. Lance, and Regina G. Lawrence. "News Icons and the Mainstreaming of Social Change." *Journal of Communication* 43.5 (1995): 20–39.

Ben-Yehuda, Nachman. *Masada Myth: Collective Memory and Mythmaking in Israel.* Madison: University of Wisconsin Press, 1996.

Berliner Zeitung. "Bloss mal übern Kudamm bummeln—und zurück!" November 11, 1989

Bhabha, Homi K. *The Location of Culture.* London and New York: Routledge, 1994.

Bild Zeitung. "Geschafft! Die Mauer ist offen!" November 10, 1989.

Bild Zeitung. "Sarah—das Baby der offenen Mauer." November 13, 1989.

Blondheim, Menahem, and Tamar Liebes. "Live Television's Disaster Marathon of September 11 and Its Subversive Potential." *Prometheus* 20.3 (2002): 271–276.

Bodnar, John. *Remaking America: Public Memory, Commemoration, and Patriotism in the Twentieth Century.* Princeton, NJ: Princeton University Press, 1992.

Boorstin, Daniel J. *The Image; or, What Happened to the American Dream.* New York: Atheneum, 1962.

Bösch, Frank. "Medien als Katalysatoren der Wende? Die DDR, Polen und der Westen 1989." *Zeitschrift für Ostmitteleuropa-Forschung* 59 (2010): 459–471.

Bösch, Frank. "Transnationale Trauer und Technikkritik? Der Untergang der Titanic." In *Medienereignisse der Moderne*, edited by Friedrich Lenger and Anskar Nünning, 79–95. Darmstadt: WBG, 2008.

Bösch, Frank, and Patrick Schmidt, eds. *Medialisierte Ereignisse: Performanz, Inszenierung und Medien seit dem 18. Jahrhundert.* Frankfurt: Campus Verlag, 2010.

Brinkmann, Peter. Personal website. Accessed September 29, 2015. http://goo.gl/ fWwgFP.

Brokaw, Tom. "It Is Permission to Leave the GDR." *NBC News*, November 11, 2009. Accessed September 29, 2015. http://goo.gl/oxldEh.

Carey, James W. "American Journalism on, before, and after September 11." In *Journalism after September 11*, edited by Barbie Zelizer and Stuart Allan, 85–104. London and New York: Routledge, 2002.

Carey, James W. *Communication as Culture: Essays on Media and Society.* New York: Routledge, 1992.

Carey, James W. *Media, Myths, and Narratives: Television and the Press.* Newbury Park, CA: Sage, 1988.

Carey, James W. "Political Ritual on Television: Episodes in the History of Shame, Degradation and Excommunication." In *Media, Ritual and Identity*, edited by Tamar Liebes and James Curran, 42–70. London: Routledge, 1998.

Cassirer, Ernst. *Language and Myth.* New York: Harper & Brothers, 1946.

Cesario, Marco. "It Was My Question That Brought the Wall Down." *ResetDOC: Dialogues on Civilizations,* November 23, 2009. Accessed September 29, 2015. http://goo.gl/XtiV5.

Chouliaraki, Lilie. "Post-Humanitarianism: Humanitarian Communication Beyond a Politics of Pity." *International Journal of Cultural Studies* 13 (2010): 107–126.

Cohen, Stanley. *Folk Devils and Moral Panics: The Creation of the Mods and Rockers.* London: MacGibbon and Kee, 1972.

Cohen, Stanley, and Jock Young. *The Manufacture of News: Social Problems, Deviance and the Mass Media.* London: Constable, 1973.

Confino, Alon. *Germany as a Culture of Remembrance: Promises and Limits of Writing History.* Chapel Hill: University of North Carolina Press, 2006.

Cottle, Simon. "Mediatized Rituals: Beyond Manufacturing Consent." *Media, Culture & Society* 28.1 (2006): 411–432.

Couldry, Nick. *Media Rituals: A Critical Approach.* London and New York: Routledge, 2003.

Couldry, Nick. *The Place of Media Power: Pilgrims and Witnesses of the Media Age.* London and New York: Routledge, 2000.

Couldry, Nick, Andreas Hepp, and Friedrich Krotz, eds. *Media Events in a Global Age.* London: Routledge, 2010.

Couldry, Nick, and Eric W. Rothenbuhler. "Simon Cottle on 'Mediatized Rituals': A Response." *Media, Culture & Society* 29.4 (2007): 691–695.

Cramer, Johannes, and Tobias Rütenik. *Die Baugeschichte der Berliner Mauer.* Petersberg: Michael Imhof Verlag, 2011.

Crary, Jonathan. "Géricault, the Panorama and Sites of Reality in the Early Nineteenth Century." *Grey Room* 9 (2002): 5–25.

Cui, Xi. "Media Events Are Still Alive: The Opening Ceremony of the Beijing Olympics as a Media Ritual." *International Journal of Communication* 7 (2013): 1220–1235.

Czaplicki, Andreas. *Die Rolle der Westmedien in der Revolution in der DDR.* PhD dissertation, Johannes Gutenberg Universität zu Mainz, 2002.

Danto, Arthur C. *Narration and Knowledge.* New York: Columbia University Press, 1985.

Darnton, Robert. *Berlin Journal 1989–1990.* New York and London: W.W. Norton & Company, 1993.

Dayan, Daniel. "Beyond Media Events: Disenchantment, Derailment, Disruption." In *Owning the Olympics: Narratives of the New China,* edited by Monroe E. Price and Daniel Dayan, 391–401. Ann Arbor: University of Michigan Press, 2008.

Dayan, Daniel, and Elihu Katz. *Media Events: The Live Broadcasting of History.* Cambridge, MA: Harvard University Press, 1992.

Dekavalla, Marina. "Constructing the Public at the Royal Wedding." *Media, Culture & Society* 34 (2012): 296–311.

Deleuze, Gilles. *Logique du Sens*. Paris: Éditions de Minuit, 1969.

Demke, Elena. "'Antifaschistischer Schutzwall'—'Ulbrichts KZ' Kalter Krieg der Mauer Bilder." In *Die Mauer: Errichtung, Überwindung, Erinnerung*, edited by Klaus-Dietmar Henke, 96–110. München: Deutscher Taschenbuch Verlag, 2011.

Derrida, Jacques. "Signature, Event, Context." In *Margins of Philosophy*. Translated by Alan Bass, 307–330. Chicago: University of Chicago Press, 1982.

Detjen, Marion. "Die Mauer als politische Metapher." In *Die Mauer: Errichtung, Überwindung, Erinnerung*, edited by Klaus-Dietmar Henke, 426–440. München: Deutscher Taschenbuch Verlag, 2011.

Die Welt. "Deutsches Volk das glücklichste der Welt." November 11, 1989.

Die Welt. "SED öffnet Grenze nach Westen: Keiner wird an Ausreise gehindert." November 10, 1989.

Dinnie, Keith. *Nation Branding: Concepts, Issues, Practice*. Burlington, MA: Elsevier, 2008.

Domansky, Elisabeth. "'Kristallnacht,' the Holocaust and German Unity: The Meaning of November 9 as an Anniversary in Germany." *History and Memory* 4.1 (1992): 60–94.

Draper, Elaine. "Risk, Society, and Social Theory." *Contemporary Sociology* 22.5 (1993): 641–644.

Drechsel, Benjamin. "The Berlin Wall from a Visual Perspective: Comments on the Construction of a Political Icon." *Visual Communication* 9.1 (2010): 3–24.

Dundes, Alan, ed. *Sacred Narrative: Readings in the Theory of Myth*. Berkeley: University of California Press, 1984.

Durkheim, Emile. *The Elementary Forms of Religious Life: A Study in Religious Sociology*. Translated by J. W. Swain. London: Allen & Unwin, 1915.

Edy, Jill A. "Journalistic Uses of Collective Memory." *Journal of Communication* 49.2 (1999): 71–85.

Eggert, Hans. "Die Mauer in Berlin wegreißen?" *Berliner Zeitung*, November 13, 1989.

Eliade, Mircea. *Myth and Reality*. Translated by Willard R. Trask. New York: Harper & Row, 1963.

Engel, Jeffrey A. *The Fall of the Berlin Wall: The Revolutionary Legacy of 1989*. New York: Oxford University Press, 2009.

Ettema, James S., and Theodore L. Glasser. *Custodians of Conscience: Investigative Journalism and Public Virtue*. New York: Columbia University Press, 1998.

Eyerman, Ron. *The Cultural Sociology of Political Assassination*. Basingstoke, UK: Palgrave Macmillan, 2011.

Eyerman, Ron. *Is This America?: Katrina as Cultural Trauma*. Austin: University of Texas Press, 2015.

Feversham, Polly, and Leo Schmidt. *Die Berliner Mauer heute / The Berlin Wall Today*. Berlin: Verlag Bauwesen, 1999.

Fiske, John. *Media Matters: Everyday Culture and Political Change.* Minneapolis: University of Minnesota Press, 1994.

Flood, Christopher. *Political Myth: A Theoretical Introduction.* New York: Garland, 1996.

Frankfurter Allgemeine Zeitung. "Die DDR öffnet ihre Grenze zur Bundesrepublik." November 10, 1989.

Friedrichs, Hanns Joachim. "'Cool bleiben, nicht kalt:' Der Fernsehmoderator Hanns Joachim Friedrichs über sein Journalistenleben [interview]." *Der Spiegel* 13 (1995): 112–119.

Frosh, Paul. "Television and the Imagination of Memory: *Life on Mars*." In *On Media Memory: Collective Memory in a New Media Age,* edited by Motti Neiger, Oren Meyers, and Eyal Zandberg, 117–131. New York: Palgrave Macmillan, 2011.

Frosh, Paul, and Amit Pinchevski. *Media Witnessing: Testimony in the Age of Mass Communication.* Basingstoke, UK: Palgrave Macmillan, 2009.

Fuchs, Anne, Kathleen James-Chakraborty, and Linda Shortt, eds. *Debating German Cultural Identity Since 1989.* Rochester, NY: Camden House, 2001.

Fulton, Mary Lou, and Rose Ellen O'Connor. "O.C. German Community Celebrates Fall of the Wall." *Los Angeles Times,* November 11, 1989. Accessed September 29, 2015. http://goo.gl/UWyCKY.

Galtung, Johan, and Mari Ruge. "Structuring and Selecting News." In *The Manufacture of News,* edited by Stanley Cohen and Jock Young, 52–63. Beverly Hills, CA: Sage, 1973.

Garton Ash, Timothy. "The Fall of the Berlin Wall: What It Meant to Be There." *The Guardian,* November 6, 2014. Accessed September 29, 2015. http://goo.gl/qh51MY.

Garton Ash, Timothy. *In Europe's Name: Germany and the Divided Continent.* London: J. Cape, 1993.

Gat, Eli. "The Warsaw Ghetto Myth." *Haaretz.* December 23, 2013. Accessed September 29, 2015. http://goo.gl/4aAH7n.

Gedmin, Jeffrey. *The Hidden Hand: Gorbachev and the Collapse of East Germany.*Washington, DC: AEI Press, 1992.

Gelb, Norman. *The Berlin Wall: Kennedy, Khrushchev, and a Showdown in the Heart of Europe.* New York: Times Books, 1986.

Gitlin, Todd. *Media Unlimited: How the Torrent of Images and Sounds Overwhelms Our Lives.* New York: Holt, 2002.

Gitlin, Todd. *The Whole World Is Watching: Mass Media in the Making & Unmaking of the New Left.* Berkeley, Los Angeles: University of California Press, 1980.

Goffman, Erving. *Frame Analysis: An Essay on the Organization of Experience.* New York: Harper & Row, 1974.

Greenberg, Bradley S., and Edwin B. Parker, eds. *The Kennedy Assassination and the American Public: Social Communication in Crisis.* Stanford, CA.: Stanford University Press, 1965.

Grimm, Von Imre. "Wer war's?" *Hannoversche Allgemeine,* June 11, 2009. Accessed September 29, 2015. http://goo.gl/1Ovvf.

Großmann, Thomas. *Fernsehen, Revolution, und das Ende der DDR.* Göttingen: Wallstein Verlag, 2015.

Guez, Olivier. "Are There Any Europeans Left?" *New York Times,* March 2, 2013.

György, Péter. *Apám helyett [Instead of my Father].* Budapest: Magvető, 2011.

György, Péter. *Néma hagyomány: kollektív felejtés és a kései múltértelmezés, 1956 1989-ben [Silent Tradition: Collective Forgetting and Late Interpretation of the Past: 1956 in 1989].* Budapest: Magvető, 2000.

Hallin, Daniel C. *"The Uncensored War": The Media and Vietnam.* New York: Oxford University Press, 1986.

Hanke, Helmut. "Das 'deutsche Fernsehen'—doch kein Null-Medium? Fernsehgesellschaft und kulturelle Chance." In *Medien der Ex-DDR in der Wende,* edited by Peter Hoff and Dieter Wiedermann, 7–23. Berlin: Vistas, 1991.

Haraszti, Miklos. *The Velvet Prison: Artists Under State Socialism.* New York: Basic Books, 1988.

Hariman, Robert, and John Louis Lucaites. *No Caption Needed: Iconic Photographs, Public Culture, and Liberal Democracy.* Chicago, London: University of Chicago Press, 2007.

Haritos, Anna. "Demonstration on Diag Fights 'Political Correctness.'" *The Michigan Daily,* November 10, 2015. Accessed November 15, 2015. https://goo.gl/VUbhdc.

Harrison, Hope M. "The Berlin Wall and Its Resurrection as a Site of Memory." *German Politics & Society* 29.2 (2011): 78–106.

Harrison, Hope M. *Driving the Soviets up the Wall: Soviet–East German Relations, 1953–1961.* Princeton, NJ: Princeton University Press, 2003.

Harrison, Hope M. "Wie die Sowjetunion zum Mauerbau getrieben wurde. Ein Superalliierter, eine Supermacht und der Bau der Berliner Mauer." In *Mauerbau und Mauerfall. Ursachen-Verlauf-Auswirkungen,* edited by Hans-Hermann Hertle, Konrad Hugo Jarausch, and Christoph Klessmann, 77–96. Berlin: Christoph Links, 2002.

Hegel, George Wilhelm Friedrich. *Vorlesungen über die Philosophie der Weltgeschichte.* Leipzig: Verlag von Felix Meiner, 1920.

Henke, Klaus-Dietmar, ed. *Die Mauer: Errichtung, Überwindung, Erinnerung.* München: Deutscher Taschenbuch Verlag, 2011.

Hepp, Andreas. *Netzwerke der Medien: Medienkulturen und Globalisierung.* Wiesbaden: VS, 2004.

Hepp, Andreas. "Transculturality as a Perspective: Researching Media Cultures Comparatively." *Qualitative Social Research* 10.1 (2009). Accessed February 12, 2016. http://goo.gl/G88nlg.

Hepp, Andreas. "Translocal Media Cultures: Networks of the Media and Globalization." In *Connectivity, Networks and Flows: Conceptualizing*

Contemporary Communications, edited by Andreas Hepp, Friedrich Krotz, Shaun Moores, and Carsten Winter, 33–58. Cresskill, NJ: Hampton Press, 2008.

Hepp, Andreas, and Nick Couldry. "Introduction: Media Events in Globalized Media Cultures." In *Media Events in a Global Age*, edited by Nick Couldry, Andreas Hepp, and Friedrich Krotz, 1–20. London: Routledge, 2010.

Hepp, Andreas, Marco Höhn, and Waldemar Vogelgesang, eds. *Populäre Events: Medienevents, Spielevents und Spaßevents*. Opladen: Leske and Budrich, 2003.

Hepp, Andreas, and Friedrich Krotz. "Media Events, Globalization and Cultural Change: An Introduction to the Special Issue." *Communications: The European Journal of Communication Research* 33 (2008): 265–273.

Hertle, Hans-Hermann. *The Berlin Wall Story: Biography of a Monument*. Berlin: Ch. Links, 2011.

Hertle, Hans-Hermann. *Chronik des Mauerfalls. Die dramatischen Ereignisse um den 9. November 1989*. Berlin: Ch. Links, 2009.

Hertle, Hans-Hermann. "Document No. 8: Günter Schabowski's Press Conference in the GDR International Press Center, 9 November 1989, 6:53–7:01 p.m. [author's transcript of television broadcast]." Translated by Howard Sargeant. *Cold War International History Project Bulletin* 12–13 (2001): 157–158. Accessed September 29, 2015. http://goo.gl/rOVFHf.

Hertle, Hans-Hermann. *The Fall of the Wall*. Berlin: Arbeitshefte der Forschungsstelle Diktatur und Demokratie am FB Politik- und Sozialwissenschaften der Freien Universität Berlin, 1999.

Hertle, Hans-Hermann. "The Fall of the Wall. The Unintended Self-Dissolution of East Germany's Ruling Regime." *Cold War International History Project Bulletin* 12–13 (2001): 131–140. Accessed November 4, 2015. http://goo.gl/TrhZd8.

Hertle, Hans-Hermann, and Kathrin Elsner. *Der Tag and dem die Mauer fiel. Die wichtigsten Zeitzeugen berichten vom 9. November 1989*. Berlin: Nicolai, 2009.

Hertle, Hans-Hermann, and Kathrin Elsner. *Mein 9. November: Der Tag an dem die Mauer fiel*. Berlin: Nicolai, 1999.

Hertle, Hans-Hermann, Konrad Hugo Jarausch, and Christoph Klessmann. *Mauerbau und Mauerfall. Ursachen-Verlauf-Auswirkungen*. Berlin: Christoph Links, 2002.

Hesse, Kurt R. *Westmedien in der DDR. Nutzung, Image und Auswirkungen bundesrepublikanischen Hörfunks und Fernsehens*. Köln: Wissenschaft und Politik, 1988.

Hirschman, Albert O. "Exit, Voice, and the Fate of the German Democratic Republic: An Essay in Conceptual History." *World Politics* 45 (1993): 173–202.

Hitchcock, William I. *The Struggle for Europe: The Turbulent History of a Divided Continent, 1945 to the Present*. New York: Anchor Books, 2004.

Hobsbawm, Eric, and Terence Ranger, eds. *The Invention of Tradition*. Cambridge, UK: Cambridge University Press, 1983.

Holt, Douglas B. *How Brands Become Icons: The Principles of Cultural Branding.* Boston: Harvard Business School Press, 2004.

Hunt, Darnell M. *O. J. Simpson: Fact and Fictions.* Cambridge, UK: Cambridge University Press, 1999.

Huyssen, Andreas. "Present Pasts: Media, Politics, Amnesia." *Public Culture* 12.1 (2000): 21–38.

Huyssen, Andreas. *Present Pasts: Urban Palimpsests and the Politics of Memory.* Stanford, CA: Stanford University Press, 2003.

Huyssen, Andreas. *Twilight Memories: Marking Time in a Culture of Amnesia.* New York, London: Routledge, 1995.

International Solidarity Movement. "Palestinians Mark the Fall of the Berlin Wall by Taking Down the Wall on Their Land." *Monthly Review,* November 9, 2009. Accessed September 29, 2015. http://goo.gl/4OVkY.

Jacobs, Ronald N. "Civil Society and Crisis: Culture, Discourse and the Rodney King Trial." *American Journal of Sociology* 101.5 (1996): 1238–1272.

Jacobs, Ronald N. *Race, Media & the Crisis of Civil Society: From Watts to Rodney King.* Cambridge, UK: Cambridge University Press, 2000.

Jarausch, Konrad H. "The Failure of East German Antifascism: Some Ironies of History as Politics." *German Studies Review* 14.1 (1991): 85–102.

Jenkins, Henry. *Convergence Culture: Where Old and New Media Collide.* New York: New York University Press, 2006.

Jericho, Dirk. "Mauerpfarrer Manfred Fischer starb im Alter von 65 Jahren." *Berliner Woche,* December 9, 2013. Accessed November 8, 2015. http://goo.gl/ftX9hU

Kaminsky, Anna. *Die Berliner Mauer in der Welt.* Berlin: Bundesstiftung zur Aufarbeitung der SED Diktatur, 2009.

Kampf, Zohar. "Blood on Their Hands: The Story of a Photograph in the Israeli National Discourse." *Semiotica* 162 (2006): 263–286.

Kampf, Zohar. "Public (Non-) Apologies: The Discourse of Minimizing Responsibility." *Journal of Pragmatics* 41.11 (2009): 2257–2270.

Kampf, Zohar, and Nava Löwenheim. "Rituals of Apology in the Global Arena." *Security Dialogue* 43.1 (2012): 43–60.

Katz, Elihu, and Daniel Dayan. "The Audience Is a Crowd, the Crowd Is a Public: Latter-Day Thoughts on Lang and Lang's 'McArthur Day in Chicago.'" In *Canonic Texts in Media Research: Are There Any? Should There Be? How About These?*, edited by Elihu Katz, John Durham Peters, Tamar Liebes, and Avril Orloff, 121–136. Cambridge, UK: Polity, 2003.

Katz, Elihu, Daniel Dayan, and Pierre Motyl. "In Defense of Media Events." In *Communication in the Twenty-First Century,* edited by Robert W. Haigh, George Gerbner, and Richard B. Bryne, 43–59. New York: Wiley, 1981.

Katz, Elihu, and Tamar Liebes. "'No More Peace!': How Disaster, Terror and War Upstaged Media Events." *International Journal of Communication* 1 (2007): 157–166.

Katz, Elihu, John Durham Peters, Tamar Liebes, and Avril Orloff, eds. *Canonic Texts in Media Research: Are There Any? Should There Be? How About These?* Cambridge, UK: Polity, 2003.

Kellner, Douglas. *Media Spectacle.* London, New York: Routledge, 2003.

Kellner, Douglas. *Media Spectacle and Insurrection, 2011: From the Arab Uprisings to Occupy Everywhere.* New York: Bloomsbury, 2012.

Kelman, Steven. *Behind the Berlin Wall: An Encounter in East Germany.* Boston: Houghton Mifflin, 1972.

Khan, Maria. "Berlin Wall Crosses Stolen to Protest EU Border Deaths." *International Business Times*, November 3, 2014. Accessed September 29, 2015. http://goo.gl/jmCsrw.

Kitch, Carolyn. "'A Death of American Family': Myth, Memory, and National Values in the Media Mourning of John F. Kennedy Jr." *Journalism and Mass Communication Quarterly* 79.2 (2002): 294–309.

Kitch, Carolyn. *Pages from the Past: History and Memory in American Magazines.* Chapel Hill: University of North Carolina Press, 2009.

Kitch, Carolyn. "Placing Journalism Inside Memory—and Memory Studies." *Memory Studies* 1.3 (2008): 311–320.

Kitch, Carolyn. "Selling the 'Authentic Past': *The New York Times* and the Branding of History." *Westminster Papers in Communication and Culture* 4.4 (2007): 24–41.

Kitch, Carolyn. "'Useful Memory' in Time Inc. Magazines: Summary Journalism and the Popular Construction of History." *Journalism Studies* 7.1 (2006): 105–122.

Kitch, Carolyn, and Janice Hume. *Journalism in a Culture of Grief.* New York: Routledge, 2012.

Klausmeier, Axel. "Ein unbequemes Denkmal mitten in der Stadt. (Interview with Axel Klausmeier by Clemens Maier-Wolthausen)." *Bundeszentrale für politische Bildung*, August 2, 2013. Accessed September 29, 2015. http://goo.gl/LSoTrN.

Klausmeier, Axel. *Hinter der Mauer: Zur militärischen und baulichen Infrastruktur des Grenzkommandos Mitte.* Berlin: Ch. Links, 2012.

Klausmeier, Axel, and Leo Schmidt. *Wall Remnants—Wall Traces: The Comprehensive Guide to the Berlin Wall.* Berlin, Bonn: Westkreuz Verlag, 2004.

Knischewski, Gerd, and Ulla Spittler. "Remembering the Berlin Wall: The Wall Memorial Ensemble Bernauer Strasse." *German Life and Letter* 59.2 (2006): 280–293.

Koch, Tom. *The News as Myth: Fact and Context in Journalism.* New York: Greenwood Press, 1990.

König, Ewald. "Die Mythen des Riccardo Ehrman." *EurActiv.de*, October 21, 2009. Accessed September 29, 2015. http://goo.gl/WriJ3.

Koselleck, Reinhart. *Futures Past: On the Semantics of Historical Time.* New York: Columbia University Press, 1985.

Koselleck, Reinhart. "Linguistic Change and the History of Events." *Journal of Modern History* 61.4 (1989): 649–666.

Kowalczuk, Ilko-Sascha. *Endspiel: Die Revolution von 1989 in der DDR.* Munich: Beck, 2014.

Kraidy, Marwan M. *Hybridity, or the Cultural Logic of Globalization.* Philadelphia: Temple University Press, 2005.

Krell, Gert. "West German Ostpolitik and the German Question." *Journal of Peace Research* 28.3 (1991): 311–323.

Kubina, Michael. "'Gesundungsgürtel' und 'Frontstadtsumpf'—Die Logik des Mauerbaus aus Sicht der SED." In *Die Berliner Mauer vom Sperrwall zum Denkmal,* edited by Winfried Heinemann, 53–71. Bonn: Schriftenreihe des Deutschen Nationalkomitees für Denkmalschutz, Band 76/1, 2009.

Kulturprojekte Berlin GmbH. "Berlin Twitter Wall." Accessed September 29, 2015. http://goo.gl/hqz8Q.

Labov, William. "The Transformation of Experience in Narrative Syntax." In *Language in the Inner City: Studies in the Black English Vernacular,* Vol. III, 354–396. Philadelphia: University of Pennsylvania Press, 1972.

Landsberg, Alison. *Prosthetic Memory: The Transformation of American Remembrance in the Age of Mass Culture.* New York: Columbia University Press, 2004.

Lang, Kurt, and Gladys Engel Lang. "The Unique Perspective of Television and Its Effect: A Pilot Study." *American Sociological Review* 18.1 (1953): 3–12.

Leavy, Patricia. *Iconic Events: Media, Politics, Power in Retelling History.* Plymouth, UK: Lexington, 2007.

Lechner, Frank J., and John Boli. *World Culture: Origins and Consequences.* Malden, MA: Blackwell, 2005.

Lee, Chin-Chuan, Hongtao Li, and Francis L. F. Lee. "Symbolic Use of Decisive Events: Tiananmen as a News Icon in the Editorials of the Elite U.S. Press." *International Journal of Press/Politics* 16.3 (2011): 335–356.

Lenger, Friedrich, and Ansgar Nünnin. *Medienereignisse der Moderne.* Darmstadt: WBG, 2008.

Levy, Daniel, and Natan Sznaider. "Memory Unbound: The Holocaust and the Formation of Cosmopolitan Memory." *European Journal of Social Theory* 5 (2002): 87–106.

Li, Hongtao, and Chin-Chuan Lee. "Remembering Tiananmen and the Berlin Wall: The Elite U.S. Press's Anniversary Journalism, 1990–2009." *Media, Culture & Society* 35.7 (2013): 830–846.

Lichtblau, Eric. "The Holocaust Just Got More Shocking." *New York Times,* March 1, 2013.

Liebes, Tamar. "Television's Disaster Marathons: A Danger for Democratic Processes?"In *Media, Ritual and Identity,* edited by Tamar Liebes and James Curran, 71–84. London: Routledge, 1998.

Liebes, Tamar, and James Curran, eds. *Media, Ritual and Identity.* London: Routledge, 1998.

Lojewski, Günther von. "Als die Mächtigen von den Medien überholt wurden." *Frankfurter Allgemeine Zeitung,* November 9, 2009.

Lojewski, Günther von. *Einigkeit und Recht und Freiheit*. München: Herbig, 2000.

Loshitzky, Yosefa. "Inverting Images of the 40s: The Berlin Wall and Collective Amnesia." *Journal of Communication* 45.2 (1995): 93–107.

Lule, Jack. *Daily News, Eternal Stories: The Mythological Role of Journalism*. New York: Guilford Press, 2001.

Lull, James, and Stephen Hinerman, eds. *Media Scandals: Morality and Desire in the Popular Market Place*. Cambridge, UK: Polity Press, 1997.

Maass, Peter. "The Toppling: How the Media Inflated a Minor Moment in a Long War." *The New Yorker*, January 10, 2011. Accessed September 29, 2015. http://goo.gl/qa3vwt.

Maier, Charles S. *Dissolution: The Crisis of Communism and the End of East Germany*. Princeton, NJ: Princeton University Press, 1997.

Major, Patrick. *Behind the Berlin Wall: East Germany and the Frontiers of Power*. Oxford, New York: Oxford University Press, 2009.

Manghani, Sunil. *Image Critique and the Fall of the Berlin Wall*. Chicago: Intellect, 2008.

Marion, Jean-Luc. *Being Given: Toward a Phenomenology of Givenness*. Translated by Jeffrey L. Kosky. Stanford, CA: Stanford University Press, 2002.

Mast, Jason L. *The Performative Presidency: Crisis and Resurrection During the Clinton Years*. Cambridge, UK: Cambridge University Press, 2012.

Die Mauer and *Stacheldraht*. [DVD]. Directed by Matthias Walden, 1961. SAD Home Entertainment, 2009.

May, Von Stefan. "Der Tag des Riccardo Ehrman." *Länderreport*, July 11, 2014. Accessed September 29, 2015. http://goo.gl/uSVzLw.

McCartney, Robert J. "East Germany Opens Berlin Wall and Borders, Allowing Citizens to Travel Freely to the West." *Washington Post*, November 10, 1989.

Melson, Robert. "Paradigms of Genocide: The Holocaust, the Armenian Genocide, and Contemporary Mass Destructions." *Annals of the American Academy of Political and Social Science* 548 (1996): 156–168.

Meyer, Michael. *The Year That Changed the World: The Untold Story Behind the Fall of the Berlin Wall*. New York: Scribner, 2009.

Meyers, Oren. "Memory in Journalism and the Memory of Journalism: Israeli Journalists and the Constructed Legacy of Haolam Hazeh." *Journal of Communication* 57.4 (2007): 719–739.

Meyers, Oren. "Still Photographs, Dynamic Memories: A Study of the Visual Presentation of Israel's Past in Commemorative Newspaper Supplements." *Communication Review* 5 (2002): 179–205.

Meyers, Oren, Motti Neiger, and Eyal Zandberg. *Communicating Awe: Media Memory and Holocaust Commemoration*. Basingstoke, UK: Palgrave Macmillan, 2014.

Meyers, Oren, Motti Neiger, and Eyal Zandberg. "Structuring the Sacred: Media Professionalism and the Production of Mediated Holocaust Memory." *Communication Review* 14.2 (2011): 123–144.

Meyers, Oren, Eyal Zandberg, and Motti Neiger. "Prime-Time Commemoration: An Analysis of Television Broadcasts on Israel's Memorial Day for the Holocaust and the Heroism." *Journal of Communication* 59 (2009): 456–480.

Mitchell, William J. T., ed. *On Narrative.* Chicago and London: University of Chicago Press, 1981.

Molotch, Harvey, and Marilyn Lester. "News as Purposive Behavior: On the Strategic Use of Routine Events, Accidents and Scandals." *American Sociological Review* 39 (1974): 101–113.

Morozov, Evgeny. *Net Delusion: The Dark Side of Internet Freedom.* New York: Public Affairs, 2011.

Moseley, Ray. "East Germans Open Berlin Wall: Citizens on Both Sides Dance atop Barrier: 'Long-Awaited Day Has Arrived.'" *Chicago Tribune,* November 10, 1989.

Neiger, Motti, Oren Meyers, and Eyal Zandberg. *On Media Memory: Collective Memory in a New Media Age.* New York: Palgrave Macmillan, 2011.

Neubert, Ehrhart. *Unsere Revolution. Die Geschichte der Jahre 1989/90.* München: Piper Verlag, 2008.

Neues Deutschland. "Hundertthausende nutzen die neuen Reiseregelungen der DDR." November 13, 1989.

Niemeyer, Katharina. *De la chute du mur de Berlin au 11 septembre 2001 – Le journal télévisé, les mémoires collectives et l'écriture de l'histoire.* Lausanne: Éditions Antipodes, 2011.

Niemeyer, Katharina. *Media and Nostalgia: Yearning for the Past, Present and Future.* New York: Palgrave Macmillan, 2014.

Nooke, Maria. "Geglückte und gescheiterte Fluchten nach dem Mauerbau." In *Die Mauer: Errichtung, Überwindung, Erinnerung,* edited by Klaus-Dietmar Henke, 163–180. München: Deutscher Taschenbuch Verlag, 2011.

Nooke, Maria. "Todesopfer an der 'Berliner Mauer' 1961–1989—Ergebnisse eines Forschungsprojektes." In *Tagung Mauer und Grenze, Denkmal und Gedenken.* Bonn: Schriftenreihe des Deutschen Nationalkomitees für Denkmalschutz, Band 76/2, 2009.

Nora, Pierre. "Between Memory and History: Les Lieux de Mémoire." *Representations* 26 (1989): 1–21.

Nora, Pierre. "Le retour de l'événement." In *Faire de l'histoire I. Nouveaux problèmes,* edited by Jacque Le Goff and Pierre Nora. Paris: Gallimard, 1974.

Norris, Pippa, Montague Kern, and Marion R. Just, eds. *Framing Terrorism: The News Media, the Government and the Public.* New York: Routledge, 2003.

Novosseloff, Alexandra. "A New Walled Order?" *The Getty Iris,* November 12, 2014. Accessed September 29, 2015. http://goo.gl/ilra4y.

Olick, Jeffrey K. "Collective Memory: The Two Cultures." *Sociological Theory* 17.3 (1999): 333–348.

Olick, Jeffrey K., and Joyce Robbins. "Social Memory Studies: From 'Collective Memory' to the Historical Sociology of Mnemonic Practices." *Annual Review of Sociology* 24 (1998): 105–140.

Olick, Jeffrey K., Vered Vinitzky-Seroussi, and Daniel Levy, eds. *The Collective Memory Reader.* Oxford: Oxford University Press, 2011.

Oltermann, Philip. "Art Group Removes Berlin Wall Memorial in Border Protest." *The Guardian*, November 3, 2014. Accessed September 29, 2015. http://goo.gl/6JKYlE.

Oplatka, Andreas. *Der erste Riß in der Mauer: September 1989—Ungarn öffnet die Grenze.* Vienna: Zsolnay, 2009.

Orlow, Dietrich. "The GDR's Failed Search for a National Identity, 1945–1989." *German Studies Review* 29.3 (2006): 537–558.

Palestine Telegraph. "Palestinians Tear down Chunk of Own 'Berlin' Wall." November 24, 2009. Accessed September 29, 2015. http://goo.gl/JX7ZoE.

Pantti, Mervi, and Johanna Sumiala. "Till Death Do Us Join: Media, Mourning Rituals and the Sacred Centre of the Society." *Media, Culture & Society* 31.1 (2009): 119–135.

Papacharissi, Zizi. "Affective Publics and Structures of Storytelling: Sentiment, Events and Mediality." Information, Communication & Society 19.3 (2015): 307–324.

Pauly, John J., and Melissa Eckert. "The Myth of 'the Local' in American Journalism." *Journalism & Mass Communication Quarterly* 79.2 (2002): 310–326.

Perlmutter, David D., and Nicole Smith Dahmen. "(In)visible Evidence: Pictorially Enhanced Disbelief in the Apollo Moon Landings." *Visual Communication* 7 (2008): 229–252.

Peters, John Durham. "Distrust of Representation: Habermas on the Public Sphere." *Media, Culture & Society* 15.4 (1993): 541–571.

Pfaff, Steven. "Collective Identity and Informal Groups in Revolutionary Mobilization: East Germany in 1989." *Social Forces* 75.1 (1996): 91–117.

Pinchevski, Amit, and Tamar Liebes. "Severed Voices: Radio and the Mediation of Trauma in the Eichmann Trial." *Public Culture* 22.2 (2010): 265–291.

Pinchevski, Amit, Tamar Liebes, and Ora Herman. "Eichmann on the Air: Radio and the Making of an Historic Trial." *Historical Journal of Film, Radio and Television* 27.1 (2007): 1–26.

Pooley, Jefferson D. "Review of 'Canonic Texts in Media Research.'" *Journal of Communication* 55.1 (2005): 199–203.

Popplewell, Richard. "The Stasi and the East German Revolution of 1989." *Contemporary European History* 1.1 (1992): 37–63.

Potter, W. James. *An Analysis of Thinking and Research About Qualitative Methods.* Mahwah, NJ: Lawrence Erlbaum, 1996.

Price, Monroe E. "Introduction." In *Owning the Olympics: Narratives of the New China*, edited by Monroe E. Price and Daniel Dayan, 1–13. Ann Arbor: University of Michigan Press, 2008.

Price, Monroe E., and Daniel Dayan, eds. *Owning the Olympics: Narratives of the New China*. Ann Arbor: University of Michigan Press, 2008.

Punathambekar, Aswin. *From Bombay to Bollywood: The Making of a Global Media Industry*. New York: NYU Press, 2013.

Rechtien, Renate, and Dennis Tate, eds. *Twenty Years On: Competing Memories of the GDR in Postunification German Culture*. Rochester, NY: Camden House, 2011.

Remnick, David. "Soviets Accept Wall's Fall, Not Reunification." *Washington Post*, November 11, 1989.

Rév, István. *Retroactive Justice: Prehistory of Post Communism*. Stanford, CA: Stanford University Press, 2005.

Ricoeur, Paul. *Time and Narrative*. Translated by Kathleen McLaughlin and David Pellauer. Chicago: Chicago University Press, 1984.

Rienhardt, Joachim. "Brandenburger Tor: der interessanteste Fleck auf unserem Planeten." *Bild Zeitung*, November 17, 1989.

Robertson, Alexa. *Mediated Cosmopolitanism: The World of Television News*. Cambridge, UK: Polity, 2010.

Roche, Maurice. *Mega-Events and Modernity: Olympics and Expos in the Growth of Global Culture*. London: Routledge, 2000.

Romano, Claude. *Event and World*. Translated by Shane Mackinlay. New York: Fordham University Press, 2008.

Rosa, Hartmut. *Social Acceleration: A New Theory of Modernity*. Translated by Jonathan Trejo-Mathys. New York: Columbia University Press, 2015.

Ross, Corey. "East Germans and the Berlin Wall: Popular Opinion and Social Change Before and After the Border Closure of August 1961." *Journal of Contemporary History* 39.1 (2004): 25–43.

Rothberg, Michael. *Multidirectional Memory: Remembering the Holocaust*. Stanford, CA: Stanford University Press, 2009.

Rothenbuhler, Eric W. "From Media Events to Ritual to Communicative Form." In *Media Events in a Global Age*, edited by Nick Couldry, Andreas Hepp, and Friedrich Krotz, 61–76. London: Routledge, 2010.

Rothenbuhler, Eric W. "The Living Room Celebration of the Olympic Games." *Journal of Communication* 38.3 (1988): 61–81.

Rothenbuhler, Eric W. "Media Events, Civil Religion and Social Solidarity: The Living Room Celebration of the Olympic Games." PhD dissertation, Annenberg School of Communications at the University of Southern California, 1985.

Rühle, Jürgen, and Günter Holzweißig. *13 August 1961. Die Mauer von Berlin*. Köln: Verlag Wissenschaft und Politik, 1988.

Sälter, Gerhard. "Die Sperranlagen, oder: Der unendliche Mauerbau." In *Die Mauer: Errichtung, Überwindung, Erinnerung*, edited by Klaus-Dietmar Henke, 122–138. München: Deutscher Taschenbuch Verlag, 2011.

Samimian-Darash, Limor, and Paul Rabinow, eds. *Modes of Uncertainty*. Chicago: University of Chicago Press, 2015.

Sarotte, Mary Elise. *The Collapse: The Accidental Opening of the Berlin Wall*. New York: Basic Books, 2014.

Sarotte, Mary Elise. *1989: The Struggle to Create Post-Cold War Europe*. Princeton, NJ: Princeton University Press, 2009.

Sassen, Saskia. *Expulsions: Brutality and Complexity in the Global Economy*. Cambridge, MA: Harvard University Press, 2014.

Scannell, Paddy. *Radio, Television and Modern Life*. Oxford: Blackwell, 1996.

Scannell, Paddy. "Review Essay: Media Events." *Media, Culture & Society* 17 (1995): 151–157.

Scannell, Paddy. *Television and the Meaning of 'Live': An Enquiry into the Human Situation*. Cambridge, UK: Polity, 2014.

Schabowski, Günter. "Erklärung." Peter Brinkmann's personal website, September 2009. Accessed September 29, 2015. http://goo.gl/jku51P.

Schabowski, Günter. *Wir haben fast alles falsch gemacht: Die letzten Tage der DDR*. Berlin: Econ, 2009.

Schmemann, Serge. "A Jubilant Horde—Berlin Wall Is Rushed by Easterners as Travel Limits Are Lifted." *New York Times*, November 10, 1989.

Schmidt, Leo. "Architektur und Botschaft der 'Mauer' 1961–89." In *Die Berliner Mauer vom Sperrwall zum Denkmal*, 53–71. Bonn: Schriftenreihe des Deutschen Nationalkomitees für Denkmalschutz, Band 76/1, 2009.

Schmidt, Leo. "Die universelle Ikonisierung der Mauer." In *Die Mauer: Errichtung, Überwindung, Erinnerung*, edited by Klaus-Dietmar Henke, 456–468. München: Deutscher Taschenbuch Verlag, 2011.

Schneider, Peter. *Berlin Now: The Rise of the City and the Fall of the Wall*. London: Penguin, 2014.

Schneider, Peter. *The Wall Jumper: A Berlin Story*. Chicago: University of Chicago Press, 1983.

Schudson, Michael. "The Anarchy of Events and the Anxiety of Story Telling." In Michael Schudson, *Why Democracies Need an Unlovable Press*, 50–63. Cambridge, UK: Polity Press, 2008.

Schudson, Michael. "Lives, Laws, and Language: Commemorative Versus Non-Commemorative Forms of Effective Public Memory." *Communication Review* 2.1 (1997): 3–17.

Schudson, Michael. *Watergate in American Memory: How We Remember, Forget, and Reconstruct the Past*. New York: Basic Books, 1992.

Schudson, Michael. "What's Unusual About Covering Politics as Usual." In *Journalism After September 11*, edited by Barbie Zelizer and Stuart Allan, 44–55. London, New York: Routledge, 2002.

Schudson, Michael, and Julia Sonnevend. "Mourning Becomes Electric." *Columbia Journalism Review*, November/December (2009): 71.

Schuller, Wolfgang. *Die Deutsche Revolution 1989.* Berlin: Rowohlt, 2009.

Schürer, Ernst, Manfred Keune, and Philip Jenkins, eds. *The Berlin Wall: Representations and Perspectives.* New York: Peter Lang, 1996.

Schwartz, Barry, Yael Zerubavel, Bernice M. Barnett. "The Recovery of Masada: A Study in Collective Memory." *Sociological Quarterly* 27.2 (1986): 147–164.

Senat von Berlin. *Gesamtkonzept zur Erinnerung an die Berliner Mauer: Dokumentation, Information und Gedenken.* 2006.

Sewell, Jr., William H. "Historical Events as Transformations of Structure: Inventing Revolution at the Bastille." *Theory and Society* 25.6 (1996): 841–881.

Sherif, Maurice. *The American Wall: From the Pacific Ocean to the Gulf of Mexico.* Paris: Maurice Sherif, 2011.

Shifman, Limor. *Memes in Digital Culture.* Cambridge, UK, and London: MIT Press, 2014.

Shils, Edward. *Centre and Periphery: Essays in Macrosociology.* Chicago: University of Chicago Press, 1975.

Siebeneichner, Tilmann. *Proletarischer Mythos und realer Sozialismus: Kampfgruppen der Arbeiterklasse in der DDR.* Cologne, Weimar, Vienna: Böhlau, 2014.

Silverstone, Roger. *Why Study the Media?* London: Sage, 1999.

Simon, Ralf. "Frage der Fragen." *Einestages: Zeitgeschichten auf Spiegel Online.* Accessed September 20, 2015. http://goo.gl/RYWJo.

Slater, Don, and George Ritzer. "Interview with Ulrich Beck." *Journal of Consumer Culture* 1.2 (2001): 261–277.

Smyser, William R. *Kennedy and the Berlin Wall: "A Hell of a Lot Better than a War."* Lanham, MD: Rowman & Littlefield Publishers, 2009.

Somerstein, Rachel. "Newspapers Commemorate 11 September: A Cross-Cultural Investigation." *Journalism: Theory, Practice & Criticism* 16.3 (2015): 359–375.

Somerstein, Rachel. "Our Anniversaries, Ourselves: 25 Years After the Berlin Wall." NPR's *On the Media*, November 7, 2014. Accessed September 29, 2015. http://goo.gl/hjho7i.

Sonnevend, Julia. "Counterrevolutionary Icons: The Representation of the 1956 'Counterrevolution' in the Hungarian Communist Press." *Journalism Studies* 14.3 (2013): 336–354.

Sonnevend, Julia. "Event." In *Digital Keywords: A Vocabulary of Information Society and Culture*, edited by Benjamin Peters. Princeton, NJ: Princeton University Press, 2016.

Sonnevend, Julia. "Global Iconic Events: How News Stories Travel Through Time, Space and Media." PhD dissertation, Columbia University, 2013.

Sonnevend, Julia. "Iconic Rituals: Towards a Social Theory of Encountering Images." In *Iconic Power: Materiality and Meaning in Social Life*, edited by Jeffrey C. Alexander, Dominik Bartmanski, and Bernhard Giesen, 219–233. New York: Palgrave Macmillan, 2012.

Sonnevend, Julia. "More Hope! Ceremonial Media Events Are Still Important in the 21st Century." In *Global Perspectives on Media Events in Contemporary Society*, edited by Andrew Fox. Hershey, PA: IGI Global, 2016.

Sonnevend, Julia. "'Symbol of Hope for a World Without Walls:' The Fall of the Berlin Wall as a Global Iconic Event." *Divinatio* (2015): 39–40, 223–233.

Stein, Mary Beth. "The Banana and the Trabant: Representations of the 'Other' in a United Germany." In *The Berlin Wall: Representations and Perspectives*, edited by Ernst Schürer, Manfred Keune, and Philip Jenkins, 333–347. New York: Peter Lang, 1996.

Steinfels, Peter. *The Neoconservatives: The Origins of a Movement*. New York: Simon and Schuster, 2013.

Steinmetz, Rüdiger. "The Opening of the Berlin Wall on 9 November 1989, and East–West Television Cooperation." *Historical Journal of Film, Radio and Television* 24.3 (2004): 465–482.

Sturken, Marita. "Memory, Consumerism and Media: Reflections on the Emergence of the Field." *Memory Studies* 1.1 (2008): 73–78.

Sturken, Marita. *Tangled Memories: The Vietnam War, the AIDS Epidemic, and the Politics of Remembering*. Berkeley: University of California Press, 1997.

Sturken, Marita. *Tourists of History: Memory, Kitsch, and Consumerism from Oklahoma City to Ground Zero*. Durham, NC: Duke University Press, 2007.

Süss, Walter. "Der 9. November." In *Die Mauer: Errichtung, Überwindung, Erinnerung*, edited by Klaus-Dietmar Henke, 227–241. München: Deutscher Taschenbuch Verlag, 2011.

Takács, Ádám. "The 'Return of the Event': Adventures of the Event in Historiographical and Philosophical Discourses since the 1970s." *Divinatio* (2015): 39–40, 129–141.

Taylor, Frederick. *The Berlin Wall: A World Divided, 1961–1989*. New York: Harper Collins, 2006.

Tebbel, John, and Mary Ellen Zuckerman. *The Magazine in America 1741–1990*. New York, Oxford: Oxford University Press, 1991.

Tenenboim-Weinblatt, Keren. "Fighting for the Story's Life: Non-Closure in Journalistic Narrative." *Journalism* 9.1 (2008): 31–51.

Tenenboim-Weinblatt, Keren. "Journalism as an Agent of Prospective Memory." In *On Media Memory: Collective Memory in a New Media Age*, edited by Motti Neiger, Oren Meyers, and Eyal Zandberg, 213–226. New York: Palgrave Macmillan, 2011.

Tenenboim-Weinblatt, Keren. "The Management of Visibility: Media Coverage of Kidnapping and Captivity Cases Around the World." *Media, Culture & Society* 35 (2013): 791–808.

Thompson, John B. *Political Scandal: Power and Visibility in the Media Age.* Cambridge, UK: Polity Press, 2000.

Thompson, John B. "Tradition and Self in a Mediated World." In *Detraditionalization: Critical Reflections on Authority and Identity,* edited by Paul Heelas, Scott Lash, and Paul Morris, 89–108. Malden, MA: Blackwell, 1996.

Thussu, Daya. "Media Identities in a 'Post-American' World." In *Global Media, Culture, and Identity,* edited by Rohit Chopra and Radhika Gajjala, 231–234. New York: Routledge, 2011.

Times Wire Services. "Berlin Wall Crumbling: Germans Begin Dismantling Sections for 18 Exits: Huge Cheers Go Up as Bulldozer Arrives." *Los Angeles Times,* November 10, 1989. Accessed September 29, 2015. http://goo.gl/p3V10i.

Torpey, John C. *Intellectuals, Socialism, and Dissent: The East German Opposition and Its Legacy.* Minneapolis: University of Minnesota Press, 1995.

Trotnow, Helmut. "Understanding the Present by Looking Back at the Past: Bernauer Strasse and the Berlin Wall Memorial Site." In *Berlin Wall: Memorial Site, Exhibition Center and the Chapel of Reconciliation on Bernauer Strasse,* edited by The Berlin Wall Memorial Site and Exhibition Center Association, 8–12. Berlin: Jaron, 1999.

Tuchman, Gaye. "Telling Stories." *Journal of Communication* 26.4 (1976): 93–97.

Tuohy, William. "East Germans Punch 1st Holes in Wall, Pledge Free Elections: East Bloc: Tens of Thousands Stream Past the Berlin Wall to the West. The Communist Regime Promises That Freedom of Travel Will Be Permanent." *Los Angeles Times,* November 11, 1989.

van Dülmen, Moritz, and Tom Sello. *Mauergeschichten—Wall Stories.* Berlin: Kulturprojekte Berlin GmbH, 2014.

Vinitzky-Seroussi, Vered. "Commemorating a Difficult Past: Yitzhak Rabin's Memorials." *American Sociological Review* 67.1 (2002): 30–51.

Vinitzky-Seroussi, Vered. "'Round up the Unusual Suspects': Banal Commemoration and the Role of the Media." In *On Media Memory: Collective Memory in a New Media Age,* edited by Motti Neiger, Oren Meyers, and Eyal Zandberg, 27–37. New York: Palgrave Macmillan, 2011.

Wagner-Pacifici, Robin. *The Art of Surrender: Decomposing Sovereignty at Conflict's End.* Chicago: University of Chicago Press, 2005.

Wagner-Pacifici, Robin. "A Manifesto for a Quantum Sociology of Events." *Divinatio* (2015): 39–40, 49–61.

Wagner-Pacifici, Robin. "Theorizing the Restlessness of Events." *American Journal of Sociology* 115.5 (2010): 1351–1386.

Walker, Marcus. "Did Brinkmanship Fell Berlin's Wall? Brinkmann Says It Did." *Wall Street Journal,* October 21, 2009. Accessed September 29, 2015. http://goo.gl/a4D2j.

Walte, Juan J. "The Wall is Gone." *USA Today,* November 10, 1989.

Waltert, Bruno. "Erst der Anfang." *Berliner Morgenpost,* November 11, 1989.

Waltert, Bruno. "Historischer Tag." *Berliner Morgenpost,* November 10, 1989.

Ward, James J. "Remember When It Was the 'Antifascist Defense Wall'? The Uses of History in the Battle for Public Memory and Public Space." In *The Berlin Wall: Representations and Perspectives,* edited by Ernst Schürer, Manfred Erwin Keune, and Philip Jenkins, 11–25. New York: Peter Lang, 1996.

Wende Museum. "Mission and Identity." Accessed September 29, 2015. http://goo.gl/Tj0d7.

Wende Museum. "The Wall Project Documentary." Accessed September 29, 2015. http://goo.gl/OYCKU.

Wentker, Hermann. "Der Westen und die Mauer." In *Die Mauer: Errichtung, Überwindung, Erinnerung,* edited by Klaus-Dietmar Henke, 196–210. München: Deutscher Taschenbuch Verlag, 2011.

White, Hayden. *Metahistory: The Historical Imagination in Nineteenth-Century Europe.* Baltimore, MD: Johns Hopkins University Press, 1973.

Widmer, Ted. "Reagan at the Wall." *New York Times,* June 11, 2012. Accessed September 29, 2015. http://goo.gl/1kd2U9.

Wiener, Jon. "Berlin, Israel, Mexico: Walls across the World." *The Nation,* November 2, 2009. Accessed November 7, 2015. http://goo.gl/aRyJEp.

Wiener, Jon. *How We Forgot the Cold War: A Historical Journey Across America.* Berkeley, Los Angeles, London: University of California Press, 2012.

Winters, Peter Jochen. "Mauer und Stacheldraht trennen nicht mehr." *Frankfurter Allgemeine Zeitung,* November 11, 1989.

Wirtz, Christoph. "Was macht eigentlich Riccardo Ehrman? [Interview with Riccardo Ehrman]." *Stern,* April 12, 2009. Accessed September 29, 2015. http://goo.gl/MoBdcd.

Wolfrum, Edgar. *Die Mauer: Geschichte einer Teilung.* München: C. H. Beck, 2009.

Yehoshua, Avraham B. *Ha-kirveha-har (The Wall and the Mountain).* Tel Aviv: Zmora-Bitan, 1989.

Ytreberg, Espen. "The 1911 South Pole Conquest as Historical Media Event and Media Ensemble." *Media History* 20.2 (2014): 167–181.

Zandberg, Eyal. "The Right to Tell the (Right) Story: Journalism, Authority and Memory." *Media, Culture & Society* 32.1 (2010): 5–24.

Zerubavel, Yael. "The Death of Memory and the Memory of Death: Masada and the Holocaust as Historical Metaphors." *Representations* 45 (1994): 72–100.

Zerubavel, Yael. *Recovered Roots: Collective Memory and the Making of Israeli National Tradition.* Chicago, London: University of Chicago Press, 1995.

Zelizer, Barbie. "Cannibalizing Memory in the Global Flow of News." In *On Media Memory: Collective Memory in a New Media Age,* edited by Motti Neiger, Oren Meyers, and Eyal Zandberg, 27–37. New York: Palgrave Macmillan, 2011.

Zelizer, Barbie. *Covering the Body: The Kennedy Assassination, the Media, and the Shaping of Collective Memory.* Chicago: University of Chicago Press, 1992.

Zelizer, Barbie. "The Parameters of Broadcast of Sadat's Arrival in Jerusalem." MA thesis, Communications Institute, Hebrew University of Jerusalem, 1981.

Zelizer, Barbie. *Remembering to Forget: Holocaust Memory through the Camera's Eye.* Chicago: University of Chicago Press, 1998.

Zelizer, Barbie. "Why Memory's Work on Journalism Does Not Reflect Journalism's Work on Memory." *Memory Studies* 1.1 (2008): 79–87.

Zelizer, Barbie, and Keren Tenenboim-Weinblatt, eds. *Journalism and Memory.* London: Palgrave Macmillan, 2014.

Zimmering, Raina. *Mythen in der Politik der DDR: Ein Beitrag zur Erforschung politischer Mythen.* Leske, Budrich: Opladen, 2000.

Žižek, Slavoj. *Event: A Philosophical Journey Through a Concept.* New York, London: Melville House, 2014.

Index

Note: Italic page numbers refer to photographs and accompanying captions.